ISBN 978-0-9790622-4-7

10 9 8 7 6 5 4 3 2 1

Softcover edition / E

Classic Bible Stories For the Modern World

The Complete Story of the Bible: Egermeier's 233 Timeless Stories Revised for Today's Readers And Richly Illustrated with Over 500 Works by The Greatest Bible Artists Of All Time

By L.B. Glisson

A Doberwarez Multimedia Publication

Gainesville, Florida USA

WWW.DOBERWAREZ.COM   WWW.BIBLEWAREZ.COM

Samson and Delilah

INTRODUCTION

There is no greater storybook than the Bible. It is so great that it is intimidating to many readers simply by virtue of its size. It is difficult for one person to grasp all of the names of the people and places and the events that make up the entire story.

Because of the influence of television and the pace of modern life, readers today have less patience for the formality and outdated language that is found in most printed editions of the Bible and most other existing Bible storybooks such as this one. Some of the storybooks include so many minor details and events that the main points can easily be lost for the less patient reader.

There already is an abundance of simpler, smaller Bible storybooks for very young children. This book should be suitable for anyone from an older child to a mature, educated adult. The language is contemporary enough for younger readers but sophisticated enough for anyone. This is a book that can be kept and reread, as it never will be outgrown.

Nearly all of the important stories and lessons of the Bible have been included. The stories "move along" at a fairly rapid pace but without sacrificing important details or events.

The illustrations are often graphic in their depictions. It is hoped that this will hold the modern, visually-oriented reader's interest, even if a few of the images may be a bit violent for the youngest readers. The images represent the works of the greatest Bible illustrators of all time, although they are primarily from the nineteenth century. Each illustration has been restored by removing defects and distortions. In nearly all cases the images have been enhanced by fixing backgrounds and borders and correcting for contrast and balance. The illustrations were selected from a larger pool based on quality and the ability to maintain continuity.

It is hoped that readers will learn that God has a plan for our lives and that we are not here due to a series of astronomical and biological accidents. Each of us is here as part of a larger purpose. God has the power to heal the sick and protect us from any enemy - if we understand and believe.

The Creation of Light

Contents

The Old Testament

Between The Old and New Testaments

The New Testament

The Garden of Eden

Stories of

The Old Testament

In Six Parts

Earth

PART A: THE PATRIARCHS
GENESIS, JOB

A-1 CREATION
GENESIS 1:1 - 2:7

We live on the planet Earth, but the planet Earth did not always exist. Nor did the sky, the sun, the other planets, and the stars. God has always existed.

One day God decided to create Earth. At first our planet was covered in water, and there was only darkness and icy cold.

The next day, God decided to make light because he was planning to create life. All life on Earth receives energy from the sun's light, especially plants, and we need plants for our food.

Then God created the atmosphere and clouds which produce rain. Next he made the waters flow into the seas and oceans. Dry land appeared as the water completely evaporated on higher ground.

Still there was no life. God started by creating the trees, flowers, and grasses. Then he made the sun, the moon, the other planets, and the stars. They produce and reflect light, allowing us to see during the day and night.

The Stars and Planets

On the sixth day of creation, God made fishes in the seas and oceans, animals on land, and birds that live mostly in the sky. God was happy with the animals, and he wanted them to be treated well.

To complete his plan for Earth, God created Adam, the first human. God wanted people to enjoy the planet's animals, plants, and oceans - and to love and worship him. God allowed Adam to name all of the animals.

The Creation of Eve

God could see that Adam needed a helper, and he decided to create the first woman. God caused Adam to fall asleep, and God removed one of Adam's ribs. With the rib he removed, God created another human.

Adam named her Eve and she became his wife. God told them that it was good to be fruitful and multiply, which means to have children.

On the seventh day, God rested. This is why we have one day of rest and worship each week, to honor God and his plan for humanity.

A-2 THE FIRST HOME
GENESIS 2:8 - 3:24

Adam and Eve lived in a large garden where four rivers flowed together. In the middle of the garden, known as the Garden of Eden, God planted the Tree of Life. Anyone who ate the fruit of this tree would live forever.

Adam and Eve were very happy, and they enjoyed the many fruits and vegetables that grew where they lived. They helped to care for the animals

Adam and Eve Enjoying the Garden

and their young. God even spoke to them sometimes, and he listened to their replies.

There was another tree in the garden called the Tree of Knowledge. God told them not to eat the fruit of this tree or they would surely die. Adam and Eve listened to God and did not eat the forbidden fruit.

Adam and Eve Disobeying God

14

Eve began to talk with a snake. The snake, or serpent, told her that God was afraid anyone eating the fruit of the Tree of Knowledge would become as powerful as him, and that was why God said not to eat of the fruit.

After listening more to the snake, Eve ate the fruit, and she convinced Adam to do the same. It didn't take long for them to realize that they had done wrong, and they tried to hide among the trees.

God called out to Adam, "Why are you hiding, Adam? Where are you? Have you eaten the fruit from the Tree of Knowledge?"

"Eve gave me some!" said Adam.

"Why did you do this?" God asked Eve.

"I listened to the snake!" she answered.

God was very angry. He told them that they no longer deserved to live in their garden home because they had sinned, or displeased God, and he placed an angel at the entrance to keep them out.

An Angel Drives Adam and Eve From the Garden

15

God told Eve that she would have pain and trouble her whole life because of her sin. During childbirth she would have to endure great suffering.

God told Adam that he would have to work in the fields for his food. Weeds, thistles, insects, and other pests would make his work more difficult. He would grow older and older, eventually he would die, and his body would become the dust that he was created from.

Adam Working to Survive

God said that even though life would be difficult and we would have to work hard, there was still hope for men and women because he would one day send a Savior to give everyone a chance to be redeemed from sin.

A-3 THE FIRST CHILDREN
GENESIS 4

Adam and Eve had to build a home for themselves outside the garden. They had to work very hard to grow food and feed themselves. It was not easy, but they managed to eat and have simple lives.

God still loved Adam and Eve. However, he could no longer walk and talk with them as he had done before they sinned against him.

Adam and Eve believed in the promise of a Savior. They confessed their sins to God, and they also offered sacrifices to God on altars. They would place wood and their offerings on the altar and then set fire to it.

Soon Eve became pregnant with her first baby. It was a boy named Cain. Her second child was a son named Abel.

Adam and Eve tried to raise their children to live without sin, but sin crept into their lives. Cain grew to have a sinful heart while Abel remained a good person who only wanted to please God.

Cain and Abel Offering Their Sacrifices

Cain was a gardener who raised fruits and grains, and Abel tended a flock of sheep. One day they both gave their offerings to God.

God was happy with Abel's offering of a fat lamb and the fire burnt very strongly. But he wasn't happy with Cain's offering of fruit from his field.

God could see that Cain was angry. God warned him not to be angry but to be sorry for his sins.

One day Cain and Abel began quarreling, and Cain killed Abel. God called to him, "Where is your brother, Cain?"

"I don't know!" answered Cain. God knew what had happened, and he was even more angry that Cain was lying.

God made Cain leave his home forever. He placed a mark on him that everyone could see, and the mark told everyone not to kill Cain because God had already punished him. Cain wandered away to a land called Nod where he lived for many years.

Adam and Eve had other children. Eventually they grew old and died as God had said they would do after eating the forbidden fruit. They all had to work to survive, and life was not that easy, but still they looked to God as their creator.

It was during this time that people began to make and play musical instruments. They often played music to praise and honor God.

Cain Killing Abel

18

Playing Music to Praise God

A-4 THE GREAT FLOOD
GENESIS 5:1 - 9:17

The children of Adam and Eve lived to be very old. Their children also lived for several hundred years. Many generations of people lived and worked together.

Sadly, many of those early people forgot about God and became sinful and wicked. There was one man who wanted to please God. His name was Enoch. Because his heart was not sinful, God talked with him as he took walks. When Enoch was 365 years old, God took him directly to heaven, without having to die first. His son Methuselah lived to be 969 years of age.

By the time Methuselah died, there were many more people living on the Earth, and most of them were wicked and did not care anything about God. God was so disappointed that he planned to destroy everything on the Earth, including the people, animals, and plants. He would cause a great flood of water to cover the Earth and drown everyone.

Then God thought of Noah. Noah had always tried to do right, and he taught his sons to live the same way. Sometimes God talked to Noah. He told him he was preparing to destroy the Earth with a flood, and he told Noah to build a great boat or ark. He was to take his family and two of every type of animal into the ark, and they all would be spared from the flood.

God told Noah how to build the ark. God told him the exact size to make it and the materials to use. Noah followed God's instructions precisely. Others laughed at Noah and his sons. Noah warned them to repent or face their imminent destruction.

Noah led all the animals into the ark, and God himself closed the door once everyone was inside. There was no way for anyone else to get inside the ark.

Soon the rain began to fall. It rained very, very hard, day after day and night after night, until the Earth was covered with water.

Entering the Ark

The Great Flood

People tried desperately to escape the waters, but there was nowhere at all to go. It rained for forty days and nights.

Trying to Escape the Waters

Soon everyone who was not in the ark drowned in the water. Only those animals that lived in the seas and oceans were able to survive.

After the rain stopped, the ark floated on the water for six months. The waters gradually began to dry. The ark stopped atop a mountain one day.

The Ark Rests Atop a Mountain

After resting there for a while, Noah opened a window and sent out a dove. She soon returned to the ark because she could not find any other place to build a nest.

The next week, the dove was sent out again, and this time she returned with an olive branch in her mouth.

Noah knew they soon would be able to leave the ark. God opened the door and told Noah, his sons, and their wives to come out of the ark, along with all the animals.

Noah made a sacrifice to God to show his thanks for sparing his life. God was pleased, and God promised never again to destroy the Earth with a flood.

God made a rainbow for Noah. He told Noah that rainbows would always represent this promise.

The Dove Carries an Olive Branch

Noah's Sacrifice and the Rainbow

A-5 THE TOWER OF BABEL
GENESIS 9:18 - 11:9

Noah's family had the Earth completely to themselves like Adam and Eve's family, with all the plants and animals. His three sons were named Shem, Ham, and Japheth. They had children, and more children, and soon many people inhabited the Earth again.

Building the Tower of Babel

In the land of Shinar where many lived, the people wanted to build a great city with a tower that would reach up into the sky. They began working very hard, making bricks and using mortar to hold them together. It didn't take long for the tower to grow tall.

God saw what they were doing and he was not pleased. They had forgotten entirely about God, and God knew they would become even more proud and sinful after the tower was completed.

Until this time, all the people had spoken the same language. God caused them all to begin speaking many different languages, and they could no longer understand each other.

They separated into small groups, and it was impossible for them to continue working together on the tower because they could not understand each other at all. The city was called Babel, but most of the people left and went to far away places where they eventually started their own nations.

25

The Confusion of Languages

A-6 A Man Who Heard and Obeyed God
Genesis 11:27 - 12:20

The people moved away from Babel, and they began worshiping different gods in their different lands. Some worshiped the sun, moon, or stars, and others worshiped idols they made of wood or stone.

Not far from Babel was the city of Ur, named after the moon god the people of that city worshiped. Near Ur lived an old shepherd who had three sons: Abram, Nahor, and Haran. Abram was a good man and he worshiped God. He made sacrifices and his prayers were answered.

One day Abram heard the voice of God. God told him to gather up his family and his possessions and prepare to leave for a far away promised land. God also promised to bless all of humanity through Abram's family.

Abram was not afraid to go. His entire family - his wife, father, brother and his wife, and nephew, along with their servants - set out on the journey. They brought tents and herds of cattle and sheep. They stopped at a place called Haran. Abram's father died there and was buried. Nahor didn't want to continue the journey, and he stayed in a settlement called Naran.

Abraham Journeying Into the Land of Canaan

27

Abram continued on with the others, heading southwest toward the land of Canaan. They traveled over mountains and through valleys. Finally they came to the plain of Moreh, and God told Abram that this was to be his land. Abram built an altar to worship God.

Abram lived away from the Canaanite people. He pitched his tents where he could find grass for his herds. The number of his cattle and sheep grew very large, and Abram became a rich man.

A famine came to the land. There was very little food and many people had to go hungry. There was no rain, and all the crops and grasses turned brown and died. God told Abram to go to Egypt until the famine was over. A few years later when the famine had ended, he returned to Canaan.

A-7 THE QUARREL BETWEEN ABRAM'S AND LOT'S SERVANTS
GENESIS 1 3

Abram returned to Canaan after the famine. He and his nephew Lot pitched their tents near each other. They both had grown to be very rich men. They not only had sheep and cattle but also large amounts of gold and silver.

They both had servants to care for their sheep and cattle. The servants got into an argument over which sheep and cattle should feed in which pastures. With the Canaanites nearby and their herds and flocks, there really wasn't enough pasture for everyone.

Abram told Lot he thought they should separate into different areas, and he allowed Lot to pick which area he wanted. Lot selfishly chose the area near the Jordan River, leaving the area to the west for his uncle.

God could see that Abram was lonely, and he reminded him that all of Canaan would someday belong to him and his children. God told Abram to explore the land of Canaan.

A-8 LOT'S DECISION
GENESIS 1 4

The land Lot selected for his sheep and cattle was close to the cities of Sodom and Gomorrah. Lot thought he had made a good business decision, since the people in these cities would buy his sheep and cattle, and he would soon have much more silver and gold. But the people in the cities were wicked and cared nothing about God.

One day, Sodom, Gomorrah, and three neighboring cities were defeated in battle, and the invading soldiers took all the people to become slaves, along with all the gold, silver, and everything else they could carry. Lot, his wife, and their children were captured and taken away as captives.

One of the captured men was able to escape and he went to Hebron, where Abram was living. He told Abram what had happened to Lot and his family. Abram, his friends, and 318 of his servants went to find them. In the northern part of Canaan, they found the enemy's camp at a place called Dan. They rushed into the camp at night, and all of the enemy soldiers ran away from their own camp, believing a great army was invading them. They left behind everything they had taken from the cities, including all the slaves.

This was a great victory for Abram, and he was celebrated as a hero in the land of Canaan. The king of Sodom went to meet him. He offered Abram as much gold, silver, food and clothing as he wanted for rescuing them, but Abram wouldn't accept anything.

The king of Salem, the city which later became Jerusalem, was a man who believed in and worshiped God. He came out to meet Abram, accompanied by the king of Sodom.

The king brought food for Abram and asked God to bless him. Because the king was also a priest of the true God, Abram gave him a tenth of everything he had taken from the enemy's camp, once the stolen goods were returned to their owners in the cities. Lot and his wife went back to the city of Sodom, and Abram returned to Hebron.

Abram and the King of Salem

29

Abram was getting old, but he still didn't have any children. God appeared to him in a vision one night. God told him not to be afraid. God said that he would soon have a son, and one day his descendants would number as many as the number of stars in the sky.

Abram's Vision

God also told him that one day his people would be taken away as slaves for 400 years. Afterward they would return to possess Canaan again.

While Abram was traveling, he brought back an Egyptian servant girl named Hagar. She became unhappy after Abram's wife, Sarai, had scolded her and she decided to run away.

An angel appeared to Hagar when she stopped to rest by a fountain in the middle of the wilderness. The angel told her to return home to Abram and Sarai and that she would soon have a son whose name would be Ishmael. He would grow up to be a strong leader.

Hagar knew she could not run from God and she returned home. Soon she had a son that she named Ishmael, which means "God hears."

God appeared to Abram again when he was nearly 100 years old. God told him that he would give him a son if he would remain faithful. God also told him that his name would be Abraham from that time on, which means "the father of many," and Sarai's name would be Sarah, which means "Princess."

It was noon one day and the sun was shining brightly. Abraham sat in the shade near his tent, and he saw three strange-looking men approaching. They appeared to be from a different land. He went out to meet them and urged them to stay and rest for a while. They agreed.

He sent for water to allow them to wash their feet. Abraham asked his wife to prepare some barley cakes, and he prepared a calf for dinner.

As they were leaving, Abraham realized they were heavenly visitors: two angels and God himself, all in the form of humans.

God said that he was going to visit the cities of

Abraham's Visitors

Sodom and Gomorrah in human form to determine whether their sins were as wicked as he had heard. Abraham was afraid for Lot's safety, since he was living in the city of Sodom.

He asked God if he would spare the city if righteous people were living there. Before he left to visit the cities in human form, God said he would spare Sodom if at least ten righteous people were living in the city.

A-11 WHAT HAPPENED TO SODOM
GENESIS 19

As Lot was keeping watch at the gates of Sodom, he saw the two angels in human form approaching. He did not know they were angels, but he knew they were not from Sodom. He invited them to his home. They wanted to stay out longer and continue to see the city, but Lot persuaded them to visit.

News traveled around Sodom that Lot had two strange-looking visitors at his home. Some of the men wanted to hurt the visitors, and they arrived at Lot's home. They tried to push past Lot when he refused to let them come inside to see the visitors.

The angels caused the men to go blind, and Lot realized then that they were angels. He figured out that they had come to destroy Sodom because it was so wicked. The angels ordered Lot, his wife, and daughters to leave. He

Lot's Flight From Sodom

hated leaving all his riches behind, but he had no choice.

The angels warned them not even to look back at the cities while God was destroying them. Lot's wife did not listen to the angels' warning. She looked back and was turned into a pillar of salt.

Lot was afraid to live in the wilderness, and he prayed to God to spare one small city named Zoar. They stayed there for a short time. They were so afraid God would destroy the city that they didn't want to stay there too long. Lot and his family ended up living in a cave in the mountains - after they lost everything they had while living among people who hated God.

A-12 THE LITTLE BOY WHO BECAME A GREAT HUNTER
GENESIS 20 - 21:21

After the destruction of Sodom and the other cities, Abraham moved away from Hebron. He journeyed south and west, and he made his home at a place called Gerar. Soon God gave Abraham and his wife a son, Isaac. His name means 'laughing' in Hebrew, because they were both so happy to have a son in their old age.

Hagar and Ishmael Leave

33

When Isaac was old enough to begin walking and talking a little, Abraham threw a party or feast for him. Many visitors came, and they could see how much Sarah and Abraham loved their baby.

Hagar and her son Ishmael were still living with Abraham and his wife. Ishmael was several years older than the young Isaac. On the day of the feast, Ishmael was very unkind to Isaac, perhaps because he was jealous.

When Sarah heard how badly Isaac had been treated, she asked Abraham to send Hagar and Ishmael away. God also told Abraham to send them away. The next morning, he gave them food and water, and he sent them on their way toward Egypt.

Eventually they ran out of water, and Hagar and Ishmael were becoming very sick. Hagar could not bear to watch Ishmael die and she walked away from him.

God sent an angel to tell her to go back and take care of Ishmael because he would become the father of a great nation. Just then water began bubbling up out of the ground and Hagar filled her water container.

Hagar Finds A Spring of Water

They did not go all the way to Egypt, but instead they decided to make their home in the wilderness. Ishmael had many sons and grandsons, and he was the father of the Arabian people.

A-13 How Abraham Gave Isaac Back to God
Genesis 22:1-20

It is God's will that people show their love for him by their actions. Abraham always tried to do what God commanded him to do.

Abraham loved his young son Isaac very much. He knew that Isaac was part of God's plan for his family. Isaac grew into a youth, and he learned to love and worship God from his father. He learned to pray and to make sacrifices.

The Journey to Moriah

God wanted to test Abraham one more time. He told him to take his son into the land of Moriah, where he was to build an altar and give him back to God as an offering. Abraham was not afraid to obey. Moriah was a long distance away, and he started on the journey with Isaac and two servants. They brought along wood and fire.

After a few days, they could see the mountain where God told Abraham to build the altar. They left the servants, and only Isaac and Abraham continued. "Where is the lamb?" asked Isaac. Abraham told him that God would provide the lamb.

God Tests Abraham's Faith

They built the altar and piled the wood on top. Abraham bound Isaac's hands and feet with cord. As Abraham was about to kill Isaac with a knife, an angel appeared and told him to stop. "It is clear now that you love God more than anything," said the angel.

The Angel Tells Abraham to Stop

Abraham looked up and saw a lamb that was caught in a thicket by its horns. He offered the lamb as a sacrifice to God.

The angel of God continued to speak to Abraham. The angel reminded him that he would be the father of many descendants, as many as the number of stars in the sky. And God would always bless his descendants and the land given to them. Isaac and Abraham returned home knowing that they were important to God.

A-14 How Abraham Found a Wife for Isaac
Genesis 23:1 - 25:18

Sarah died when she was 127 years old. Abraham bought some land with a cave on it and buried her there. It was time for Isaac to get married, but Abraham did not want him to marry one of the idol worshipers from Canaan.

Abraham remembered his brother Nahor who lived in Haran. Nahor had twelve sons and other family. Abraham thought Nahor could help him find a woman who wanted to obey God. He called his trusted servant, Eliezer, and asked him to journey to Haran and try to find a wife for his son Isaac.

The Burial of Sarah

Eliezer knew that the journey might be dangerous and would take several days, but he agreed to go. With ten camels, many servants, and precious gifts, they set out on the journey. Finally they were getting close to Haran, and they came to a well.

Eliezer trusted in God, and he asked God to give him a sign: a woman who would be kind enough to offer water not only for him, but also for his

Eliezer and Rebekah

camels; she would be a good wife for Isaac. A woman did arrive, and she kindly offered to fill pitchers for everyone, including the camels.

She was Rebekah, the granddaughter of Nahor. Eliezer gave her some of the beautiful gifts they had brought. She offered to let them stay at her father's house.

Once there, Eliezer explained why he was there and how God had

Isaac and Rebekah Meet

brought Rebekah to him to be the wife of Isaac, the son of Abraham. He told them Isaac was very rich, and Abraham didn't want him to marry an idol worshiper.

Everyone agreed that Rebekah would go. After a big feast, Eliezer, Rebekah, and the servants set out on the return journey. Before long, Isaac and Rebekah were married.

Abraham died at the age of 175. Ishmael heard the sad news and came to help bury Abraham in the cave next to Sarah.

A-15 Two Boys and Their Father's Blessing
Genesis 25:19 - 27:41

Isaac and Rebekah had two sons. Esau, the older child, had red hair, and he had much hair all over his body.

Jacob was the younger son. He didn't have much hair on his arms, legs, and the rest of his body like Esau had. Isaac favored Esau because they hunted together, and Isaac enjoyed eating venison cooked by Esau.

Firstborn children were entitled to a "birthright," or larger inheritance than the other children in a family because they were the oldest. Jacob knew Esau was to be granted this birthright, and he was jealous of his brother. Jacob tricked Esau into selling his birthright to him in exchange for some food on one occasion when he was very hungry. Esau later regretted this.

Many years later, Isaac's eyes had grown dim with age and he could no longer see. He wanted to give his inheritance to his family before he died. He called Esau to him. He told Esau to go into the woods, catch a deer, and prepare the venison the way that he liked so much, and then he would receive his birthright.

Rebekah overheard this conversation, and she did not think that Esau deserved to receive the birthright because he was not a very righteous man.

Jacob Receives His Father's Blessing

41

She cooked some lamb with the same spices Esau always used, and then she sent Jacob to deliver the meal to Isaac.

Jacob dressed as Esau and wore the skin of an animal on his arms and hands to simulate Esau's body hair. Isaac was surprised that his son had returned so soon with his food. He felt the animal skin on Jacob's hands, and he thought it must be Esau. He gave Esau's inheritance to Jacob.

Then Esau returned. His father was very upset to learn he had given the birthright to the wrong son. But it was too late. Esau was enraged and planned to kill Jacob after their father died, which would have left everything to him.

A-16 JACOB'S JOURNEY AND DREAM
GENESIS 27:42 - 29:12

When Rebekah heard of Esau's intention to kill his brother Jacob as soon as Isaac should die, she sent for Jacob. She told him that he was to go and stay with her brother Laban in Haran until Esau was no longer angry with him.

Rebekah did not tell Isaac about Esau's plan to kill Jacob. She said that Jacob needed to meet a woman who worshipped God, not an idol worshiper like the two women Esau had married. Isaac agreed that this was a good plan, since he wanted Jacob's children to love and worship God.

Jacob set out alone for Haran. When night fell, he became tired and stopped to sleep. He had a dream: a ladder that reached all the way up into heaven. He saw angels climbing up and down the ladder, and he saw God at the top of the ladder.

God spoke to him and told him the land he promised to Abraham's descendants was now to be the land of his many descendants, and through his family all the people of the Earth would be blessed. God promised to stay with him and protect him always.

Jacob awoke. He was alone, but he felt the presence of God.

Later on during his journey, he saw some men taking care of their sheep. They told Jacob they were from Haran, and he knew his uncle was not far away.

Jacob Meeting Rachel

Jacob's Dream

Jacob met a beautiful young woman named Rachel who turned out to be his cousin. Rachel hurried home to tell her father, Laban, that his sister's son had arrived.

A-17 HOW LABAN DECEIVED JACOB
GENESIS 29:13 - 31:55

Laban hurried out to meet his nephew. Jacob helped his uncle with his work for many days. Laban offered to pay him for his help, and he asked Jacob to tell him how much he wanted. "I will work for you for seven years if you will give me your beautiful daughter Rachel to marry," Jacob told him.

Jacob Working for Laban

44

Jacob worked for the full seven years and then the wedding was arranged. The bride's face was covered by a veil, as was the custom in that part of the world. Jacob thought he was marrying Rachel, but it turned out when the wedding was over that he had married Leah, Rachel's older sister.

He was not happy that he had married Leah instead of Rachel. Laban explained that the oldest daughter must always be married before the younger daughters.

Jacob asked if he could work another seven years and then marry Rachel, as he originally planned. Laban agreed, since men were allowed to have more than one wife at that time. Jacob did marry Rachel after seven more years. Laban did not want him to leave, but Jacob knew he had to go back to Canaan. Once again Jacob had a dream, and this time an angel spoke to him. The angel told him to prepare to leave for Canaan at once.

Jacob Returning to Canaan

Fearing that Laban wouldn't let him leave, he left in secret with Leah and Rachel. Laban learned that they had left and he started to pursue them.

Then God spoke to Laban and warned him not to interfere with Jacob's plans. The warning from God caused Laban to become less angry by the time he found their encampment.

Jacob, Laban and the other men gathered stones together to form a pillar and also a large pile of rocks. This was called a Mizpah, or "watchtower." Laban wished Jacob and his family well, and he turned back toward Haran. Jacob, his wives, and their children continued on their journey to Canaan.

A-18 WHY JACOB'S NAME WAS CHANGED TO ISRAEL
GENESIS 32 - 35

Jacob's Prayer

Twenty years had passed since Jacob left Canaan, but he didn't know whether Esau had forgiven him for taking his inheritance. Jacob prayed to God and asked for help, and God sent angels to comfort him and give him courage.

Jacob sent some messengers to find Esau and tell him that he would be arriving soon. Esau had moved from Canaan to Edom, and he was planning to bring 400 men to meet Jacob.

This worried Jacob, and he didn't know whether Esau still planned to kill him. He divided his family into two groups, and he sent a gift of camels, oxen, sheep, and asses on ahead for his brother.

Jacob Wrestling the Angel

When it became dark, someone grabbed Jacob and wrestled with him. They wrestled all night, but neither gained an advantage over the other.

In the morning, Jacob could see that he had been wrestling with an angel. The angel told him his name was now "Israel," which means "A prince of God."

Jacob and Esau Meet

Jacob joined everyone else, and soon he saw his brother coming toward him. They bowed and embraced each other. Jacob told Esau how he had been blessed in Haran, and he introduced his wives and children. Esau accepted his gift of camels, oxen, sheep, and asses.

After visiting for a while, Esau returned to Edom, and Jacob bought some land near Bethel and set up an altar. God appeared to him again, telling him that he should only be known as Israel from that time forward and that his descendants would include kings.

From Bethel, they traveled toward Hebron, where Isaac still lived. Rachel died before they arrived, leaving a tiny baby boy, Benjamin. Jacob buried her and they continued on toward Hebron.

Isaac was overjoyed when Jacob returned with twelve sons and a daughter. But Isaac did not live much longer. He soon died at the age of 180. Esau returned home to help Jacob bury their father.

A-19 HOW JACOB'S FAVORITE SON BECAME A SLAVE
GENESIS 37

Joseph was Jacob's favorite son out of twelve sons. Unlike his brothers, he was always careful to do right. Jacob made Joseph a special coat of many colors to show him how much he loved him. It was more beautiful than any of his brothers' coats.

His brothers became jealous because they knew their father favored Joseph the most. When Joseph told Jacob about some of their wrong actions, they disliked their little brother even more.

Joseph's Second Dream

Joseph was now about seventeen years old. He had a dream and told his brothers about it. "We were together in the field binding sheaves," he said, "and my sheaf stood upright while yours bowed down around it." His brothers thought this meant he would rule over them one day, and they hated that idea.

Joseph had another dream in which the sun, moon, and eleven stars all bowed down before him. He told his father and brothers about the dream. Jacob believed it meant that he would someday bow before his son, and this thought displeased him.

Jacob was living at Hebron, where Abraham had lived with his flocks and herds. There was not enough land for all of the animals to feed, and Abraham sent his ten eldest sons to Shechem with their cattle and sheep.

Joseph Is Thrown Into a Pit

After several weeks Jacob sent Joseph to learn whether they had found suitable land for the animals.

When Joseph arrived at Shechem, he could not find his brothers. A man told him his brothers had gone to Dothan, where the pastures were better. Joseph then traveled on to Dothan to continue searching for his brothers.

The brothers saw him coming in his brightly colored coat. Most of them wanted to kill him because they were jealous of the way he was treated.

They decided to throw him into a pit and let him die. First they tore off his coat. His oldest brother, Reuben, intended to go back and rescue him.

Joseph Is Sold by His Brothers

While Reuben was working in a different part of the field, some Ishmaelite travelers passed by, and the other brothers ended up selling Joseph as a slave for twenty pieces of silver.

Reuben tried to find Joseph, and he discovered that he was gone from the pit. He felt very bad that he had allowed something terrible to happen to his little brother.

The brothers decided to dip Joseph's coat in goat's blood and tell their father that a wild animal had killed him. Jacob believed their story and he was very sad, believing that his most beloved son had died a painful death.

Showing Joseph's Coat to Their Father

A-20 Joseph a Prisoner in Egypt
Genesis 37:36 - 40:23

The Ishmaelites arrived in Egypt with Joseph after a long journey. The Egyptians wore unfamiliar clothing, spoke an unrecognized language, and worshiped idols. It must have seemed like a very strange world to Joseph.

They took Joseph to the city where the king lived, and they sold him to an officer in the king's army. Joseph realized that he should try to do his best to please his new master. He remembered the dreams he had and he knew that God must still have a plan for him.

Potiphar was the name of the Egyptian officer who bought Joseph as a slave. He was very rich and owned many other slaves. Joseph soon learned the Egyptian language. He stood out among all the slaves because of his cheerful attitude, good character, and business sense. Potiphar soon made him responsible for the finances and management of the entire household.

Joseph in Prison

Potiphar's wife wanted to get Joseph in trouble after he refused her efforts to seduce him, and she falsely accused him of immoral behavior.

He was thrown in jail because Potiphar believed his wife's lie. In prison, Joseph kept his cheerful and helpful attitude. Soon he was given responsibility over the other prisoners.

Joseph helped to interpret the dreams of the other prisoners, the chief butler and the chief baker. He made many friends there.

A-21 Joseph a Ruler in Egypt
Genesis 41

One morning Pharaoh called all of the wise men of Egypt together to tell him the meaning of two strange dreams he had. None of them could tell him. The chief butler, who had been in prison with Joseph, told Pharaoh about Joseph's ability to interpret dreams, and Pharaoh sent for Joseph.

Joseph shaved and put on clean clothes before going to see Pharaoh. Pharaoh anxiously asked him for help with the meaning of his two dreams. Joseph explained that the power to interpret the dreams came from God, and he said he would ask his God for help.

Joseph Interpreting Pharaoh's Dreams

Pharaoh said he was standing by the Nile River in his first dream, and he saw seven fat cattle come up out of the river and feed in the green meadow. Later he saw seven other cattle that were very lean come up out of the water. They thin cattle ate the fat cattle, but still they were lean.

In his second dream, he saw seven ears of corn growing up out of a stalk. Then seven more ears grew next to them, but they were withered and thin. The thin ears devoured the healthy ears.

Joseph explained that the dreams meant there would be seven plentiful harvests followed by seven years of famine. God was warning him to begin saving food for the famine; otherwise every living creature would die.

Pharaoh thought Joseph must be a very wise man and that his God must be powerful, and he decided to make Joseph ruler of all of Egypt. Pharaoh dressed him in royal robes and a gold chain.

Pharaoh gave him his second-best chariot, and he rode through the streets of the city to be honored by everyone. He was still a kind man with a good heart, even after he had so much power and wealth. Joseph and his wife had

Joseph Dressed in Royal Clothes

Joseph in Pharaoh's Chariot

two sons.

When the seven years of prosperity had elapsed, the famine began. The Egyptians survived because of Joseph's careful planning and storehouses filled with food. He worked very hard as ruler and gained much respect.

A-22 HOW JOSEPH'S DREAMS CAME TRUE
GENESIS 42

In the land of Canaan the famine was having an effect. Jacob and his sons were rich in gold but they were running out of food. They had heard grain could be bought in Egypt, and Jacob sent his ten eldest sons to buy food.

The youngest son, Benjamin, stayed at home with Jacob. The older brothers regretted what they had done to Joseph and they were kind to Benjamin, even though their father cared for him the most.

In Egypt, Joseph was the person who sold food to anyone who wanted to buy it. His ten brothers bowed before him humbly, hoping he would grant their request. Joseph's brothers did not recognize him, but Joseph recognized his brothers, and he knew that his dream from long ago had come true.

Joseph wanted to learn whether his brothers' hearts were still wicked. In the Egyptian language, he accused them of being spies. He said he would keep one of them in jail, Simeon, the second-oldest, and the other nine would have to return later with their youngest brother Benjamin before Simeon would be freed and allowed to return home.

Joseph Accuses His Brothers of Being Spies

Joseph's brothers didn't know he spoke their language, and he heard them talking about how they were being punished for the way they treated their brother they had sold into slavery. Joseph was very glad and relieved to hear that they were sorry for what they had done to him years earlier.

Unpacking the Moneybags

They returned to Canaan, but Jacob refused to allow them to take Benjamin to Egypt. The brothers discovered that their empty moneybags had been replaced with different moneybags that were filled with money, even though they had spent all their money on the food they purchased. They were afraid that they would be accused of stealing when they returned.

A-23 Joseph Makes Himself Known to his Brothers
Genesis 43:1 - 45:24

The famine continued in Canaan. There was not a drop of rain or even dew on the parched grass. Every source of water dried up. Eventually all of the food that Jacob's sons had brought from Egypt was nearly eaten. Jacob told them to go to Egypt again and buy more food.

Judah told Jacob they would never get more food until they brought their youngest brother, Benjamin, to the ruler in Egypt. Jacob was angry that they had even mentioned their younger brother. He was unwilling to let Benjamin go with the other brothers even though their food supply was running out.

Judah begged Jacob to let them leave with Benjamin. Reuben, the oldest brother, told Jacob to kill his own two sons if they did not return safely with Benjamin.

Finally Jacob agreed to let them go, and they prepared for the journey. They gathered presents for the leader in Egypt, and this time they brought twice as much money in case they were accused of stealing during their previous visit.

Joseph was pleased when he saw that they had returned to Egypt with their youngest brother Benjamin. He ordered his servants to prepare a feast at his home for all of them.

The brothers did not understand what was going on because they did not speak the Egyptian language, and they were afraid that they were being accused of stealing. A servant told them not to be afraid and that nothing bad would happen to them. Simeon was brought out of prison and they were all told they were going to have dinner with Joseph.

Joseph arrived to meet them at his home, and he asked if their father was still alive. He was happy to see Benjamin, and he had to restrain himself from hugging him. The brothers were beginning to feel more comfortable. They were glad Simeon was well, and they hoped they would soon all be returning to their father with the food supply that they so badly needed.

Three tables were set. Joseph sat by himself at one table, other guests sat at the second table, and the third table was for the brothers. They were all assigned places according to their ages, from oldest to youngest, and the brothers thought it was strange that Joseph apparently knew their ages.

Joseph sent food to them from his table, but Benjamin's portion was five times as large as the other brothers' portions. Perhaps Joseph wanted to see if they would be jealous of Benjamin, as they had been jealous of him. Joseph told his servant to fill their bags with corn and to put their money back in their moneybags, as he had done before. This time Joseph told the

Putting the Silver Cup in Benjamin's Bag

servant to put his own silver cup in Benjamin's bag.

The brothers began to leave for home the next morning. Joseph sent his servant to recover the silver cup, and he accused the brothers of stealing it. They pleaded with him and explained that they tried to pay back the extra money they had in their moneybags after their first visit.

They even said that if one of them had the cup, that brother should die, and all the rest of them would become servants in Egypt. Joseph's servant said that would not be necessary: if the cup were found in someone's bag, that brother would remain in Egypt as a servant, and all the others could return home.

The search began with Reuben, the oldest brother, and ended with Benjamin. The cup was found in Benjamin's bag where Joseph's servant had put it. All the brothers were astonished at the discovery. They didn't know what to do, and they thought someone was trying to get them in trouble.

They knew they couldn't return home without Benjamin, and they returned to Joseph and begged him to let Benjamin return home to see his father. Joseph said that wouldn't be possible, but all the others could leave. Joseph was testing them to find out whether they would be willing to let Benjamin suffer.

Finding the Cup in Benjamin's Bag

Judah fell on his face at Joseph's feet. He explained how their old father did not want to let Benjamin go with them, but they convinced him to do so. Judah said their father would probably die of grief if they returned without Benjamin. Judah begged Joseph to let him stay in Benjamin's place; otherwise their dear father would die.

Judah's words touched Joseph's heart deeply. He sounded so much different compared to how he sounded when he wanted to sell little Joseph to the Ishmaelites as a slave. Joseph realized that all of the brothers were better people now, and he longed to hug them. He quickly ordered his Egyptian servants to leave the room. Turning to his brothers, he said to them in their own language, "I am your brother Joseph. Is my father still alive?"

The brothers were so surprised and afraid that they could say nothing. Joseph told them everything that happened was part of God's plan to keep their family alive. He explained that the famine would continue for five more years and that they would have to move all of their families to Egypt where they would be provided with food. He then embraced all of his brothers.

Joseph's servants told Pharaoh that his brothers were in Egypt, and Pharaoh urged Joseph to send for his father also. Joseph's brothers began their journey home, this time with a gift of twenty asses loaded with food as a gift from Joseph to his father.

Joseph Reveals His Identity to His Brothers

Joseph gave each of his brothers a gift of Egyptian clothes. He gave Benjamin five times as much as he gave to the others, and he also gave Benjamin a gift of three hundred pieces of silver.

Jacob had been waiting anxiously for his sons for what seemed like a long time. At last a messenger arrived at his tent and told him that they had all returned safely, along with great treasures from Egypt.

Jacob did not know what he meant, so he hurried out to see for himself. He saw wagons loaded with provisions, and more provisions were being carried by a herd of asses. Jacob did not care so much about these things when he saw that Benjamin had arrived home safely.

Jacob Sees Everyone Arriving With the Gifts

Many of the men began to tell everyone how their lost brother Joseph was now the ruler of Egypt and how Joseph wanted them to return along with their wives, their children, and of course their father. Jacob could hardly believe what he heard. Then he saw the gifts Joseph had sent for him, and he believed.

He decided that he should go and see his lost son before he died. Jacob, his sons' wives, and all the children rode in the wagons Joseph had sent, while the men drove the herds of animals.

One night they made camp at Beersheba, where Abraham and Isaac had lived many years before. Jacob offered sacrifices to God, as his father and grandfather had done. God spoke to him in a dream and told him not to be afraid to go to Egypt; that his family would grow to be very powerful and one day would be returned to the land promised to Abraham; and that he would soon see his lost son Joseph in Egypt.

Jacob Travels to Egypt to See His Son Joseph

After this time, Jacob was called Israel, the name God gave to him when he wrestled with the angel. His children were called Israelites. The Israelites numbered sixty-seven when they arrived in Egypt. When Joseph and his two sons were included, the Israelites numbered seventy.

Before entering the city, they decided to make camp and send Judah to tell Joseph of their arrival. Joseph sent a guide to lead them into the land of Goshen. He prepared his royal chariot, and he rode into Goshen to meet his father and relatives.

Both Jacob and his son Joseph wept with joy when they saw each other. Joseph decided to bring five of his brothers and his father to see Pharaoh, the king.

Joseph Meeting His Father

Pharaoh was glad to see them. When he learned that they were shepherds, he told them they could live in the land of Goshen, which was very fertile land. While the famine lasted Joseph continued to provide food for his family and their herds.

After a while, the Egyptian people had spent all of the money they had saved to buy food. Joseph told them to sell their cattle to Pharaoh, and they all did this. Then they ran out of money again. Joseph told them to sell their lands and farms to the king, and they did this also. When that money finally ran out, they were forced to sell themselves as servants to Pharaoh.

64

Joseph Presenting His Father to Pharaoh

When the seven years of famine had ended, Joseph sent the farmers back to the fields with seed to plant. He told them to care for their crops, just as they had done before. When they harvested, one-fifth was to go to Pharaoh, and the other four-fifths could be kept for food and used to plant the following year.

After the famine ended, Joseph's people continued living in Goshen. Israel was 130 years old when he left Canaan, and he lived seventeen more years in Goshen. Before he died, he asked his sons to bury his body in Canaan, at the cave of Machpelah, where Abraham and Isaac were buried. Then he gave each of his sons a parting blessing.

Joseph brought his two children, Manasseh and Ephriam, to see their old grandfather and to receive his blessing also. Israel said he was so lucky to see the faces of his grandsons, after he thought Joseph had been killed. He blessed the younger grandson with more than his older brother, telling Joseph this wasn't a mistake and that the younger son would become greater.

Israel gave each of the boys some of the inheritance that was to have been for his own sons.

After Israel died, Joseph commanded the Egyptian physicians to embalm his father's body for burial. This would take forty days to complete. The people spent seventy days mourning Israel's death. Joseph asked Pharaoh for permission to go to Canaan and help bury his father.

When everyone returned to Goshen to help bury Jacob, who was called Israel, the brothers were afraid that Joseph had treated them well only because his father had been alive. They thought he might still punish them for selling him into slavery.

They sent a messenger to Joseph, begging forgiveness. Joseph wept when he heard this message. He knew his brothers feared he might harm them now that their father had died. He called the brothers to him, and he told them that only God should punish people. He told them that he planned only to care for them and their children.

Embalming Jacob

Over time, Joseph's family increased in number until they became a strong nation. Joseph cared for them as long as he lived. He knew his life was nearly over when he reached the age of 110.

He called the old men of Israel together and told them he was going to die. He told them God would protect them and eventually lead them back to the land of their fathers, and he asked to be buried in Canaan. The men wept when they heard this, and they promised to obey his wishes and trust in God.

Job was a good man who lived in the country of Uz, which was to the east of Egypt. He had many thousands of camels, cattle and asses. He was very rich and had many servants. Job had seven sons and three daughters.

Job

Even though Job was rich and had many possessions, he always tried to do the right thing and he often thought about God. Many of his neighbors worshiped the sun and the moon, but Job believed that God created all that we see, including the sun and the moon. He built altars and made sacrifices to God. He prayed and asked God to forgive his sins and bless him.

Everyone respected Job as the greatest man in his country. The young, the old, and the poor all stopped to ask for his help because they knew that he would help people who were in trouble.

After Job's sons were grown, they had homes of their own where they often had great feasts. They always invited their brothers and sisters to the feasts. Job wondered whether they loved God as he did, and he prayed for God to forgive their sins as well as his own.

God blessed Job with much health and happiness. He gave him many friends and great honors. God blessed Job because he knew Job's heart was

Job Hears of His Ruin

pure and true.

One day Satan began to speak against Job. He said, "Job serves God only because God blesses him. If he had troubles instead of riches, he would quickly turn away from God."

God did not believe Satan's words because he knew better. Satan wanted to trouble Job. He sent bad men from other countries to steal many of his animals. They even killed his servants. Then a great storm came and killed all of Job's sons and daughters while they were attending a feast.

When Job heard about all of this, he tore his clothes as a sign of grief and fell down on his face. But he continued to praise God as he always had done before.

Satan planned to cause even more trouble for Job. Satan wanted Job to be so miserable that he would want to die. Many people believed their troubles were punishment from God for their sins.

Job and His Three Friends

Satan thought Job would believe this, and he caused large, ugly sores to break out all over Job's body. The sores were very painful. They were so horrible that even Job's wife hoped he would die instead of continuing to suffer.

Three rich men who had been friends

Job's Friends Blame Him for His Troubles

of Job's for many years came to see him. They had heard about his troubles and they wanted to comfort him. At first, they didn't even recognize him because of the sores covering his face and body.

They sat down next to him, but they didn't say anything to him for several days because they thought God must have been punishing him for something. Finally they told him to confess his sins to God instead of trying to hide his sins. This made Job even sadder.

Then God spoke to Job out of a whirlwind, and Job bowed down and worshiped. He didn't think he was great or good in the eyes of God. God told Job he was pleased with him, but he was not pleased with his three friends. God told those three men to make sacrifices for their sins and to ask Job to pray for them. God caused Job's sores to become dry, and soon his body was well again.

God blessed Job in many ways. Every year he grew richer, until soon he was twice as rich as he had been before Satan started to trouble him. And God gave him seven sons and three daughters again. Those daughters were the most beautiful women in the country.

Once again God blessed Job with health, happiness, friends and riches. He lived to be a very, very old man, and he always continued to try to help those in need.

Job Restored to Health and Prosperity

PART B: MOSES
EXODUS, LEVITICUS, NUMBERS, DEUTERONOMY

B-1 HOW MOSES LIVED IN THE KING'S PALACE
EXODUS 1:1 – 2:10

The Israelites, who were all descendants of Jacob, had been living in Goshen for a long time. They had grown very large in number, and the current Pharaoh was not friendly toward them as the Pharaoh of Joseph's time had been.

Israelites Working

71

Pharaoh worried that eventually the Israelites would be able to overtake the Egyptian army if they kept growing in number. However, Pharaoh did not want them to leave Goshen; if they left, he wouldn't be able to use them as slaves any longer.

He made them work very hard building new cities, but the Israelites only grew stronger and were not discouraged. He passed a new law, stating that all Israelite baby boys must be thrown into the Nile River. He hoped this would keep their population from growing too large for him to control.

Moses Left in the Nile

When Moses was born, his mother believed in God and thought it would be wrong to kill a baby. She hid Moses for three months. She made a waterproof basket to hide him in, and she placed the basket with Moses inside among the grasses and bulrushes in the river.

One day, Pharaoh's daughter and her friends were by the river's bank. She found baby Moses. She knew that he must be an Israelite baby, but she did not agree with her father's command to kill all the baby boys. She decided to adopt Moses and raise him as her own son.

Pharaoh's Daughter Finds Moses

The Child Moses

The princess allowed Moses's mother to nurse him until he was old enough to go to the palace. He went to the best schools and was prepared to someday occupy the Egyptian throne.

B-2 WHY MOSES LIVED IN THE WILDERNESS
EXODUS 2:11-25

When Moses grew into a young man, he did not forget that he was an Israelite. Sometimes he would go out into the fields where his people worked. He felt sad, seeing them treated cruelly, but he thought that God had spared him from death so that he might someday help the Israelites.

Moses Sees an Egyptian and an Israelite Fighting

One day, Moses saw an Egyptian and an Israelite fighting. He killed the Egyptian and buried him in the sand. After this incident, it became clear to Moses that the Israelite people were not grateful and did not respect him or look to him for help. They did not even keep the death of the Egyptian a secret, and Moses feared that Pharaoh would find out and punish him.

Moses decided to hide in the wilderness. He came to a well where seven sisters were gathering water. Some wicked shepherds came along and tried to drive them away. Moses stood up for the sisters and they were grateful.

Moses was invited to the home of the sisters, and eventually he married one sister. He became a shepherd and worked there for many years.

A new Pharaoh became the king of Egypt. He was even crueler to the Israelites than the previous Pharaoh had been. The Israelites prayed for God to ease their suffering. God heard their prayers, and he remembered his promises to Abraham, Isaac, and Jacob.

Forty years had passed since Moses went away to the wilderness. His brother Aaron still thought Moses was going to be a hero to his people, after the way God had saved him from death when he was young. Aaron went out into the wilderness, hoping to find his brother and somehow help his people.

B-3 How God Spoke to Moses From a Burning Bush
Exodus 3, 4

One day, Moses was taking care of his father-in-law's sheep, and he saw a flame coming from a bush on the mountainside. He watched as the bush continued to burn and the fire did not burn out. He continued to watch it and then he moved closer.

A voice spoke to him, "Do not come near the bush, and take off your shoes, for you are standing on holy ground." Moses understood at once that God was speaking to him. He removed his sandals and was afraid to look directly at the bush.

"I am the God of Abraham, of Isaac, and of Jacob," the voice continued, "and I have seen the suffering of my people the Israelites here in Egypt. Now I am ready to deliver

The Burning Bush

them from the Egyptians and return them to the land I promised to their fathers."

The voice told Moses that he was to go to Pharaoh to lead his people out, and that God would be with him the whole time. Moses was afraid his own people would not believe it.

God told him, "Tell them that my name is I AM, the one who is always living." They were to ask Pharaoh to be allowed to go into the wilderness for three days to worship their God. At first he would refuse, God said, but eventually Pharaoh would want them out of his land.

Moses still doubted that his own people would believe him. God told him to throw down his rod. It instantly turned into a snake. Moses ran, but God told him not to be afraid. God said to pick up the snake by the tail. Moses grabbed the snake's tail and it turned back into a rod.

Moses's Rod Turns Into a Serpent

God told him to put his hand inside his pocket. When he removed it, his hand was covered with leprosy and Moses became frightened. God told him to put his hand back inside his pocket and take it out again. When he did this, his hand was completely healed. God told Moses that he could use the signs of the snake and the hand with leprosy to make his own people believe.

Moses still doubted his own ability to speak in public. God told him not to worry and that he was the one who gave all men the ability to speak. God said he would send his brother Aaron with him. Moses was surprised to hear from God that Aaron was on the way to meet him.

Moses returned the flocks of sheep to Jethro, his father-in-law, and he told him he had to go and see his people. Jethro told him that he could go. Moses took his wife and sons and started traveling toward Goshen, where the Israelites lived. On the way, he met Aaron and the two continued together.

The elders of the Israelite people believe Moses was to be their deliverer after seeing the signs and hearing what God had said to him. They were happy that God was answering their prayers.

B-4 Moses and Aaron Talk With Pharaoh
Exodus 5:1 – 7:24

One day a messenger came to Pharaoh and told him that two men wanted to see the king. Pharaoh agreed to see them.

Moses and Aaron told Pharaoh that God wanted the Israelite people to worship him in the wilderness and that he must let the Israelites go. Pharaoh said he did not know the God of the Hebrews, and he had no reason to obey.

Moses and Aaron Before Pharaoh

Moses and Aaron told Pharaoh that the Egyptians would be plagued with terrible diseases and problems if he did not let the Israelites go into the wilderness for three days to worship God. Pharaoh still did not take them seriously, and he sent them away.

He commanded the taskmasters to make the slaves work even harder. They were making bricks, and Pharaoh said that now they would have to gather their own hay to go into the bricks instead of having it brought to

The Israelites and Their Egyptian Taskmasters

them. They were whipped when they could not make enough bricks in a day, and the people began to doubt the ability of Moses and Aaron to help them.

God told Moses to return to Pharaoh. He said to show the signs and God would perform other miracles. Moses began to understand that he would have to speak to Pharaoh more than one time before his people would be released.

Moses and Aaron went to see Pharaoh a second time. Moses threw down his cane and it turned into a snake. Some other sorcerers made their canes turn into snakes. The snake that had been Moses's cane ate the other snakes and turned back into a cane. Pharaoh was impressed, but still he sent them away.

The next morning, Moses and Aaron met Pharaoh near the bank of the Nile River. Pharaoh was becoming irritated at being bothered so often, but

Moses's Cane Turns Into a Snake

Moses and Aaron were not afraid. Moses told Pharaoh that God had commanded them to show him another sign. Aaron waved his rod over the waters, and the entire Nile River turned from water into blood.

Moses's Snake Eats the Others

All the fish died and a terrible odor filled the air. Aaron stretched his rod toward the other rivers, lakes, and streams and they all turned to blood as well. Pharaoh's magicians were able to change water in a glass to blood, and then the king turned away and went back to his palace. The people were alarmed because they had no water at all.

B-5 Pharaoh Sees God's Signs and Miracles
Exodus 7:25 – 10:29

A full week passed before God lifted the plague of blood from the waters of Egypt. Then Moses and Aaron went to see Pharaoh again.

They told him that God was preparing another plague. Aaron stretched out his rod over the waters of the Nile, and millions of frogs came hopping out of the water and covered much of the land.

Moses Warns Pharaoh

They went inside people's homes, including the palace. Pharaoh's magicians were able to make a few frogs hop out of water, but not many.

Pharaoh was very troubled. He hid his fear about the blood, but the frogs were too much for him to take. He told Moses and Aaron that he would let the people go into the wilderness to make sacrifices if God would stop the frogs. The next day, all the frogs died.

But Pharaoh did not keep his promise. He grew stubborn and refused to let the people go. This time, Aaron struck his rod on the ground, and lice and fleas appeared everywhere. Even Pharaoh's magicians could not repeat this miracle when they tried. Still Pharaoh would not listen.

Then Moses and Aaron warned Pharaoh that flies would fill all of Egypt, except the houses of the Israelites, if he did not let them go. When the flies came, Pharaoh told Moses to have his people make sacrifices in Goshen.

Moses explained that this was not what God wanted and that they must take a journey of three days' time.

The next plague was a disease that killed the animals of the Egyptians, but the animals which belonged to the Israelites were not harmed. After that, boils appeared on all the Egyptians, and the magicians could no longer stand before Pharaoh because of the painful boils on their feet.

The Disease That Killed the Egyptian Animals

Moses warned Pharaoh that the greatest trouble he had ever seen in Egypt would come the next day if Pharaoh had not let the Israelites go by then. Moses and Aaron told the Israelites to shelter and protect all of their possessions including their animals.

The next day, a storm of giant hailstones and non-stop lightning destroyed anything that was not protected. Pharaoh begged Moses to make it stop, but again he broke his promise and refused to let the Israelites leave.

God told Moses that more plagues would be necessary before Pharaoh would let the Israelites leave Egypt. The next plague would be locusts, and they would eat up every living crop. Moses stretched out his hand, and clouds of locusts soon covered everything.

82

The Plague of Hail (above) and The Plague of Frogs (below)

The Plague of Locusts

The next plague was three days and nights of darkness. It was completely dark except for inside the homes of the Israelites. Pharaoh offered to let the Israelites leave - but only if they would leave their flocks and herds behind. Moses said they would take everything with them when they left Egypt.

Pharaoh became very angry and said that he would kill Moses if he ever saw him again. Moses told Pharaoh that he would never see him again, but he would let the Israelites go after one more terrible plague.

B-6 THE DEATH ANGEL VISITS PHARAOH'S PALACE
EXODUS 11 – 13

God told Moses to tell the Israelites to prepare to leave Goshen on short notice. That night, each family was to kill a lamb and sprinkle the blood around their door. The wives were to cook vegetables to be served with the lambs. Moses told them God said an angel was to pass over at midnight, and the angel would enter any house without the blood around the door. The angel would kill the oldest child in the house. They were to eat the lamb and vegetables at midnight. This would give them energy for the long journey they would soon start.

The Destroying Angel

None of the Egyptians sprinkled blood around their doors, and the eldest child was killed in every home. Even Pharaoh's oldest child was dead when Pharaoh went to check on him. Screaming and crying could be heard from homes all over Egypt. Pharaoh knew this was the result of the Hebrew God.

Pharaoh's Own Son Is Killed

85

The Israelites Leave Goshen

He sent a messenger to tell Moses and Aaron to have their people leave Egypt at once and to take everything with them. The Egyptians were so eager to have them leave that they gave them money, gold, and jewels.

Early that morning, the 600,000 Israelites set out from Goshen with all of their animals and possessions. They also carried the coffin of Joseph, who had asked to be buried in Canaan. God led their path during the day with a cloud that they could all see, and at night he guided their way with a pillar of fire.

B-7 God Shows His Power at the Red Sea
Exodus 14:1 – 15:21

After they left Goshen, the cloud led the Israelites to the edge of the Red Sea, where they camped. Suddenly someone cried out that Pharaoh's army was approaching. The people were very frightened since they were not trained or prepared to fight. They blamed Moses for their predicament.

Moses prayed to God for help. God told him to stretch out his rod over the water. Suddenly the water was parted into two halves, with a dry path

The Egyptian Army in Pursuit

allowing the Israelites to cross. They crossed the Red Sea with the army close behind. When the Egyptian army was crossing, God caused the waters to return and Pharaoh's soldiers were all drowned. The people felt truly delivered, now that their oppressors had been destroyed.

The Red Sea Closes and Kills the Egyptian Army

B-8 THE WILDERNESS OF SHUR
EXODUS 15:22-27

After crossing the Red Sea, the Israelites began marching across the Wilderness of Shur. The land was very dry, and they were running out of water. Finally they found a spring at a place called Marah. They tasted the water and it was too bitter to drink. Once again, they were ready to blame Moses for their troubles.

Moses asked God for help. God told him what to do. Moses cut down a tree and threw it into the spring. The water became sweet. Everyone including all the animals had plenty to drink. God promised that the people would not suffer from the diseases the Egyptians had suffered from if they would trust in him.

After leaving there, the Israelites found another stopping place called Elim. It had twelve wells of water and beautiful palm trees. The Israelites were happy to have a pleasant place to camp.

B-9 HOW GOD FED THE PEOPLE IN THE WILDERNESS
EXODUS 16

After staying at Elim for several days, the cloud began to slowly move away. The people understood it was time for them to leave. They entered

Gathering Manna

a great desert. They could not find any food, and they blamed Moses and Aaron. Some even said that they wished they had stayed in Egypt.

God said he would send them meat in the evening and bread in the morning. Quails flew into the camp and were captured for the evening meal.

The next morning, the ground was covered with a strange white bread which they called manna. God continued to give them manna six mornings per week, every morning except the Sabbath day, until they reached Canaan.

B-10 GOD SHOWS HIS POWER AT REPHIDIM
EXODUS 17, 18

After they left the wilderness, the Israelites arrived at a place called Rephidim. The cloud stopped moving and hovered, telling the Israelites that they should stay there and camp.

Even though the people had plenty of bread, there was no water and they began to complain. They asked Moses to help but he couldn't do anything himself. Moses prayed to God for help with finding water.

God told him to take the leader of each tribe to Mount Horeb. Moses was to strike a certain rock with his rod while the men watched. When Moses struck the rock with his rod, water sprang forth and flowed down the mountain, all the way down to where the people were camping.

Water Flows From the Rock After Moses Strikes It

Water Flowing From the Rock to the Camp

There was enough water for everyone in the camp, and they all filled their water containers to have water for the future. Once again God had helped the Israelites.

Aaron and Hur Helping Moses

Near where the Israelites were camped lived a barbaric people called the Amalekites. They attacked the Israelites and tried to steal their belongings. Moses chose a brave young man named Joshua to lead the army of Israel against the enemy.

While they were fighting, Moses stretched out his arms and prayed for God to help his people win. In one hand he held the rod he had used to perform miracles. The Israelites were winning the battle, but Moses began to grow tired and couldn't hold up his arms any longer. When he dropped his arms, he could see that the enemy started to win.

Aaron and Hur were with him, and they helped to hold up his arms until Joshua and his men had won the battle. Everyone returned to the camp and knew that God had helped them to drive away their enemies that day.

B-11 A Voice From a Smoking Mountain
Exodus 19 – 24

Moses moved the camp to the wilderness near Mount Horeb, which was also called Mount Sinai. While the people were busy arranging their tents and preparing food, Moses climbed the mountain to talk with God. God told Moses to tell the people to wash their clothes, and God would speak to them from the mountain in three days. The people listened and were busy gathering water and washing their dirty clothes.

On the third morning, a thick, dark cloud rested atop Mount Sinai. The whole mountain shook with thunder and lightning. A voice said not to touch the mountain because it was holy, or whoever touched it would die. Much smoke started coming from the mountain, and God's voice could be heard speaking the Ten Commandments.

The Smoking Mountain

The people were afraid, but Moses told them not to be frightened. Moses went closer into the smoke, and he wrote down all of the laws and commands from God into a book. When Moses returned to the others, they all said they would obey the laws.

Early the next day, Moses built an altar and oxen were sacrificed to God. He read from the book of laws, and the people again promised to obey God's laws. He sprinkled some of the blood from the oxen on the people as a symbol of their covenant with God.

Moses Reciting the Law

Most of the people went back to the camp. Moses, his two sons, Aaron, and seventy of the old men went with him, back up the mountain. They saw the glory of God and were not afraid.

Later, Moses went back up the mountain and took Joshua with him. He commanded the people to be obedient to Aaron and Hur until he returned. For forty days he listened to God's words, and God gave him two stone tablets on which he had written the Ten Commandments:

Thou shalt have no other gods before me.
Thou shalt not worship any graven images.
Thou shalt not take the name of the Lord in vain.
Keep the sabbath day holy.

93

Honor thy father and mother.

Thou shalt not kill.

Thou shalt not commit adultery.

Thou shalt not steal.

Thou shalt not bear false witness against thy neighbor.

Thou shalt not covet thy neighbor's house, wife, or anything else that belongs to him.

B-12 THE STORY OF A GOLDEN CALF
EXODUS 32

While Moses was up on the mountain, the people below could see fire and smoke, and they knew God was talking to Moses. After weeks passed, the people grew restless. They demanded that Aaron give them a god to show them the way.

Aaron was not a good leader and was afraid the people might kill him. He told them to gather all of the gold earrings the Egyptians had given them. He threw them into a fire and melted them into the shape of a calf, which the Egyptians often worshiped. He set the calf idol in the middle of the camp. The Israelites had a great feast and began to dance around the golden calf. They even said it was the golden calf that had rescued them from Egypt.

The Golden Calf

94

God was very angry when he saw what was happening. Moses did not know exactly what they were doing, but God told him he would destroy the Israelites and start over with his own children. Moses begged God not to do this. He hurried back down the mountain with Joshua, carrying the stone tablets.

Moses saw the people dancing around the golden calf and offering sacrifices, and then he understood why God was so angry. He threw the stone tablets down and they broke into pieces. He destroyed the golden calf by grinding it into dust and throwing it into everyone's drinking water. Moses was also angry with Aaron.

Moses Coming Down From Mt. Sinai

Moses Breaking the Stone Tablets

95

Moses called to the people, saying whoever was on God's side should stand with him. Many of them did stand with Moses. He then told those men to take their swords and go through the camp, killing anyone who still wished to worship idols. Over three thousand people were killed that day.

Moses tried to have God take his own life as a sacrifice for his people's sins, but God told Moses the people would have to suffer for their own sins. God told Moses to bring two more stone tablets onto the mountain, and once again God wrote the Ten Commandments for Moses.

B-13 How God Planned to Live Among His People
Exodus 34 – 39; Numbers 1 – 5

The People Presenting Their Gifts to Moses

The Israelites were glad when they heard that Moses was coming down from Mt. Sinai with two stone tablets for the second time. Although he had been gone another forty days and nights, no one had complained or wanted to worship idols, and the people wanted to learn the Ten Commandments.

When the people first saw him, they ran from him. Moses could not understand why the people were frightened. The leaders of the tribes went with Aaron to meet Moses. They told him why everyone was so frightened of him: the skin on his face was shining brightly like the sun. He put a veil over his face, and then the Israelites weren't afraid to be near him. But when he talked about God, he took the veil off.

God wanted the people to know that he was living there with them in the camp, and he wanted to have a special place for them to worship him. God told Moses how to build a place of worship. The people were glad to hear of the plan. They brought gold, silver, furs, and other offerings to be used in the place of worship, which was to be called a tabernacle.

Everyone began to help with building the tabernacle. Because the people were living in tent-homes that could be moved easily, God told Moses to use a similar type of construction for the tabernacle. It was to have board walls and a top made of cloth and animal skins. God told them exactly how to make it and what to put inside.

Building the Tabernacle

When everything was finished, the tabernacle was set up in the middle of camp. The tribe of Levi, which Moses and Aaron belonged to, was selected to care for the tabernacle. God told Moses to divide the tribe of Levi into three groups. One group would camp on the north side, one on the south side, and one on the west side of the tabernacle. Moses and Aaron camped on the east side.

He divided the tribe of Joseph into two groups, named after Joseph's two sons. The way the tribes were divided, there were always twelve tribes ready to go to war if necessary.

The tabernacle, where the Israelites worshiped God, was surrounded by an uncovered space called a court. Curtains enclosed the court. A great altar stood near the entrance to the court. It could be moved when it was time to move the whole tabernacle. A large basin or laver stood near the altar. This would be filled with water and used by the priests for washing their hands and feet. Priests burned incense on the incense altar.

ALTAR OF INCENSE.   ALTAR OF BURNT OFFERING.   LAVER.

Near the altar was the tabernacle itself. It was covered with four curtains and divided into two rooms. The first room was called the "holy place," and the second room, which it led to, was called the "holy of holies."

In the first room were three objects: a table, a golden candlestick, and a small altar. Everything was made of gold or covered with gold. Bread was placed on the table by the twelve tribes, and incense was burnt on the small altar.

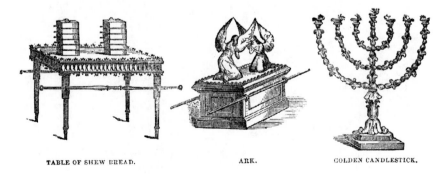

TABLE OF SHEW BREAD.   ARK.   GOLDEN CANDLESTICK.

The second room contained only the "Ark of the Covenant" which was a chest covered entirely in gold. The lid of the box was called the "mercy seat." It was made to look like two angels. The two stone tablets containing the Ten Commandments were placed inside the Ark of the Covenant.

During the day, the cloud always hovered above the tabernacle. At night, a flame of fire leaped from its roof. The people saw these things, and they knew that God was always nearby.

B-15 How the People Worshiped at the Tabernacle
Leviticus 1 – 10:7

After the tabernacle was set up, Moses no longer needed to climb Mt. Sinai to talk to God. Now he only needed to enter the tabernacle.

Prior this time, everyone had to make their own sacrifices. Now the people were able to bring their sacrifices to the entrance of the court, and the priests would make the sacrifices for them on the altar.

Aaron was the high priest and his sons were his priests. When the tabernacle was finished, God told Moses to anoint Aaron and the other priests with oil, and they were to wear beautiful robes.

A lamb was used for their first sacrifice, and God started the fire himself. Every day, one sacrifice was made in the morning and another in the

Moses Anointing Aaron and His Sons

A Priest Burning Incense

evening. The fire in the altar was never allowed to burn out. The priests added fresh wood every morning. When the tabernacle was moved, they made sure to move the fire that God started.

Every day, incense was burned on the smaller altar. God commanded that it be lit with the fire from the larger altar. Every Sabbath morning, the loaves of bread from the twelve tribes were changed. Only the priests could eat this bread.

One day, two of Aaron's sons didn't use the fire from the altar to light the incense. They fell over dead as punishment for disobeying God's command. This was a great lesson to Aaron and his other sons. They saw that God's instructions must be carefully obeyed.

Death of Two of Aaron's Sons

B-16 THE JOURNEY FROM SINAI TOWARD CANAAN
NUMBERS 9 – 12

One year after the Angel of Death had passed over them in Egypt, God reminded Moses that the Israelites were to have a Passover supper to remember what had happened and to celebrate their freedom from Pharaoh. Each Israelite family prepared a meal according to Moses's instructions.

A few days later, the people noticed the cloud was beginning to move to the north. They had lived for nearly a year under the shadow of Mt. Sinai, and they were glad to be starting the journey toward Canaan again. They packed up their tent homes and the tabernacle, and they began to travel.

Traveling With the Tabernacle

After a few days the cloud stopped, and some of the people began to complain. A great fire broke out in the camp, and many of the people who had been complaining were killed. Moses prayed and God stopped the fire.

Then the cloud led the Israelites further north. The people stopped again and made their camp. This time they complained that they were tired of manna and wanted to eat meat instead of birds. Both God and Moses knew the Israelites were acting like spoiled children, and they didn't like it.

Still, God sent many birds for them to eat. They caught the birds and ate them, but the people were not all grateful. God made many of the ungrateful people die of a sickness, and they were buried there.

The cloud started to move again, and it stopped at a place called

Hazeroth. Miriam and Aaron, the sister and brother of Moses, were not happy because Moses had married a woman who was not an Israelite.

They were jealous of Moses's power and questioned why God chose him to lead everyone. God was angry with Miriam and gave her a dreadful disease called leprosy. Aaron realized they both had been wrong, and he asked Moses to pray for Miriam. She was cured after seven days.

When the cloud left Hazeroth, it did not stop until it reached the Wilderness of Paran, which lies just outside the promised land of Canaan.

B-17 TEN MEN WHO SPOILED GOD'S PLAN
NUMBERS 13, 14

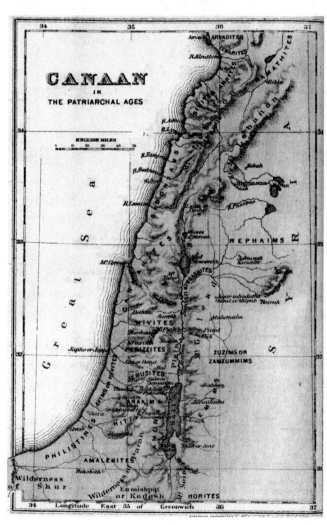

The Israelites were now in the land of Kadesh in the Wilderness of Paran, and they were very close to the land of Canaan. But they were afraid to enter immediately even though they had always followed the cloud before. They wanted to have more information about what lay ahead of them.

God told Moses to choose one man from each of the twelve tribes and to send them to search the land carefully. Moses told these men, whom he called spies, that God would take care of them. They were to bring back some fruit from the land of Canaan.

The Spies in the Land of Canaan

The spies searched the land for forty days. They saw strong cities and small towns. They saw fields of grain and large vineyards of grapes. They could see that the Israelites would have plenty of food there.

They returned with samples of the fruits that grew in Canaan, including a large cluster of grapes that two men carried. The spies said that indeed there was much food in Canaan, but walls surrounded the cities and many of the people were like giants. They did not believe the Israelites could ever take the land by force.

Two of the spies, Caleb and Joshua, had faith in God. They tore their clothes to show their sorrow because of the other spies who didn't have

God Talking to Moses

faith. Instead of listening to Caleb and Joshua, the people wanted to throw stones at them and kill them.

Suddenly a bright light flashed from the tabernacle and God spoke to Moses. He wanted to kill all of the Israelites with a terrible disease and start over with Moses's family. Moses begged God to forgive the Israelites. God said he wouldn't kill them all, but no one over twenty years of age would ever be allowed to enter Canaan. They would have to stay in the wilderness until every man who had complained against God had died, and only their children would see the Promised Land.

Some of the Israelite men decided to try to enter Canaan on their own. They were quickly defeated in battle because God was not helping them.

B-18 The Earth Swallows Some Israelites
Numbers 16, 17

A man named Korah began to think wrong thoughts about Moses and Aaron. He told others about his ideas, and soon many people shared in his incorrect ideas and beliefs.

Korah was a member of the tribe of Levi, the only tribe that helped to care for the tabernacle. Only the high priest Aaron and his sons, the priests, were allowed to enter the tabernacle, and Korah was jealous of this. He and 250 other men went to see Moses. They told Moses they wanted to be as important as he was. Moses knew that God had chosen him to be their leader, and he was only obeying God. He also knew God had chosen Aaron to be the high priest.

Korah and His Followers Swallowed

Moses told all of them to return the following day with offerings of incense. Aaron would also give his offering, and God would show whom he wanted to be the high priest.

The next day, they arrived at the tabernacle. God was greatly displeased, and he told Moses to leave the area because he was going to kill all of the Israelites. Moses fell to the ground and begged God not to kill them. God told Moses he would spare the Israelites if they ran away from Korah and his friends. When the people heard this, they ran away from Korah.

Moses then said, "If the earth opens up and swallows these people, then we shall know that God has decided that I am to be the ruler." The ground opened up under the feet of Korah and his friends. They fell screaming into the depths of the earth.

The next day, some of the Israelites began to blame Moses and Aaron for the deaths of Korah and his friends. God decided to kill many of them, regardless of Moses and Aaron pleading for him to stop. He sent a terrible disease that killed many people.

Aaron's Rod With Buds

Soon after this, God commanded each of the twelve tribes to send Moses a rod. And he commanded Moses to write on each rod the name of the tribe that had sent it. God said Aaron's name was to be written on the rod from the tribe of Levi. God said to leave the rods in the tabernacle next to the Ark until the next day. The rod that grew would be the man God chose to be his priest.

The next day, eleven of the twelve rods looked the same. But the one with Aaron's name had grown and had blossoms on it. Moses showed these rods to the people, and they could see that God had chosen Aaron to be the high priest. Aaron's rod was kept in the tabernacle in case the people ever forgot God's decision.

B-19 The Forty Years in the Wilderness
Numbers 20; Deuteronomy 2:1-15

For nearly forty years, the Israelites wandered about in the wilderness. They waited for the time to come when God would lead them into the Promised Land. Miriam, the sister of Moses and Aaron, died and was buried in the wilderness.

There was a drought, and the people began to complain to Moses. As God told him to do, Moses took all the people to a large rock. God had told Moses to speak to the rock and it would produce water. But Moses was angry with the people and struck the rock twice with his rod. God caused water to come out, but he decided to punish Moses and Aaron by not letting them enter the Promised Land before they died.

Moses Brings Water From the Rock

Moses planned to lead the people through Edom, and he asked the king for permission. He promised that the people would not enter the fields or vineyards, and they would pay for any water they used. The king was afraid to allow so many people to pass through his country, and he sent word to Moses that he would attack anyone entering his kingdom.

Moses did not want to fight with the king and he changed his plans. The Israelites passed by Mount Hor. On the mountain, God told Moses to take off Aaron's priestly robes and to put them on Aaron's son, Eleazar. Moses consecrated him as the new high priest. Aaron was too old to be high priest any longer, and he died up on the mountain that day.

Moses Consecrating Eleazar to Succeed Aaron

B-20 THE BRASS SERPENT ON A POLE
NUMBERS 21:4-9

After the Israelites left Mount Hor, they entered a desert country. The ground was very hot and scorched their feet. The people complained that the manna no longer tasted good, and they could find no water at all.

While they were complaining, God caused fiery venomous serpents to crawl into the camp and bite many people. The venom burned like fire. The young people knew they had done wrong, and they asked Moses to pray that God would take away the fiery serpents.

Moses prayed, and God told him to make a serpent of brass resembling one of the fiery serpents, hang it on a pole, and set the pole in the middle of the camp. God told Moses that anyone who was bitten could look toward the brass serpent; he or she would be cured of the venom and not die. Those who believed in God and looked to the brass serpent for help were saved.

The Brazen Serpent

B-21 How God Helped the Israelites When They Trusted in Him
Numbers 21:12 – 22:2

After the Israelites left the camp where the fiery serpents had bitten them, they came to a wilderness near the land of Moab. They had no water, but they had learned to trust in God and they did not complain. God told Moses to gather the people together in one place and he would give them water.

Moses told the chief men of the tribes to dig a well in the sand. The people sang songs as they dug, and soon they found bubbling water. God was pleased that the people had learned to trust him better.

The Amorite people lived nearby, and Moses asked their king for permission to pass through his land. The Amorite people were idol worshipers and generally wicked people. The king not only refused Moses's request, he sent out his army to attack the Israelites.

God gave the Israelites a great victory. The king was killed, and they drove all the Amorite people from the land and took it for their own.

Then the Israelites marched into the land of Bashan. They did not even ask Og, the king, for permission. He was another wicked king and his people were idol worshipers. When Og heard that the Israelites were coming, he took his army to meet them. God told Moses not to be afraid, and once again they conquered their enemies.

Now the long journey of forty years had come to an end. All of the old men except Moses, Joshua, and Caleb had died in the wilderness. The Israelites had once again reached the border of Canaan, and they could look across the Jordan River and see the Promised Land.

B-22 A Wise Man Who Tried to Disobey God
Numbers 22:1-35

While the Israelites were setting up their tents on the plains of Moab, the king of that country was becoming concerned about them. He had heard about what happened to the Amorites. The king thought the Israelites would conquer his army in battle and take his country away from him.

This king, whose name was Balak, decided to send for a wise man from Midian to come to him and help him. He asked for help defeating a large number of invaders from Egypt. The princes of Moab delivered the message to the wise man, whose name was Balaam.

Balaam wanted to wait until the following day before deciding whether to go. That night, God told Balaam not to help Balak because the Israelites were his chosen people.

Balak's Agents Appeal to Balaam

When Balak heard Balaam's answer, he sent more princes with a large sum of money to offer to Balaam for his help. They again stayed the night at his home, and God told Balaam that he could help if the men awakened him in the morning. But he was to speak only the words God told him.

Balaam was eager to go, and he did not wait for the men to awaken him in the morning. He got up and prepared to leave. God was angry that Balaam did not follow his instructions exactly, and he sent an angel to trouble him. Balaam's ass could see the angel in his path while Balaam could not. Twice the ass moved off the road, and twice Balaam hit the ass. The second time, the ass crushed his foot against a wall.

Then the ass saw the angel for a third time. She sunk down, fearing what might happen. Balaam hit her for a third time. God gave a voice to the ass, and she asked Balaam what she had done to deserve being hit three times. Balaam said if he had a sword, he would kill her for behaving badly. The ass reminded him that she had always protected him. Just then, God allowed Balaam to see the angel.

Balaam was very frightened and fell down before the angel. The angel asked why he was beating the ass when she saved him from death. Balaam was very sorry, and the angel told him to go on to Moab, but to say only what God told him to say.

Balaam Sees the Angel in His Path

B-23 HOW BALAAM TRIED TO PLEASE THE KING
NUMBERS 22:36 – 32:9

Balak rushed out to meet Balaam as soon as he arrived. Balaam told him that he couldn't promise to help, but he would say the words God told him to say. Balaam wanted to earn the money Balak was offering him for helping, but he remembered the angel's warning.

The Arrival of Balaam

Balak took Balaam to the top of a mountain and they made sacrifices. Balaam listened for God's voice, and God told him to say that God blessed

113

Balak's Sacrifice

the Israelites. Of course Balak was angered by this. Balaam reminded him
that he could only say what God told him.

Balaam was hoping the king might still reward him. They went to a
different location and offered more sacrifices. Still God told Balaam the
same thing - that he blessed the Israelites.

After a third time, the king was angry and he told Balaam to return
home without any money. Balaam suggested that he and his people try to
cooperate with the Israelites.

That is what the king decided to do. Soon many Israelites married the
idol worshipers, and the Israelites began to worship idols also. This angered
God, and he sent a plague into the camp that killed many of the young
people. Then the Israelites went to war against the Moabites and Midianites
and killed many of their people. And Balaam was killed in his own land for
causing the people to sin because of his greed.

B-24 The Last Journey of Moses
Numbers 27:12-23; Deuteronomy 34

Moses was now a very old man. He had lived in the palaces of Egypt for the first part of his life. Then he lived as a shepherd in the wilderness for many years. The last part of his life was spent leading his people out of Egypt and to the Promised Land.

Moses knew that he would have to die before the people could enter Canaan with God's protection, and he asked God to select another man to lead the people in. God chose Joshua.

The high priest, Eleazar, laid his hands on Joshua, and the people could see that he was given a position of leadership. Moses wrote down everything the people needed to know before entering the Promised Land, which is part of the book of Deuteronomy in the Old Testament.

Moses and Joshua at the Tabernacle

Everyone knew it was time for Moses to die. He climbed Mount Nebo to get a final view of the Promised Land. He closed his eyes and folded his arms, and God took his spirit. God buried his body somewhere in the plain near the mountain. The Israelites wept for thirty days after the loss of their leader.

Moses on Mt. Nebo

PART C: JOSHUA AND THE JUDGES OF ISRAEL
JOSHUA, JUDGES, RUTH, 1 SAMUEL 1-8

C-1 HOW A WOMAN SPOILED THE PLAN OF AN EVIL KING
JOSHUA 1, 2

Jericho was a large city across the Jordan River from the Israelites' camp. A high wall with a gate surrounded the city. The people inside Jericho had heard how God helped the Israelites many times by protecting them during battles, and they were afraid that God would help the Israelites defeat them.

Joshua believed Jericho would have to be captured before the Israelites could control Canaan. He sent two men into the city to find out more about it. They entered through the open gate and began to talk to a woman named Rahab. Others in the city reported the two strangers to the authorities. The king believed they were from the camp of Israel, and he sent his men to Rahab's house to catch the spies and kill them.

Rahab Hiding the Spies

Rahab hid the men on her roof under piles of flax and they were not found. The king believed they had already escaped, and he sent his men to chase after them. He closed the gate, and the spies were trapped at Rahab's house. Rahab asked that she and her family be protected when the Israelites would take over the city, and in exchange she would help the spies to escape.

Because she believed in God, the spies agreed. They told her to tie a cord to her window-frame so that they would know to protect her. Rahab let them out a window on the wall, and they climbed down a rope.

117

The Spies Escape From Jericho

As Rahab had told them to do, they hid in the mountains for three days until the king's troops stopped searching. Then they returned to the Israelite camp. They told Joshua that the people of Jericho were afraid of the Israelites.

C-2 How the Israelites Crossed a Dangerous River
Joshua 3:1 – 5:1

Joshua, the leader, ordered everyone to prepare to move forward. The tabernacle and the Ark were prepared for traveling. The people came to the Jordan River, and they discovered it was too flooded to cross easily. After three days, God told the people to have faith and to march forward.

The Priests Carry the Ark

The waters parted, the same way that God had parted the Red Sea. The Israelites marched across the dry ground.

Crossing the Jordan River

119

Setting Up the Memorial Stones

God wanted the Israelites to remember how he had helped them cross the Jordan River. He ordered a man from each of the twelve tribes to gather a stone from the dry riverbed, and the stones were to be placed into a heap at their next camp.

After they gathered the stones and crossed the riverbed, God allowed the waters to return. The people of Canaan heard about the Israelites in their land with the help of their God, and they were very afraid.

C-3 THE STONE WALLS OF JERICHO
JOSHUA 5:13 – 6:27

The Israelites made their camp at Gilgal. Joshua went out to see the city of Jericho for himself. He could see that the gates were tightly locked and he wondered what to do. Then he saw an angel standing nearby with a glowing sword. Joshua asked him who he was, and he said that he was the Captain of the Lord's Army. He told Joshua to remove his shoes because he was standing on holy ground.

The Angel Appears to Joshua

The Captain of the Lord's Army told Joshua how the Israelites would achieve victory over Jericho. Joshua told the people about the holy visitor. The people were ready to follow the plan told to Joshua by the angel.

Every day for a week, they marched around the city one time. Soldiers were followed by seven priests blowing ram's horns, and behind them

121

The Walls of Jericho Falling Down

followed other priests carrying the Ark of the Covenant. The people of Israel followed last.

On the seventh day, the people awakened early, and they marched around the city seven times instead of one time, as they had been doing. After the seventh time, all the people turned toward the walls and shouted loudly as the priests blew their horns. The walls collapsed, which was a great miracle.

Joshua Spares Rahab

The soldiers killed most of the wicked people in the city, but Rahab and her family were spared when the soldiers saw the cord on her window-frame. All of the gold, silver, and other metals were brought to the tabernacle at Gilgal, as God had commanded. The soldiers set the city on fire and nothing was left but ashes.

C-4 A Buried Sin
Joshua 7, 8

The Israelites brought all the gold, silver, iron and brass from Jericho to the tabernacle. Most of them were pleased at the victory God had given them, and they did not mind bringing the metals to the tabernacle.

One man, Achan, decided to keep a beautiful garment and some pieces of silver and gold he had found. He buried the items under the floor of his tent. He thought no one would ever know.

Achan Stealing

Soon the Israelites sent 3,000 troops to invade the city of Ai, a city much smaller and weaker than Jericho. But the troops came rushing back after some were killed.

Joshua prayed to God for help. God told him that there was a wicked person in the camp who had kept something from Jericho, and that person would have to be destroyed before God would ever protect the Israelites again. Joshua questioned everyone, and eventually he learned what Achan had done.

Achan's Family Is Stoned

The next day, Achan and his family were stoned, and everything they owned was burned. Stones were piled on the ashes for the people to remember what happens to those who sin against God.

God then told Joshua how to invade Ai. Some men sneaked into the area at night and hid behind the city. When the troops came marching up, as before, the gates were opened and the soldiers of Ai came out to fight them off. As God had told them to do, the Israelite soldiers pretended to be frightened, and the soldiers of Ai chased after them.

Then the men who were hiding went into the city and set fire to everything. More Israelite troops arrived, and the Israelites won the battle. The gold, silver, and cattle were taken by the Israelites, and this time God allowed the people to keep everything.

Joshua Burning the Town of Ai

C-5 The Altar With God's Law
Deuteronomy 27,28; Joshua 8:30-35

After the victory at Ai, Joshua led the Israelites further north into the land of Canaan, where Abraham had built an altar to worship God. Before he died, Moses had commanded Joshua to lead the people there. Joshua was to build an altar of unbroken stones and offer sacrifices to God.

All of the people went into a valley between two mountains. Six tribes stood on one mountain-slope, and six tribes stood on the other. They built the altar and offered sacrifices in the valley, between the two slopes.

They read the laws of God from the book Moses had written. They read aloud the blessings God promised to the people for following his laws - and also the curses they would suffer if they didn't obey. Then the people returned to the camp at Gilgal.

C-6 The People Who Fooled Joshua
Joshua 9:3 – 27

One afternoon, some visitors arrived at the camp at Gilgal. They wore old, dirty clothes with holes and carried sacks containing only bits of moldy bread. They asked to speak with Joshua. They said that they were from far away, and they wanted to be allowed to live in peaced without being harmed.

The Gibeonite Visitors at the Camp of Israel

127

Believing they were from far away because of their tattered clothes and moldy bread, Joshua agreed to let them live. He did not pray and ask God for advice, which was a mistake.

Soon the Israelites were battling the Canaanites again. The troops came to where the Gibeonites lived, which was not far from Gilgal. Then they learned the strange visitors with moldy bread and old clothes were from Gibeon. They had tricked the Israelites into believing they had been on a long journey.

The Gibeonites Negotiating With Joshua

Joshua sent for the men who came to Gilgal. He asked them why they wanted to do this. They said they were afraid the Israelites wouldn't promise to let them live if they knew they lived so close. Joshua said that because they had tried to deceive him, they would be allowed to live, but they would have to be the slaves of the Israelites. Every day they would have to gather wood and water and bring it to the Israelites' camp.

C-7 THE DAY THE SUN AND MOON STOOD STILL
JOSHUA 10 – 12

Not far from where the walls of Jericho had stood was the city of Jerusalem. The people there did not believe in God and were very wicked. There were other cities near Jerusalem. All of the kings of those cities were angered that the Gibeonites had become servants of the Israelites. The king of Jerusalem sent messages to four other kings suggesting that they all go to war against the Gibeonites.

The Gibeonites heard about this plan and they were frightened. They sent a message to Joshua, asking for his help. The five kings were greatly surprised to see the Israelites ready to protect the Gibeonites. Many of the enemy soldiers began to run from the Israelites, and God sent hailstones to kill them. The kings and some of their soldiers hid inside a cave. Some-one saw them go inside the cave and told Joshua. Joshua ordered that large stones be put in front of the entrance of the cave to keep them trapped inside.

Many of the enemy soldiers who escaped the hailstones were hiding in the woods, and Joshua believed God wanted the Israelites to kill all of them. Joshua asked God to make the sun and the moon stand still so that there would be more time in the day to find all of the enemy soldiers.

Joshua Commands the Sun to Stand Still

The people in the woods were killed, and all the people inside the caves, including the five kings, were also killed. One by one, the Israelites captured the cities of thirty-one kings. Then they rested from war in their camp at Gilgal.

C-8 HOW THE LAND OF CANAAN BECAME THE LAND OF ISRAEL
JOSHUA 13 –19

Casting Lots for the Tribes

Joshua was beginning to grow old after the Israelites had destroyed thirty-one kings in Canaan. Still there were more wicked people living in Canaan, and God was not pleased that the Israelites had stopped fighting.

God told Joshua to divide the land among the twelve tribes, and each tribe would drive out anyone who didn't worship God. Lots were cast to

Caleb Pledges His Daughter

decide who should get which lands.

Joshua and Eleazar, the high priest, divided the land among the twelve tribes. From that time on the land of Canaan was known as the land of Israel.

Caleb, one of the spies that had been sent into Canaan over forty years earlier, went to see Joshua. He asked to be given land which Moses had promised to him. He wanted the mountains and cities where the giants lived, and he said he would be able to conquer them with God's help. Caleb pledged that his daughter would marry the one who helped him gain victory over this land.

Joshua was glad to give him the land of Hebron, where the giants lived. Caleb drove the giants out of the area and forced them to go near the seashore, close to their enemies. Then Caleb and his whole family moved into Hebron.

The tabernacle had been at Gilgal for many years and it was moved to Shiloh, closer to the center of Israel. The people of Israel came to the tabernacle three times every year to worship God. Some of the priests and Levites stayed at the tabernacle all of the time, as God had commanded.

C-9 How God Planned to Use Some Cities
Joshua 20, 21

The Levites were given the job of educating the other tribes about God and the law. Many Levites lived in forty-eight different cities throughout Israel. Other Levites had the job of staying with the tabernacle year-round.

God told Joshua to choose six "cities of refuge." If someone accidentally killed another person, he or she could run to a city of refuge where they would decide that person's guilt or innocence.

The person could stay safely inside the city gates if found innocent. Otherwise he or she would be turned over to his or her accusers.

Safely Reaching a City of Refuge

C-10 THE ALTAR BESIDE THE JORDAN RIVER
JOSHUA 22

Before everyone left Shiloh and went to their own territories, Joshua talked to the leaders of the tribes and told them not to forget the commandments and laws that Moses had given to the Israelites. He sent Levites with each tribe to continue to educate them about the laws, and he gave each tribe a share of the gold, silver, and cattle that had been taken from their enemies.

Joshua Talking to the Tribe Leaders

The tribes east of the Jordan River built an altar like the one at Shiloh. Since God had commanded that sacrifices be made only at the tabernacle, some of the other tribes were concerned, and they sent visitors to see them.

They asked them why they had made their own altar after God had commanded that the Israelites worship only at the tabernacle. The tribes who had built the altar explained that it was only a reminder that they too worshiped at the tabernacle, even though they lived across the Jordan River.

The coffin of Joseph was still being carried by the Israelites. Finally they buried his body at a place called Shechem, which was near Shiloh.

C-11 JOSHUA'S LAST MEETING WITH THE ISRAELITES
JOSHUA 23, 24

Joshua was growing very old, and he wanted to talk to all the people of Israel one more time before he died. All the people from all of the tribes came together at Shechem, near Shiloh, where Joseph was buried.

Joshua Making a Covenant With the People

Joshua talked to the people about all the victories God had given them. God had kept all of his promises and driven away all of their enemies. He reminded the Israelites that God would punish them if they turned away from him and started to worship other gods or idols.

Joshua told the people about Abraham and his sons, and the history of his family. He wanted them to understand how much God had helped them. He told the people that they had to decide whether to worship God or the gods of the Canaanites. They all cried out, "We will worship God." Joshua told the people they must not keep any of the idols from the Canaanites in their homes. The people promised to go on obeying the laws of God.

Joshua left a giant rock where he spoke as a reminder about that day for the people. Soon both Joshua and Eleazar died. Eleazar's son Phinehas was made the new high priest. The people continued to remember how God had helped them.

C-12 How God Helped the Israelites
Judges 1:1 – 3:14

After Joshua was dead, the Israelites remembered their promise to obey God. They fought against the wicked people who lived nearby. God helped them in battles, but after many years they grew tired of fighting. They even became friendly with many Canaanite people who worshiped idols, and they allowed their children to become friends with the Canaanite children.

God was angry that his people were not following his wishes, and he sent an angel to tell them this. The angel told them God would no longer protect them against the Canaanites, and the Canaanites would always be a worry for the Israelites. God would bless them if they didn't worship idols but punish them if they did.

Soon many of the Israelites were bowing down to idols and worshiping idols with sacrifices. God allowed invaders from the east to rule over and enslave them for eight years. Many of the Israelites prayed to God for help, and he heard their prayers. God spoke to a young man named Othniel, and he was made their military leader. He led the Israelite soldiers to victory.

For forty years, Othniel ruled the Israelite people as a judge. After he died, the people again turned back to worshiping Canaanite gods. God allowed invaders from Moab to rule over the Israelites for eighteen years because they had forgotten about him again.

C-13 The Left-Handed Man Who Judged Israel
Judges 3:15-31

The Israelites were unhappy during the eighteen years they were ruled by the king of Moab, King Eglon. Every year they had to give much of their food to the king and they received nothing in return. They remembered the days when God had protected them, before they started worshiping idols again. They decided to offer sacrifices on the great altar at Shiloh and they prayed to God for help.

God selected a second judge, Ehud from the tribe of Benjamin. As God told him to do, Ehud took a present to King Eglon. When he was meeting with him, he told the king he had a secret message for him. The king told his servants to leave the room. Ehud stabbed the king with a small dagger he had under his clothes and the king died. Ehud locked the doors and left without being seen. Hours later, the servants discovered their dead king.

The servants knew Ehud had killed King Eglon, and they sent the Moabite soldiers to find him. The Israelite soldiers were prepared to fight the Moabites, and they won the battle.

Ehud and King Eglon

The third judge of Israel was Shamgar. With God helping him, he helped the Israelites defeat the Phillistines by killing 600 enemy soldiers with only an ox bone for a weapon.

C-14 Two Brave Women Who Helped the Israelites
Judges 4, 5

Deborah lived in the land of Israel, near the settlement of Shiloh. Unlike many of the Israelites who worshiped idols, she loved the true God and worshiped him. God sometimes spoke to her and told her things that would happen. The people began to consider her a true prophetess because the predictions she made were accurate. Deborah became the fourth judge of Israel.

Many of the Israelites had turned away from God, and he allowed a hard-hearted king named Jabin to rule over them. His soldiers rode in chariots and shot at their enemies with arrows. For twenty years the Israelites suffered under King Jabin's tyranny. Finally Deborah asked God for help, and God

Deborah

told her exactly what to do.

She sent for Barak, a brave man who lived in the north near King Jabin. She told him what God had told her. Barak feared the other Israelites would not fight with him unless Deborah also went, and he made her agree to go. Soon 10,000 Israelites were ready to fight near Mount Tabor. Deborah predicted a woman would be responsible for the Israelites' victory.

Jael and Sisera

Sisera, the leader of King Jabin's army, heard about the Israelite troops massing, and he went with his soldiers to Mount Tabor. From the camp at Mount Tabor, Deborah and Barak could see King Jabin's army approaching. They saw hundreds of iron chariots, which the Israelites feared. Deborah told them that God would help them to win the battle and to go and fight.

As Barak's men went down to fight, God put great fear into the hearts of

Sisera's men and they all ran away. God caused the river to flood, and many of his men were drowned as they ran away. Sisera himself left his iron chariot and ran like a coward.

Sisera ran to the tent of Jael, believing that she would hide him from the other soldiers. She gave him some milk and he fell asleep. Knowing he was a very evil man, she killed him while he slept. Then she left her tent and saw Barak. She told him the man they were seeking was inside her tent.

Deborah's prediction about a woman giving the Israelites victory had come true. After Sisera was killed, King Jabin no longer had enough strength to rule over the Israelites, and the Israelites were a free people again.

C-15 How a Brave Man Destroyed the Altar of Baal
Judges 6

Deborah judged Israel for forty years, and during that time the people were no longer troubled by any enemies. But after she died, they grew careless and began to worship idols again.

The Israelites began to have trouble with the Midianites. The Midianites were camped near the land of Israel, and soon they started to cross the border. They began to rob the Israelites of food, and eventually they were stealing most of what the Israelites grew. The Israelites prayed to God for help, even though they had turned away from him and he stopped listening to their prayers. God sent a prophet named Gideon to remind them of why they were having such difficulty.

An Angel Appears to Gideon

When Gideon was threshing wheat one day, an angel appeared to him and told him that he would deliver the Israelites from their enemies. At first Gideon did not believe that this could be true, and the angel told him that God would help him. Gideon still doubted the words of the angel, and the angel gave him a sign by setting a plate of meat and bread on fire. Then the angel disappeared.

Baal was the idol most of the Israelites worshiped. In the middle of the night, Gideon did as God commanded and tore down the altar of Baal. Then he built an altar to God and made a sacrifice.

Gideon Destroying the Altar of Baal

At first the people were angry with Gideon, and then they realized that the idol had no power. Gideon sent messengers to the different parts of Israel to gather soldiers to drive the Midianites away.

Gideon wanted to make sure God was on his side, and he asked God for another sign. He left a piece of fleece on the ground, and he asked God to make only the fleece wet with dew and leave the ground dry. The next morning, the ground was dry and the fleece was wet with water.

Gideon still lacked confidence, and he asked God not to be angry with him for wanting another sign. He asked God to make only the ground wet with dew and leave the fleece dry, and that was what happened. Now Gideon was convinced that God was ready to help him.

Gideon Wringing the Fleece

C-16 HOW THE MIDIANITES WERE SURPRISED AT MIDNIGHT
JUDGES 7:1 – 8:28

Gideon's message to the people of Israel brought 32,000 troops ready to fight. They made their camp on Mount Gilboa, and the Midianites were camped in the valley below.

God told Gideon that he didn't need so many men, otherwise the Israelites would believe they had won on their own. God told Gideon to send home any man that was afraid, and two-thirds of the soldiers left.

Still God thought there were too many men. He told Gideon to take the men to the water's edge. Those soldiers who put down their weapons while drinking would be sent home, while those who held their weapons in one hand and drank with the other hand could remain.

Now only 300 men remained. But Gideon knew God had promised to help and he wasn't afraid. God told Gideon to sneak into the enemy's camp with only one servant, and he would hear something there that would make him even more confident. Gideon heard one Midianite telling another about

Gideon Chooses His Soldiers

Gideon Hears the Midianites Talking About a Dream

Gideon and His Followers Surprising the Midianites

a dream, and the Midianites decided it meant that Gideon's army soon would drive them away.

Gideon returned to his camp, and he divided the men into three groups, with 100 men in each group. Next he gave each man a trumpet to blow at the time of the attack. He told every man to carry an empty pitcher with a burning torch hidden inside the pitcher. With their trumpets in one hand and pitchers in the other, Gideon's men marched quietly toward the enemy's camp. They all took their places and waited for Gideon's signal.

At midnight, when all of the Midianites were sleeping, Gideon gave the signal. All of the Gideon's soldiers blew their trumpets and broke their pitchers at the same time. Then they yelled loudly on every side of the camp, "The sword of the Lord and of Gideon!"

The enemies were very surprised and ran away. Many of them died from being trampled by each other. The Israelites killed the two Midianite kings, and the Midianites troubled them no longer.

The Israelite people wanted to make Gideon their king, but he refused. He served as judge for forty years.

Chasing Away the Midianites

C-17 THE MAN WHO MADE HIMSELF KING OF ISRAEL
JUDGES 8:32 – 10:5

After Gideon refused to become king, he returned to Ophrah, the place where God first spoke to him. Many people went there to seek his advice.

When Gideon died, one of his sons, named Abimelech, wanted to be king, even though his father had refused. In the city of Shechem, not far from Ophrah, Abimelech hired some wicked men to kill his brothers. All of his brothers were killed except Jotham, and he ran away and hid in the mountains.

Then Abimelech returned to Shechem. The men from the city took him to a place in the country and crowned him king. When Jotham heard that Abimelech had been made king after killing his brothers, he knew that God would be angry. He stood in a place where the people of Shechem could hear his words, and he told them a parable about the trees:

The trees decided one day to select a king. First they asked the olive tree to rule over them, but the olive tree said it was more important for him to make oil for everyone than to be a ruler.

144

Death of the Sons of Gideon

Then they asked the fig tree. He said it was more important for him to produce figs for everyone to eat than to be a ruler.

They asked the vine. He said it was more important for him to do the work God intended and produce grapes.

Finally they asked the bramble, and he agreed, saying he would be king if they would trust in him – but if they didn't trust in him, fire would destroy

Death of Abimelech

them all.

Then Jotham explained the meaning of the parable. He said the men of Shechem were like the trees that wanted a ruler. Abimelech was like the bramble-bush on which sharp thistles grew, and he would cause great grief for the people.

After telling the story, Jotham ran away and hid in another part of the land. He knew Abimelech would be looking for him then more than ever.

For three years Abimelech ruled as king. Then God caused an evil spirit to trouble him and his people. They no longer felt kindly toward each other. The Shechemites planned to kill Abimelech. When the governor heard about the plan, he sent a messenger to warn Abimelech, and Abimelech secretly left the city.

Abimelech returned to Shechem with an army and destroyed the city. While invading a nearby city, Abimelech was preparing to set fire to a tower in which some people were hiding. A woman in the tower threw a big stone that hit him on the head. He commanded one of his own soldiers to kill him, rather than slowly dying from the stone thrown by the enemy woman.

The men of Shechem and King Abimelech were killed as cruelly as Abimelech had killed his brothers. After Abimelech's death, Tola was the judge for twenty-three years. Then Jair was the judge for twenty-two years.

C-18 How a Girl Suffered from Her Father's Promise
Judges 10:6 – 12:7

In the land of Israel east of Jordan lived a man named Jephthah. His brothers despised him and drove him away from their father's home, and he moved to the land of Tob. He became a strong man with a good reputation, and eventually even his own brothers heard news of his success.

At this time the Israelites had turned away from God and were worshiping idols again, including the idols of their enemies. The Ammonites came from the east and the Philistines invaded from the west, and they ruled over the Israelites. They took their riches and even threatened to take their homes. This was a very unhappy time for the Israelites.

After eighteen years of rule by their enemies, the Israelites cried to God for help, remembering how he had helped them in the past. But God refused, saying that he would not help them again since they had never kept their promises to remain loyal to him after they no longer needed his help. God told them to ask their idols for help.

The Israelites became very regretful about turning away from God, and they tore down the idols and false gods they had built. They began to worship the true God again and confess their sins to him.

Eventually God began to see that the Israelites were really sorry for their sins, and he began to pity them. He saw them gather their soldiers together at a place called Mizpeh to fight against the Ammonites, but they had no leader.

Someone suggested that Jephthah should be the leader since his brave deeds were legendary at that time. They sent for Jephthah, but he refused to come until his brothers promised to treat him kindly. Jephthah prayed for

147

Jephthah's Daughter Comes Out To Greet Him

help, since he knew they would not win without God's assistance. Jephthah promised that he would offer as a sacrifice whatever should come out of his door to meet him when he returned home.

The Ammonites tried to take the land east of the Jordan River, and the Israelites won the battle when led by Jephthah. Jephthah's daughter came out to greet him. Jephthah should have asked God to forgive him for making

Mourning the Death of Jephthah's Daughter

such a promise, but he did as he said and offered his daughter as a sacrifice.

The women of Israel were very sad and mourned for Jephthah's daughter. Jephthah judged Israel for six years after the victory over the Ammonites, and then he died.

C-19 THE STORY OF A STRONG MAN WHO JUDGED ISRAEL
JUDGES 13 - 16

The Israelites worshiped God for about twenty-five years before once again turning to idol worship. The younger Israelites made idols like those their neighbors worshiped, and they bowed down to them and worshiped them. There were only a few Israelites who still worshiped God.

Dagon

149

The Philistines began to trouble Israel. They worshiped an idol named Dagon who had the body of a fish and the hands and face of a man. For forty years the Philistines ruled over those Israelites who lived near their country.

One of the tribes who lived near the Philistines was the tribe of Dan. A man named Manoah belonged to this tribe, and Manoah and his wife served God. They had no children. One day an angel appeared to Manoah's wife and told her that God would give her a son. The angel said their son would be a great man and would begin to deliver the Israelites from the Philistines.

Samson Killing a Vicious Lion

Manoah and his wife named the child Samson. The angel told them never to allow Samson to drink wine and never to cut his hair because he was to become a Nazarite.

A Nazarite was someone given to God to do a special work. Other people recognized a Nazarite by his long hair, and a Nazarite would continue to be blessed by God only if he did not cut his hair and did not drink wine.

When Samson grew up, his body was very strong and he had a very determined personality. Sometimes he behaved like a naughty child, and his behavior got him into trouble on several occasions.

Samson spent time with the Philistines, and he wished to marry a Philistine woman. His parents did not want him to do this because they feared Samson and his children would worship Dagon instead of God.

Before he was married, he went with his parents to see his future wife. A lion attacked Samson, and Samson was able to kill the lion easily with his great strength.

Samson's troubles began soon after he was married. His wife's friends displeased him, and he decided to return to his old home. After he was gone for several days, his father-in-law gave his wife away to another man.

Samson became less angry with his wife and her friends. He decided to return to his home. He even brought a gift for her. Samson was enraged to learn that his wife had been married to another man.

Samson captured 300 foxes and tied their tails together in pairs. He placed a torch between each set of foxes and he released all of them. They burned up all of the Philistines' corn and grains, and the fires destroyed most of their orchards and vineyards.

The Philistines learned that Samson had set these fires because he was angry with his father-in-law for giving away his wife. They set fire to his father-in-law's house and killed him and his daughter. When Samson heard that his wife and her father had been killed, he became angry and returned to kill many of the Philistines.

The Philistines chased him into the land of the tribe of Judah. Samson hid there, and the Philistines invaded with 1,000 soldiers. When the leaders of the tribe of Judah asked the reason that their army was there, the Philistines said they had to bind Samson and bring him to their land to be punished. The men of Judah bound Samson with cords and turned him over to the army.

Just when everyone thought Samson was under control, he broke free of his cords and picked up an animal bone, the jawbone of an ass. With this bone he hit and killed many of the Philistines who were around him. Samson prayed to God for water to drink and God answered his prayer.

151

Samson Destroying the Philistines With the Jawbone of an Ass

Samson visited the city of Gaza, and the gates were locked to keep him inside. He tore the gates from the walls in the middle of the night and carried them many miles to a hill in the land of the tribe of Judah. The people of the city of Gaza were surprised to learn that their prisoner had taken their city gates with him.

Samson Carrying Away the Gates of Gaza

C-20 How Samson Was Killed
Judges 16:4-31

Although Samson knew the Philistines hated him, he dared to go among them anyway. Most of the women hated and feared him because of the problems he had caused for his former wife and her family. However, he soon met another Philistine woman that he loved. Her name was Delilah.

When the rulers heard that Samson frequently visited Delilah, they offered her money to find out the secret of his great strength. Delilah did not love Samson that much and she wanted the money. Eventually she asked Samson to tell her the secret of his strength. Samson told her that he would be powerless if tied with seven green twigs.

Delilah sent a message to the rulers. In the morning, the Philistines tied Samson with seven green twigs while he was still asleep. Delilah awakened him. He escaped from the twigs like it was nothing at all.

Later Delilah said she was disappointed Samson had lied to her. This time he told her that he would be powerless if bound with new ropes. So the same

Samson and Delilah

thing happened again. The Philistine soldiers bound Samson with new ropes, Delilah awakened him, telling him that the Philistines were upon him, and he broke through the cords like it was nothing at all.

The next time, Samson told Delilah that if his hair should be woven in a loom, he would be powerless. The Philistines tried this while he was asleep, and he was not weakened at all by his hair being put into a loom. He tore the

Samson's Hair Is Cut

loom apart.

Finally Samson told Delilah the real secret: he was a Nazarite, and God would protect him only if he kept his hair long. Delilah believed this was the truth, and once again her messenger delivered her news to the Philistine rulers. Some soldiers cut Samson's hair and Delilah awakened him. This time he had no strength, and the soldiers took him away.

Samson in Prison Turning a Millstone

Samson's Death

The soldiers took him to a prison, and his eyes were poked out to make sure that he would not escape. The blinded Samson was forced to turn a millstone, work normally done by oxen and mules.

Samson was very depressed, and he realized that he had done the wrong thing by paying too much attention to Delilah and not enough attention to God. He promised God to once again become a Nazarite even though he was blind. God heard his prayer.

156

The rulers were planning a celebration both for the capture of Samson and to honor their god Dagon. Samson was led into the court of the temple of Dagon, where thousands of people had assembled. Samson's hair had grown while he was in prison, and once again he was very strong. As he was praying while standing between the pillars that supported the roof, Samson pushed the pillars apart with his hands, destroying the temple and killing most of the people there including himself.

C-21 THE YOUNG WOMAN WHO GAVE UP WORSHIPING IDOLS TO SERVE GOD
RUTH 1 – 4

A Fire-God Idol

Ruth was a young girl who lived in the country of Moab. The Moabites worshiped an idol named Chemosh, a fire-god. The idol consisted of a brass image containing fire inside a hollow chamber in the interior, and sacrifices were placed into the outstretched arms after they became red-hot from the fire.

Some people from the land of Israel came to live near Ruth's home when there was a famine in Israel. She met them and learned they worshiped a God different from Chemosh. The man from Israel died, leaving his wife Naomi and two sons all alone in a strange land.

The sons grew up and both married women from Moab. One wife was named Orpah, and the other son married Ruth. Both Ruth and Orpah went to live with Naomi, their mother-in-law. They learned to worship the true God and lost interest in worshiping Chemosh.

Ten years passed by and Ruth's husband died. His brother also died, leaving his mother alone with the two daughters-in-law. Naomi was very sad, and she decided to return to her own people in Israel. Orpah and Ruth decided to go with Naomi. Naomi tried to convince them both to turn back and return to Moab. Eventually, Orpah did decide to return to her own home and people. But Ruth swore never to leave Naomi. Together they approached the city of Bethlehem, where Naomi had once lived.

Her friends greeted her, and they noticed she did not look as well as she once had. She told them to call her Mara, which means bitter, instead of Naomi, which means pleasant. She said to do this because her life had been so sorrowful after the loss of her husband and sons.

Ruth Gleaning

At that time the grain was ripe in the fields and the reapers were busy gathering it. It was the custom to leave some stalks of grain for the poor people, and Ruth went out to glean what she could for herself and Naomi.

A rich man named Boaz noticed Ruth gathering the leftover grain. He asked his servants who she was, and they explained that she was from Moab and had arrived with Naomi. They told him how she had forsaken idol worship to worship the true God and how she had been kind to her mother-in-law. Boaz liked her so much that he invited her to glean grain every morning, and he told his servants to make sure to leave some grain behind just for her. He even invited her to eat lunch with the servants.

Ruth and Boaz

Ruth bowed before him and thanked him for his kindness. "Why are you so kind to a stranger?" she asked. Boaz told her that she deserved to be blessed for worshiping God and taking care of her mother-in-law.

Later, Naomi explained to Ruth that Boaz was a relative of her husband's, and Naomi told her to glean grain there until the harvest was over. Boaz continued to treat Ruth well, and soon they were married.

Boaz Meets With the Elders

Boaz met with the elders of the city, and they all thought the marriage to Ruth was a good plan. After they were married, Naomi came to live with Boaz and Ruth, and she helped to take care of Ruth and Boaz's baby boy, Obed.

C-22 THE MOTHER WHO LENT HER LITTLE BOY TO GOD
1 SAMUEL 1:1 – 3:18

Hannah Prays at Shiloh

Elkanah was a man who lived in the land of Israel, not far from Shiloh. Every year, he and his family went to the tabernacle at Shiloh where he took offerings and his whole family worshiped God together.

Elkanah's wife, Hannah, was unhappy because they had no children. One year when she went to Shiloh, she prayed for a male child, and she promised to have the child serve God if he granted her prayer.

160

The Dedication of Samuel

Soon Hannah was pregnant, and she had a baby boy named Samuel. Samuel means "asked of God." When he was a young boy, she took him to the high priest Eli at Shiloh. She told the priest about her promise to God, and she asked Eli to train young Samuel to learn about the tabernacle and to be a helper to the high priest. Eli was glad to help, and Samuel remained there while his family returned to their own home.

Every year Elkanah and Hannah visited young Samuel when they visited Shiloh. Every year Hannah brought a new coat for Samuel. She was always glad to hear about the many things Samuel was learning. God also gave Hannah two more children.

Eli had two sons who were both priests at the tabernacle and they both were wicked men. The people dreaded going to Shiloh because they didn't want to go near them. Eli told his sons to behave like priests, but they would not listen to their father any longer.

One day God sent a prophet to warn Eli that both and he and his sons would be punished for their wicked deeds, and no one in his family would ever serve in the tabernacle again.

After the prophet went away, God spoke to Samuel, which was the first time God had spoken to any man or woman in a very long time. Samuel thought Eli was calling him when he heard the voice of God, but Eli told him he hadn't called him. This happened two more times, and Eli realized that God might have been trying to speak to Samuel. He told Samuel to say, "Speak, for your servant is listening" the next time God called to him.

When God called to him again, Samuel did as Eli had told him and said, "Speak, for your servant is listening." God told Samuel everything he was going to do to punish Eli and his sons: no one from their family would ever be a priest in the tabernacle again. Samuel told Eli about this. Eli said God's will was not to be questioned and his family would have to accept God's punishment.

C-23 THE STOLEN ARK
1 SAMUEL 3:19 – 4:22

God spoke to Samuel many times as he grew older. And Samuel always told the people what God had to say to them. He became known as a prophet of God.

Some of the Israelites were faithful to God, but many had returned to worshiping idols and God was not pleased with these people. When the Philistines attacked, a large number of the Israelites were killed. Seeing that God was no longer protecting them, some of the Israelite men had an idea: to move the Ark of God at Shiloh into their camp. God had always protected the Ark, and they thought God would always continue to do so.

The Israelites brought the Ark and the priests to the camp, and everyone

The Arrival of the Ark in the Camp

celebrated, even though they had been defeated in battle. The Philistines soon learned the cause of all the shouting and celebration. The Philistines worshiped idols, and they thought the Ark must be like an idol with powers to protect. The Philistines believed that the Ark must be very powerful and they were afraid.

Still the Philistine leaders decided to fight the Israelites and they used all their forces. Eli's sons were carrying the Ark and they were both killed. Many Israelite men and the other priests were killed, and the Ark of God was taken away from the Israelites.

Losing the Ark seemed like the worst thing that could happen to the Israelites. Every soldier who was left alive fled in fear. When a messenger returned to the city, Eli heard what had happened to his sons but he did not cry or even react. When he heard that the Philistines had taken the Ark, he fell backward and died. He had judged Israel for forty years and had been the high priest.

The Ark is Taken by the Philistines

C-24 HOW THE ARK TROUBLED DAGON'S WORSHIPERS
1 SAMUEL 5:1 – 7:2

The Philistines rejoiced over their victory. They believed their own god to be stronger than the God of the Israelites. They carried the Ark into one of their cities and set it up in the temple beside Dagon, the fish-god.

Troubles soon began for Dagon and his worshipers. The next morning, Dagon was found tipped over with his face down. The people returned him to his normal position and went away. The morning after that, Dagon was tipped over and his head and hands were broken off his body. The people of the cities developed boils and sores that caused them all much suffering.

Dagon Is Found Face Down

The people where the Ark was being kept decided to send it away to a different Philistine city since they believed the Ark to be the source of their boils and other troubles. The people of the city where the Ark was sent soon began to have the same boils and sores all over their bodies. Some even died.

It was transferred to a third city, and people there began to get sick and die. The Philistines decided to try to return the Ark to the Israelites. They set the Ark on a cart pulled by two young cows. The cows headed straight for the country of Bethemesh. The Philistines hoped the Israelites' God would stop punishing them since they no longer had the Ark.

The Return of the Ark

The men of Bethemesh saw the Ark coming down the road and they were overjoyed to see it, seven months after it had been stolen. The men removed the Ark from the cart. They built a fire with the wood from the cart, and they sacrificed the two young cows.

Even though they knew God had commanded that no one should look inside the Ark except the priests, the men looked inside anyway, and many of them died. The Ark was kept safe for twenty years at the house of a man named Abinadab, and eventually his son took care of it. Samuel returned to his parents' home at Ramah, and he became the last of Israel's fifteen judges.

C-25 HOW SAMUEL JUDGED THE ISRAELITES
1 SAMUEL 7, 8

After Eli's sons and Eli had died, no one remained at the tabernacle to offer daily sacrifices, and eventually the tabernacle at Shiloh was no longer used at all. Samuel was living back in Ramah.

The Israelites were suffering under the rule of the Philistines. Some of them remembered Samuel and how he was considered a prophet, and they

165

hoped he would find a way to help them.

Samuel visited people in different parts of the land. He told them if they wanted help from God that they first would have to tear down their idols and start worshiping the true God again. The people began to tear down all the idols, including those of Baal and Ashtaroth. Samuel told the people to gather in a place called Mizpeh.

The Philistines heard that the people were meeting at Mizpeh. They assumed the Israelites were gathering to fight against them. The Philistine army prepared to fight and marched toward Mizpeh. The Israelites saw the Philistines approaching, but they had brought no weapons with them. They begged Samuel to ask God for help. Samuel sacrificed a lamb and prayed to God.

God answered his prayer by sending a terrible thunderstorm to drive the Philistines away. They dropped their weapons and ran in every direction. The men of Israel picked up their weapons and killed many of them. It was a great victory for the Israelites.

The Philistines Are Defeated

To celebrate the victory, Samuel set up a stone pillar on the battlefield and called it Ebenezer, which means "The Stone of Help." Israel became free of Philistine rule under Samuel, and the Philistines stopped bothering the people of Israel as long as Samuel was judge.

Ebenezer

The last of the fifteen judges, Samuel continued to live at Ramah where he had his own altar. But much of his time was spent traveling to other parts of the land to talk with people. When Samuel became very old, his two sons began to settle disputes for him and perform his other duties. Sadly, they were not honest and did bad things such as accepting bribes.

The people were dissatisfied and told Samuel that they wanted a king. God told Samuel to let them have a king but that the people would be sorry since they were forsaking God's wishes. Samuel told the people that God said that they would be punished for wanting a king, but still they wanted one.

Samuel Anointing Saul

PART D: THE THREE KINGS OF UNITED ISRAEL
1 SAMUEL, 2 SAMUEL, 2 KINGS, 2 CHRONICLES

D-1 ISRAEL'S FIRST KING
1 SAMUEL 9, 10

Instead of trying to select a king himself, Samuel waited for God to help him. Eventually God gave Samuel an answer. God told him that a man from the tribe of Benjamin would come to see him the next day. God said that this man would be the new king and military hero who would lead the Israelites to victory over the Philistines.

Saul was the man chosen by God. He was a young man. His father, Kish, owned much land and cattle, and he was very rich. One day, some of the asses that belonged to Kish wandered away and became lost in the woods. Saul and a servant searched for them for two days. Saul wished to return home at that time, but the servant wanted to seek the help of the prophet they had heard about, to help find the asses. The servant had money to give the prophet as payment, and Saul agreed that they would ask him for help.

Two girls helped Saul and his servant find Samuel, the prophet who was also judge. They told him Samuel would be attending a feast where he was to bless the food. On their way, Saul and his servant met an old man and they asked him for directions. It turned out that Samuel was waiting for Saul at the gate, where the feast was being held.

Samuel told Saul that he must come to the feast with him, and then he would be ready to lead the people and become their king. Saul did not know what Samuel was talking about or even believe him, but he went to the feast. He was seated with important people and given the best food. The next day Samuel told Saul that he was to be the new king, and Samuel anointed Saul with oil.

Samuel promised to give Saul three signs to remove any doubts he had about God wanting him to be king. First, two men would meet him at a certain place and tell him that his missing asses had been found; they would also tell him that his father was sad because he had been gone for so long. Further down the road, three men would meet him and give him two loaves of bread. Lastly, he would meet a group of prophets whom he would talk with. Samuel said God would change Saul into a different man.

The three signs happened just as Samuel had predicted. On his way home, Saul stopped to make a sacrifice, and he met his uncle there. His uncle wanted to know where they had been, and they told him about the visit with Samuel – but they did not tell the uncle that Saul was the new king, the first king of Israel.

Samuel called all of the elders of Israel together, and he told them that God was giving them a king because they wanted one, even though that was not God's wish. All the tribes passed by, and eventually Samuel chose Saul from the tribe of Benjamin.

Everyone wanted to see the new king, but he was hiding and wanted to be alone. God told the people where to find him and they brought him out. Saul told the people what type of king he would be, and then he went home, accompanied by men who wanted to serve the new king.

Some of the people were not satisfied with the man God chose. These men were idol-worshipers who did not fear God, and they wanted to choose a king for themselves. They looked with anger at Saul. Saul pretended not to notice them, and he continued working in his fields as he had always done, even though he was the new king.

D-2 HOW THE EYES OF SOME OF SAUL'S PEOPLE WERE SAVED
1 SAMUEL 11, 12

Not long after Saul became king of Israel, the king of the Ammonite people and his army threatened to invade Jabesh, an Israelite city near the Jordan River. The people of Jabesh begged the king to spare their lives, and they promised to accept his rule. The king sent a message saying he would send his troops in seven days to put out - or poke out - the right eyes of all the people of Jabesh.

Soon Saul heard about the threat to the people of Jabesh. He killed two oxen and divided their bodies into twelve parts. He sent one part to each of the twelve tribes, saying their oxen would be cut up into pieces if they did not send men to help the people of Jabesh defend themselves. Soon many men gathered together and prepared to fight the Ammonites. The battle lasted from morning until noon. The Ammonites were defeated, and they no longer returned to bother the people of Jabesh.

During the journey home, the Israelites stopped at Gilgal, and King Saul helped to perform sacrifices. The people now accepted him as their king. Samuel gave up his position as judge, but he continued to be a prophet among the people. Some of the people wanted to kill the wicked men who were angry that Saul was king, but Saul did not permit it.

Samuel warned the people that they had displeased God by asking for a man to be their ruler instead of God. Samuel told them that he would pray,

Samuel Prays for a Storm

and God would demonstrate his anger by sending a great storm. Samuel prayed, and very strong thunder and lightning began. The people were frightened, but Samuel told them that God would continue to protect his people as long as they were careful to serve him.

D-3 KING SAUL'S PEOPLE IN TROUBLE
1 SAMUEL 13

After Saul had been king for two years, he chose 3,000 soldiers to be ready for battle at any time. He took 2,000 soldiers to a place called Michmash, and he left 1,000 at Gibeah with his son Jonathan.

The Philistines had begun to cause much trouble again in the land of Israel. They were not afraid of King Saul and his army. They even placed some of their own soldiers throughout the land, to rule over the Israelites.

Not far from Gibeah was a ruling Philistine garrison, or fort. Jonathan and his soldiers fought against the garrison and drove the Philistines away. The other Philistines heard what had happened, and they gathered an army of thousands of chariots to fight against King Saul. The Philistines had taken away most of the weapons owned by the Israelites, and only a few Israelites were prepared to fight.

Samuel prayed and asked God what to do. He continued praying for several days as more Philistine soldiers arrived. The number of Philistine soldiers was so large that many of the Israelite soldiers became frightened and did not want to fight them. Some hid in caves, and others ran away to Gilead by crossing the Jordan.

Saul became afraid that all his men would leave before Samuel returned. Not knowing what to do, he offered a burnt sacrifice, which only a priest or Levite was permitted to do. God did not want Saul to do such a thing even though he was king of Israel.

Samuel returned while the sacrifice was still burning, and he was disappointed to see what Saul had done. Saul said he was forced to do it, but Samuel knew he wasn't forced to do anything. Samuel told Saul that because he was disobedient to God, he would someday lose his kingdom to another man who would obey God.

Instead of telling Saul what to do to defeat the Philistines, Samuel turned and walked away. Saul realized that he had only 600 troops, and he marched back home instead of fighting. The Philistines camped near Michmash.

Samuel Reproves Saul

Jonathan and His Armor-Bearer Attack the Philistines

Saul's son, Jonathan, and the young servant who carried Jonathan's sword and shield both sneaked into the Philistine camp. They began attacking and killed about twenty Philistines. God caused the earth to tremble, and the Philistines believed a massive army was approaching and preparing to attack them. The Philistines were so frightened that they attacked each other.

Saul and his army were watching the Philistine camp and they realized something wasn't right. Soon they noticed Jonathan and his servant were missing and probably fighting against the Philistines. King Saul's men marched to fight the Philistines, but his troops ran away and wouldn't fight.

King Saul had ordered that no Israelite should eat until evening or that person would be put to death. Many of the troops were too hungry to fight the enemy, which was why they fled. Jonathan had not heard his father's order, and he ate some wild honey he found. When Saul heard what had happened, he decided to put his own son to death. The people would not allow it since God had helped Jonathan as he fought against the Philistines.

D-5 How King Saul's Sin Cost Him His Kingdom
1 Samuel 14:47 – 15:35

The Philistines were no longer a problem for the Israelites, and King Saul went out to fight against the other nations that had been troubling his kingdom. God helped him to be victorious in those battles, and his soldiers began to honor him as a brave leader. King Saul was always watching for strong, young Israelite men to add to his army.

As Saul's army grew larger, he began to be too proud of himself, and he forgot God was the reason he was in charge. One day, Samuel told Saul that God wanted him to go out to battle against the Amalekites. He said God had not forgotten the Amalekites' sins when they fought against the Israelites, after they had left Egypt. God wanted all of them destroyed, including all of their animals.

The Death of King Agag

Saul gathered an army of 210,000 men and began to march toward the Amalekites. He sent messages to the Kenites, who were living among the Amalekites, telling them to leave or be destroyed. During the battle, all of the Amalekites were destroyed except for the king, King Agag. The king was taken to a safe place. The soldiers took the best cattle, sheep, and lambs, and the rest were killed. With the animals and King Agag, the soldiers returned to the land of Israel.

God told Samuel that King Agag and the animals were still alive, and that was not what God had wished. Saul tried to lie to Samuel and told him that everyone had been killed. But Samuel could not be fooled so easily. He asked why the animals were there. King Saul told him that the animals would be sacrificed to God, and he made it sound like his soldiers were to blame. Samuel told him that God had already spoken to him and told him the real truth, but still Saul persisted with his lies.

Samuel told him it is better to obey God than to sacrifice to him. Saul admitted that he had sinned, but only because he had listened to the people. Samuel told Saul that God had taken away his kingdom already. Samuel and Saul made one last sacrifice together, and King Agag was killed. Samuel no longer visited Saul after this.

D-6 WHY GOD SENT SAMUEL TO BETHLEHEM
1 SAMUEL 16:1-13

Samuel was sad because he felt his work had ended, and he was sad for King Saul. One day God told Samuel to stop mourning for Saul and that he had already chosen a new king. God told him to fill his empty horn with oil and go to Bethlehem where he would anoint the new king.

At first Samuel was afraid to go, fearing that Saul might kill him if he went. God told him to take an offering for a sacrifice and prepare a feast for the people of Bethlehem. He was to invite an old man named Jesse, and one of Jesse's sons would be the new king.

Samuel was no longer afraid. He filled his horn with oil and started on the journey to Bethlehem. The rulers of Bethlehem were afraid when they saw the prophet Samuel coming. Samuel showed them the offering for the sacrifice, and he invited all of them, including Jesse, to the feast.

Jesse had eight sons, but the youngest stayed home to take care of his father's sheep while he played his harp in the field. One by one, Jesse brought his sons before Samuel. God told him none of them were the new king. Samuel asked Jesse if he had another son. Jesse told him about his youngest son.

Samuel Anointing David as the New King

Samuel told him to send for the youngest boy at once because God had chosen him to do great work. David was surprised to hear that he was wanted at the feast. He was afraid something might be wrong, and he went as quickly as he could.

When David entered the room, God told Samuel to anoint him as the new king. David understood he was to be the new king, and he wanted to be a good king. Samuel no longer grieved, and he was happy Israel had a better king than Saul.

D-7 WHY JESSE SENT DAVID TO VISIT KING SAUL
1 SAMUEL 16:14-23

Saul kept ruling the people for as long as he lived, even after Samuel told him God no longer considered him the king. He wanted to rule until he died.

David wrote many beautiful poems, which we call the Psalms, while he was living as a shepherd-boy, waiting to be king. David sang very well and played the harp.

One day, Saul's servants suggested he could have his own musician to play for him whenever he wanted his spirits lifted. Saul believed this was a

David Playing His Harp While Shepherding

good plan, and he ordered his servants to find a musician. One of his servants had heard about the musician David, the son of Jesse. He told Saul about David, and Saul sent for him to come to the king's palace.

David went to see Saul, carrying a gift from his father. Saul liked David's music so much that he asked Jesse if he could remain with him for a while as his personal musician.

David played music daily for Saul, and eventually the bad mood that had been troubling Saul began to be replaced by a feeling of happiness. Once he was feeling better, he allowed David to return to his home in Bethlehem. Of course Saul did not know that David was to be the king to replace him or he might have tried to kill him.

David Working as Saul's Musician

The Philistines had begun to trouble Israel again, and they were preparing to fight against King Saul and his army. The Philistine army camped along the side of a mountain, and King Saul's army camped nearby, ready to fight.

The Philistines were not eager to fight immediately. They sent out one of their men to talk to the men in the Israelite army. The Philistine man was a giant named Goliath. He was much, much taller than an ordinary man.

Goliath told the Israelites that he would fight any one of them, and the winner of that fight would decide the outcome of the battle. If Goliath won, the Israelites would be the slaves of the Philistines. If the Israelite won, the Philistines would be their slaves. For forty days Goliath continued to make this challenge, but no Israelite soldier responded.

David was busy caring for his father's sheep while this was going on. God gave him the strength to kill a lion that was attacking him when he had to rescue one of his sheep. God also protected David against a bear. Three of David's brothers were soldiers in the army. Jesse sent David to the camp to learn of any news from his brothers and also to take them some grain and loaves of bread.

When David arrived, the soldiers were forming a line for battle. David quickly found his brothers and gave them the food from their father. Just then, Goliath approached, wearing full armor so that no one could hurt him. King Saul's soldiers began to tremble and ran away.

David saw what was happening, and God gave him the courage to act. David said he would kill the giant, but his brother Eliab tried to stop him. A messenger arrived, telling David that King Saul wanted to see him. David hurried away to speak with the king.

David Prepares to Fight the Giant

178

King Saul was not impressed when he saw David dressed as a shepherd-boy. David told King Saul how he had killed the lion and the bear with God's help, and he said that God would help him kill the Philistine, who was an enemy of God's people.

The king tried to give David his own armor, clothes, and sword, but David said that he did not need them. David went to a stream to find some smooth stones. He took out his leather sling and prepared to meet the giant.

Goliath became angry when he saw the shepherd-boy with only his staff and sling. He thought the Israelites were making fun of him. David told him that he was going to kill him with God's help because he was an enemy of God's people.

David put a stone in his sling and shot the stone at the giant. The stone hit Goliath on the forehead, and he fell to the ground, stunned.

David hurried to the place where Goliath lay, and he killed him with Goliath's own sword. The Philistines did not wait to see what would happen because they knew that God was protecting the Israelites. All of the Philistines ran away, leaving their belongings at the camp.

Goliath Is Stunned With David's Stone

David Kills Goliath

D-9 HOW SAUL BECAME DAVID'S ENEMY
1 SAMUEL 17:55 – 18:30

Saul did not remember that David was the musician who had played for him, and he wondered where the brave young shepherd who killed Goliath had come from. Saul asked David who his father was. When he heard the name Jesse, he began to remember.

Saul told David he was placing him in command of a thousand men in his army, and David would live in the king's palace at Gibeah. David stopped working as a shepherd, and he no longer lived with his father.

Jonathan, Saul's son, was glad to hear that David would be staying. He was very fond of David and promised to always help him and be his friend. David's soldiers liked and respected their commander, and they were glad to obey his orders. Even the servants at the palace loved David.

The evil spirit that had made Saul feel unhappy once again troubled him. He was jealous that David was given credit for the victory over the Philistines. Saul began to worry that God might think David a better man than him and give his kingdom to David. While David was playing music for him, suddenly Saul threw the javelin he was holding at David, intending to kill him. David saw it coming toward him and stepped out of the way.

Saul Tries to Kill David

King Saul was afraid to try to kill David after that because he thought God was with him and protecting him. Saul had a plan. He told David he would allow him to marry his older daughter if he could once again defeat the Philistines in battle. Saul thought the Philistines surely would kill David, but David was victorious once again. When David returned, the daughter had already been married to a different man.

Saul also had a younger daughter. He promised to allow David to marry her if David would kill one hundred Philistines. Instead of killing only one hundred, David killed two hundred. This time Saul kept his promise and David was married to his younger daughter, Michal. Saul still was very fearful that God would kill him and give his kingdom to David.

D-10 How Jonathan and Michal Saved David's Life
1 Samuel 19:1 – 20:2

Eventually, Saul's anger grew and he became bolder. He called Jonathan and his servants together, and he told them to kill David. Jonathan cared too much for David to let this happen. He told David to hide, and he would send for him later, after he had a chance to talk to his father and get him to change his mind. Saul listened to his son Jonathan, who told him that David had never done anything except help the Israelites. Saul became ashamed of his jealous feelings and ordered that David should not be killed. David returned, and Saul did not try to harm him.

Again Saul Wants to Kill David

Once again Saul sent David to fight against the Philistines, and once again David returned victorious and with great honors. Soon the evil spirit of jealousy crept back into Saul's heart.

One day when David was playing his harp for Saul, the king picked up a javelin and prepared to throw it at David. Seeing what he was doing, David quickly stepped out of the room. The king was determined to get him.

Saul sent soldiers to his house, but David's wife Michal heard them coming. She urged David to escape at once. He left through a window and went out to the country.

When morning came, the soldiers told Michal that her father had sent for David. She said he was sick and could not go. The night before, she had put an image of David in his bed and covered it with sheets. The soldiers brought the bed with the image to King Saul, and he realized that his daughter had tricked him because she loved David.

David ran away to Ramah, where Samuel lived. Samuel took him to a place called Naioth, where the young prophets were studying. King Saul sent messengers to return David to him. But the messengers liked Naioth so much that they decided to stay there. The same thing happened when more

David Escapes Through a Window

messengers were sent. Finally King Saul went to Naioth himself. He saw the others praying and worshiping God, and he had no strength to harm David. The king stayed more than one day at this place. While he was there, David left to meet with Jonathan.

David and Jonathan Talking

Jonathan had a young boy assist him while shooting arrows in the country. The boy did not know it, but David came out of hiding and talked to Jonathan whenever he was off picking up arrows.

David told Jonathan that he couldn't attend the upcoming feast because he was afraid that Saul would try to kill him again. Jonathan told David that he would know Saul wanted to kill him if Saul was angry because he wasn't at the feast. If Saul wasn't angry, David would know it was safe to return, and Jonathan would send a message to him.

David and Jonathan Parting

When he saw that David wasn't at the feast, Saul was so angry that he nearly threw his javelin at Jonathan. Jonathan returned the next day to give David the bad news.

Jonathan and David were sad to leave each other. David promised to always be kind to Jonathan and his children. Then David returned to hiding in the wilderness in the land of Israel.

Nob was a small city in the land of Israel. It was where the tabernacle was being kept since the Philistines had stolen the Ark. The priests continued to care for the tabernacle and offer sacrifices there even though there was no Ark. Ahimelech was now the high priest.

One day Ahimelech saw David approaching. He knew that David was a military hero and a member of the king's family, but he did not know the king wished to kill David. David asked Ahimelech for some food and a sword. Ahimelech gave him five loaves of bread and Goliath's sword.

When David was talking to Abimelech, he saw a man named Doeg watching him. He knew Doeg worked for Saul and would tell him that he had seen David there, and Saul would send soldiers to find him. David left secretly and hid in the city of Gath in the land of the Philistines.

Achich was the king of Gath and his servants knew David. David overheard the men talking about a plan to keep him prisoner there, and he decided that he must find a way to escape. He began to act like a crazy person, and King Achich was frightened of him and told him to leave.

David Feigning Madness

From Gath, David went to a place known as the wilderness of Judah. He lived there in a cave for many days. His friends and his family all came to visit him in the cave. His parents and brothers went to live with him there in the cave because they were afraid of King Saul's men, and they also feared the Philistine soldiers who were occupying Bethlehem.

David felt sorry for his own parents, and he took them to the land of Moab, where his great-grandmother Ruth had lived. He asked the king of that country to look after them until he could find a better place for them.

David Pours Out the Well Water

Other men from around Israel kept coming to join David, and soon he had an army of about 400 soldiers. A few of the men heard David talking about how he wished he could have some water from a certain well in Bethlehem, but he knew the Philistine soldiers would recognize him. The three soldiers went there that night and brought water from the well. David was thankful, but he poured the water on the ground as a sacrifice to God.

D-13 A WICKED SERVANT AND A WICKED KING
1 SAMUEL 22:6-23

King Saul started out feeling jealous because of the attention David received. Then he became angry and eventually wanted to kill David. It's no wonder he felt unhappy with the feelings he had. No one wanted to help him find David, and this made him feel even worse.

Eventually King Saul learned that David and a small army were living in the cave known as Adullam. Saul feared that David must be planning to take over his throne, yet no one was willing to help him capture David.

Doeg told Saul that he had seen the high priest, Ahimelech, give food and Goliath's sword to David in the city of Nob. King Saul sent for Ahimelech and the other priests from Nob. They had no knowledge of where David had gone. They did not even know that David was running from the king.

When Saul asked him why he had helped an enemy, Ahimelech defended David. This made King Saul even angrier. Saul ordered his soldiers to kill all of the priests from Nob. He did not stop to think that these were God's men. Saul's soldiers did not obey him, saying they could not kill God's priests.

Then King Saul told his wicked servant Doeg to kill all of the priests. Doeg killed them all, and then he went to Nob and killed every man, woman and child he could find in the city.

One of Ahimelech's sons, named Abiathar, fled from the city and found David, telling him what had happened. David made Abiathar the high priest. He stayed there with David where he was safe from King Saul's men.

King Saul and His Soldiers

David's Army Liberating Keilah

Not far from David's hiding place was the city of Keilah, and the Philistines had been troubling the people there. David heard this news, and he prayed to ask God whether he should take his army there to help them.

God told him to take his army and go to help the people of Keilah. His soldiers were afraid to go when he gave the order to leave. David prayed a second time, and God gave courage to all of his men.

David and his men liberated Keilah. King Saul heard about this, and he thought he had a chance to capture David inside the city. God warned David to leave the city, and he hid in some nearby woods.

Jonathan found him there. He told David that God would not let his father kill him because he was to be king of Israel. They talked about old times and Jonathan left after a short visit. Soon after this last meeting, Jonathan was killed in a battle against the Philistines.

David Sparing Saul's Life

Saul's soldiers moved from place to place searching for David, and eventually they decided to rest in the cave where David was hiding; but they did not know that David was there. David and his men saw King Saul lie down and go to sleep. David sneaked up and cut off a piece of his robe. Then he went back into the shadows and waited for Saul to awaken.

David's soldiers wanted to kill Saul, but David knew God did not want that to happen. When Saul awoke, David called to him. He showed him that he had cut off a piece of his robe. King Saul realized that David could have killed him if he had wanted to do so. He knew David did not want to kill him and should not be treated like an enemy. King Saul was sorry and told David that someday he would be the next king of Israel.

Saul took his army and returned home to Gibeah. The evil spirit that had made Saul jealous soon crept back into his heart, and once again he wished to kill David. Saul was looking for him yet again, and David was afraid to return home.

David was hiding in the country that belonged to the Ziphites, and they had sent word to King Saul that David was there. King Saul sent an army of 3,000 men and they camped nearby. David sent spies to find out more about the troops, and the spies told him that the troops were King Saul's men.

David Showing Saul That He Had Spared His Life

David wanted to prove to Saul again that still he was no threat. He and his servant sneaked into the camp and stole the king's spear and water bottle. Once they had left, they called to the king's captain, Abner, and told him he was not fit to protect the king. King Saul and everyone awoke at the sound of David's voice.

Saul did realize that David was no threat when he saw David had his belongings. Once again he said he was sorry and promised not to harm him. David remembered the other times King Saul had said the same thing, and he was afraid to believe him. David and his soldiers lived in the land of the Philistines, waiting until he heard about Saul's death before leaving there.

D-15 THE UNHAPPY END OF SAUL'S LIFE
1 SAMUEL 28:3 – 31:13

King Saul's troubles began when he started disobeying God. He became more and more unhappy because of his sinful thoughts, and he was miserable by the time he was an old man.

The Philistines were causing much trouble for him at this time. They were taking from his people and even conquering entire cities of his. The Philistines were growing bolder, and Saul knew that he was not able to drive them out of his land. He wished that he could send David into battle, but he had only himself. Saul gathered his men but he was afraid. He had killed all the priests and could not ask them to pray for victory. Samuel the prophet was dead, and of course God did not want to speak directly to Saul.

The Witch of Endor Contacting the Spirit of Samuel

192

Saul thought he might be able to speak to the spirit of Samuel. He knew of a woman in the village of Endor who said she could speak to the spirits of the dead. Saul dressed like a poor man, and he went there with two of his men to visit her.

She was frightened when the strangers asked her to contact the spirit of a dead man. She told them King Saul would kill anyone who did this. Saul told her that she would not be punished.

When she tried to call Samuel's spirit, she saw something that frightened her badly. She knew at once that King Saul was the man with her, and she didn't like being fooled by him.

The king learned from the witch of Endor that he and his three sons would be killed the following day on the battlefield, and then the Philistines would gain victory over his people. Saul didn't know what to do. The woman prepared some food for Saul, and then the three men left.

The Death of Saul

The next day, Jonathan and his two brothers were killed on the battlefield, and Saul himself was wounded. When he feared the Philistines would capture him, he fell on his own sword and died. The Philistines put his armor in the temple of their idol Dagon, and they hung the bodies of Saul and his sons on the city wall.

Recovering the Bodies of Saul and His Sons

When some Israelites living nearby heard what was done with Saul's body, they went to the city wall at night and took the bodies down. They burned the bodies of Saul and his sons in the city of Jabesh and buried the bones under a tree.

David had become friendly with Achish, the king of Gath, while he was living with the Philistines and hiding from Saul. God caused the king to be kind to David and his men. At the time of Saul's death, David and his men were living in Ziklag. King Achish wanted David to lead his men in battle against King Saul, but they had returned to Ziklag because the king's men didn't entirely trust David to fight against Israel. They found that an enemy had burned the city. Everything was gone, even the women and children.

Ziklag

David called Abiathar, the high priest, and asked him whether he should take his men and pursue the enemy. God told Abiathar to tell David to go after them. David found an Egyptian who was almost dead from lack of food and water. After he regained his strength, this man told him that it was the Amalekites who had burned Ziklag. David promised to protect the Egyptian from the Amalekites if the Egyptian would help him to find them, and the Egyptian joined David's men.

The Amalekites were camped in a valley and enjoying a feast when David and his soldiers located their camp. David's men rescued the women and children, found many of their stolen possessions, and killed many

Amalekite soldiers. Others ran away.

Ziklag had been burned, and David and his men had no homes. A messenger arrived, telling David of the death of Saul and his three sons. The messenger was an Amalekite, and he claimed to have killed King Saul himself, even though this was not true. This made David angry, and he ordered his men to kill the stranger.

David grieved for Saul, Jonathan, and Saul's other two sons. He asked God what to do, now that Saul was dead. God told him to return to his own land. David took his family to live in Hebron, in the land of Judah.

D-17 THE SHEPHERD BOY BECOMES KING OF ISRAEL
2 SAMUEL 2:4 – 6:18

Many years had passed since Samuel anointed David as the new king. Over those years, David had become a great military leader and hero – with God's help.

While David was living at Hebron, the men of Judah anointed him as their king. After a few years, the other tribes all decided to make David their king when they saw how greatly God was blessing him. Then he truly was the king of Israel.

David Anointed King of Israel

He set up his kingdom in Jerusalem. He built his royal palace on the hill called Mount Zion.

The Philistines were not pleased when David took his throne, and they were still ruling many places in Israel. They brought an army to fight David into a valley near Jerusalem. David first asked God what he should do, and God told him to go out and fight. With his men he defeated the Philistines easily. David and his men burned the idols they had left behind.

David's Army Defeating the Philistines

197

David Waiting With His Men

After the battle, the Philistines returned to fight David. This time, God told him not to fight but to have his army wait under the mulberry trees for a sign from God. When he heard a sound in the tops of the trees, he was to go out to battle. David and his men followed God's instructions, and the Philistines were defeated. Never again did they return while David was king.

Transporting the Ark

David decided to return the Ark of God to Jerusalem. He started by rebuilding the tabernacle. Thirty thousand men went to help move the Ark from its resting place at Kirjathjearim.

The Ark on a Cart

God had commanded that only priests should touch or move the Ark, but the people had forgotten this commandment, and they moved it on a cart.

The Driver of the Ark is Killed

When one of the oxen pulling the cart started to stumble, the driver grabbed the Ark to keep it from falling. He immediately fell down dead.

Arrival of the Ark Carried By Levites

David knew God must be displeased, and he decided to leave the Ark at the home of a man who lived nearby. Then David tried to figure out what to do.

David soon learned that the Ark was only to be carried by priests on their shoulders, according to God's laws. The Ark was then moved to Jerusalem. This time the Levites carried it, which was the way God wanted. The Ark was placed in the new tabernacle, and the priests made offerings to God.

D-18 WHEN THE LITTLE LAME PRINCE GREW UP
2 SAMUEL 4:4 – 9:13

Mephibosheth was the name of Jonathan's little boy. When the Philistines killed Jonathan, Mephibosheth was only five years old. Everyone in his house hurried away, fearing the Philistines would come there to kill all of them, and Mephibosheth left with them.

The servant who was carrying the little boy stumbled and fell, injuring Mephibosheth. He was hurt so badly that he was never able to walk normally again. A man who lived on the other side of the Jordan River cared for him until he grew up and became a man.

Mephibosheth Meeting David in Jerusalem

David remembered his promise to always care for Jonathan's children. He heard where Mephibosheth was living and he sent for him. Mephibosheth had a wife, and he was a bit frightened to appear before King David. David told him not to be afraid and said he wanted only to show kindness to him.

David told him that he could live in the palace and also have all of the land that had belonged to his grandfather, King Saul. David had servants care for Mephibosheth's land. Mephibosheth's wife and his son Micha came to live with him at the palace. David was always kind to them, remembering the promise he had made to always take care of Jonathan's family.

D-19 DAVID'S SIN AND HIS PUNISHMENT
2 SAMUEL 11:1 – 12:26

David was a wise man, and he loved God. But sometimes he was tempted to do wrong things. One day he forgot that God could not only see what he was doing, God also knew his thoughts. He tried to deceive God by hiding his thoughts.

God sent a prophet to tell the king that he was sinning. The prophet told him that he would have many troubles because of his sin, including the death of his son.

The Prophet Nathan With David

David Prays for His Son

David was sorry for his sin and prayed for God to forgive him and help him change. God heard his prayer, and God wanted to help him because he was truly sorry.

The baby became sick, and David thought it was because God was punishing him. David didn't eat for seven days and prayed most of the time, but still the baby died.

When David heard that the baby had died, he dressed in his kingly clothes and went home to eat. The servants were surprised that he was no longer grieving, but David had accepted God's punishment. Soon David and his wife had another son and they named him Solomon. God told David that someday Solomon would be the king of Israel.

D-20 THE PRINCE WHO TRIED TO STEAL HIS FATHER'S KINGDOM
2 SAMUEL 15 – 17

Absalom was a very handsome prince, but he was not kind like his father, David. He thought only about the time when his father would die and he would take over as king.

He grew tired of waiting for his father to die, and he wanted to take over the kingdom while his father was alive. He did many favors for people in different parts of the land. These people began to like him, especially since he was young and handsome. Many thought he would make a great king.

One day Absalom asked his father for permission to go to Hebron to worship God there. David told him to go. David didn't know it, but Absalom planned to have the people of Israel make him king at Hebron, and he would return to Jerusalem and take over his father's throne.

A messenger told David what was really going on at Hebron. David took his family and servants and fled from the palace, fearing that Absalom would return and try to kill him.

Trying to Find David

David was sad that his own son was plotting against him, but he remembered that God had told him he would have future troubles because of his past sins. David and the servants cried as they left the palace.

Some priests tried to follow David with the Ark. But David told them to return the Ark to the tabernacle.

He asked the priests to send him information about what Absalom was doing. David asked another man, Hushai, to return to Jerusalem and help gather information about Absalom for the priests.

Absalom allowed Hushai to remain in his court because he thought Hushai was very wise. Hushai pretended that he wanted to work for Absalom and would keep his secrets. Soon Absalom said he wished to send some men to kill David.

Hushai told him that David fought very bravely and that it would take a large army to kill him. He said this to give David more time to get away. The priests sent messengers to tell David to go across the Jordan River because men were going to try to kill him.

A young man saw the messengers leave and he told Absalom. Absalom sent soldiers to find the messengers, but they hid in a well until the soldiers had gone back to the city. Then they delivered the message, and David fled to the city of Mahanaim on the other side of the Jordan River.

D-21 HOW THE WICKED PRINCE WAS CAUGHT IN A TREE
2 SAMUEL 18, 19

Absalom led his men to try to find David. David was hiding in Mahanaim, and his men would not let Absalom's men find him. David divided his men into three groups, and he sent them into the woods to find Absalom's men. David urged his men to be kind to Absalom since he still loved him the way a father loves his son.

David's servants were winning the battle. Many of Absalom's soldiers had been killed, and others were lost in the thick woods. Absalom became caught in a tree when his mule ran under a bough. One of David's servants found Absalom, and he told Joab, a military commander.

Joab Intends to Kill Absalom Who Is Entangled in a Tree

David Mourning for the Death of Absalom

Joab did not listen to David's wish that Absalom be treated kindly, and he killed him. Joab's men buried his body and covered the grave with stones. Absalom's men ran away when they heard that their leader had been killed.

David was very sad to learn of Absalom's death and he mourned for the loss of his son. Soon David returned to Jerusalem, and all the people there welcomed him home.

Under David's rule, Israel grew into a very strong, powerful nation. David began to trust more in his own army than he trusted in God, and God did not like this.

David wanted to know how many soldiers he had in his army, and he ordered that all of his troops be counted. Early one morning, a prophet found David and told him that God planned to punish the people because he didn't like David counting all the soldiers in Israel. David understood that he was wrong, and he prayed for forgiveness.

David Instructing Joab to Count the Soldiers

Another prophet visited David and told him that he must choose a punishment for the people: a famine of seven years, a war of three months, or a pestilence lasting three days. David chose the three days' pestilence.

Many people were killed, and David even saw an angel carrying a sword. David cried out that the angel should kill him instead of any more people. God felt sorry for him and no more people were killed.

The Plague of Jerusalem

God told David to build an altar where he had seen the angel standing. A man named Araunah owned the land, and he offered to give it to King David after he explained why he needed it. But David refused to accept it for free, and he paid the full price that the land was worth. After building the altar, David laid down offerings, and God sent fire down to burn up the sacrifices.

Araunah Offering His Land to David

With the help of his son Solomon, David planned to build a temple for God at this place, called Mount Moriah. God was pleased with David's plan.

D-2 3 WHY SOLOMON RODE THE KING'S MULE
1 KINGS 1:1 – 2:12

David was an old man, and he could no longer go out among his people. He stayed in his palace, in bed most of the time, waiting to die. His people had been blessed while he led them, but it was time to select a new leader.

One of Solomon's brothers assumed that he would rule the kingdom after David died. Adonjah led fifty men through the streets of Jerusalem, believing he would impress the people. Then he called his friends together for a great feast. The captain of David's army and the high priest were there, and they planned to make him king as soon as the feast was over.

The prophet Nathan was troubled when he heard this because he knew God had planned for Solomon to be the next king. Nathan told Bathsheba, Solomon's mother, about the feast in the valley just outside the city wall. Bathsheba asked David if he wanted Adonjah to be king, and she told him that God had chosen Solomon to take the throne. Nathan arrived, and he told King David about the feast and the plan to make Adonjah the next king.

David Tells Solomon He Will Be the Next King

David remembered the troubles that his wicked son Absalom had caused, and he feared that Adonjah would cause much trouble, too. He arranged to have Solomon anointed as king by the priest, and the servants would blow their trumpets and announce "God save King Solomon!"

The king's orders were carried out, and the people saw King Solomon riding on a mule. They were rejoicing so loudly they could be heard in the valley. Joab, the captain of David's army, heard the trumpets, and he wanted to go to Jerusalem to investigate. Before he could leave, a messenger arrived and told them what had taken place.

Everyone left the feast in fear and returned to their homes. Adonjah was afraid to return home because Solomon could have had him killed for what he had done. He ran to the tabernacle and put his arms around the altar of God. Solomon would not be angry with him as long as he behaved himself, and the servants told him this. He soon returned home.

David did not live much longer. He called Solomon to his bedside and asked him to always obey God. He told him about the many plans God had, including building the temple in Jerusalem. David had ruled as king for forty years when Solomon was made king.

D-24 How God Spoke in a Dream to Solomon
1 Kings 3:3-15; 4:29-34; 10:1-13

Solomon was not arrogant and proud like his brothers Absalom and Adonjah. He realized that he needed God's help to rule wisely over the people. Soon after he became king, Solomon made 1,000 burnt sacrifices to God at the great altar in Gibeon. They burned all day long.

He really wanted to speak to God, but he finally fell asleep. He had a dream, and God told him to ask for anything he wanted. Solomon could have asked God for anything, but he asked for an understanding heart and the ability to know right from wrong, in order to be able to rule his people wisely. God was so pleased with his request that he decided not only to give him great wisdom but also to give him honor and riches.

The Judgment of Solomon

211

Solomon awoke and knew he had been dreaming, but he believed what God said to him in the dream. He offered more sacrifices. At once his wisdom was obvious, and the people grew to respect him more and more. When two women both claimed to be the mother of the same baby, Solomon solved the problem by preparing to cut the baby in half. The real mother cried out, saying to stop and let the other woman have the baby. Solomon knew that the baby belonged to her.

The Queen of Sheba Visits Solomon

212

The wisdom of Solomon was talked about in other countries. Visitors came from other lands to see him, including from Egypt. Many came to hear the wise proverbs and wonderful songs he wrote. These are found in the Bible in the books of Proverbs, Ecclesiastes, and the Song of Solomon.

One day the Queen of Sheba came to see Solomon. She had heard about his wisdom, and she wanted to see for herself whether it was true. When she saw all of the riches of Solomon's kingdom and heard the wisdom of the answers he gave to her questions, she was glad she came and she was convinced that Solomon was indeed very wise. They gave gifts to each other, and she returned by camel to her homeland.

D-25 SOLOMON BUILDS THE TEMPLE ON MOUNT MORIAH
1 KINGS 5:1 – 9:9

David planned to build a temple much like the tabernacle, except it would be made of wood and stone instead of like a tent. However, God did not want David to build the temple because he had fought in too many battles.

God told David that his son Solomon would build the temple when the time was right and that Solomon would be a man of peace. Before he died, David carefully explained the plans for the new temple to Solomon.

David Tells Solomon How to Build the Temple

Cutting Down Trees for the New Temple

Solomon contacted Hiram, the king of Tyre, and asked for permission to buy trees to use as wood for the new temple. King Hiram had been a friend of David's and he was glad to help. Solomon's men helped Hiram's men cut down trees. Then the trees were floated in water to a place near Jerusalem, where they were cut into boards.

Making a Sacrifice While Beginning Work on the Temple

While this was going on, other men were digging great stones to be used as the foundation of the new temple. Solomon ordered that all the stones should be cut to fit in place, so that no further cutting would be necessary.

Solomon Oversees the Construction

SOLOMON'S TEMPLE—FRONT VIEW.

The task was so great that thousands of men were involved. They worked for seven years on the building before it was completed.

The temple stood on top of Mount Moriah, where David had seen the angel with the drawn sword stretched out over the city. There was a great altar built of rough stones, as God had commanded.

SOLOMON'S TEMPLE—INTERIOR.

Only the priests were allowed inside the inner rooms of the temple, but a wide outer court was built around this area, and all the men of Israel were permitted inside the outer court. Only Jews were allowed inside the building.

When the construction of the building was finished, Solomon called the men of Israel to come to Jerusalem from every part of his kingdom. He went with them to the temple and offered many sacrifices on the great altar.

The Ark of God was brought there and placed in the holy of holies, the inner room behind the great curtain where only the high priest was allowed to enter. Other furniture from the tabernacle was put in the temple just as God had commanded it to be placed. When the Ark was moved to the temple, a cloud hovered over it, just as God had made a cloud hover over the tabernacle many years before. All the people knew that God was pleased with Solomon's temple when they saw this sign.

Dedicating the New Temple

Solomon prayed that God would bless the new temple and hear the prayers of anyone who prayed there. Then the people returned home.

God spoke to Solomon in a dream once again. God told him he would bless him and his children if he kept the law, but he would curse him and his family – and cause him to lose his kingdom – if he did not keep the law.

D-26 KING SOLOMON'S LAST DAYS
1 KINGS 11

Solomon ruled Israel for many years after the temple was built. His leadership earned great fame for him and great power for his country.

However, his behavior during his last days was not his best behavior. He married women from other lands and brought them to live in Jerusalem. Instead of worshiping God, they worshiped idols that they had brought from their own countries. Solomon felt obligated to build temples for their idols, and he even bowed down to the idols himself.

God was angered by his actions. God allowed Solomon's enemies to rise up against him, and he told Solomon that the kingdom of Israel would be taken away from him forever. God also said that Solomon's son would be the leader of only one of the twelve tribes.

Solomon's Last Days

Solomon taxed the people to pay for large storehouses for fruits and grains. Many of the people felt that the taxes were too high.

Jeroboam was one of Solomon's servants. Solomon respected his hard work so much that he made him the overseer of all the building workmen. One day a prophet spoke with Jeroboam as he was leaving Jerusalem.

Ahijah, the prophet, met Jeroboam in a field outside Jerusalem and stopped to speak with him. The prophet tore his cloak into twelve pieces, and he gave ten pieces to Jeroboam. He told Jeroboam the ten pieces represented the ten tribes God was giving to him because Solomon had turned to idol worship. God was leaving one tribe for Solomon's son because God had promised David his children would sit on the throne in Jerusalem.

Solomon heard what the prophet had told him, and he became angry and wanted to kill Jeroboam. Jeroboam heard that the king was sending men to kill him. He ran away to Egypt and lived there until he heard that King Solomon had died.

Part E: The Divided Kingdom
1 Kings, 2 Kings, 1 Chronicles, 2 Chronicles, Jonah, Jeremiah

E-1 The Foolish Young Prince Who Lost His Father's Kingdom
1 Kings 12:1-24

Solomon's son, Prince Rehoboam, grew up when Israel was a powerful and wealthy country. He had lived near the temple and saw many people coming there to worship God, but he had never learned to honor and worship God himself. His mother had not taught him the religion of the Israelites, and he worshiped idols as she did.

After Solomon died, the men of Israel were not sure who should be the next king. At first they brought Jeroboam back from Egypt. The men of Israel decided to consider making Jeroboam their leader.

Then they met with Rehoboam. They told Rehoboam they wanted to know what type of ruler he would be, and then they would decide whom to

Rehoboam Refuses to Listen to the Old Men

make king.

Rehoboam was not ready to give an answer immediately. He did not have his father's wisdom, and he knew nothing about what it was like to be poor and work hard to survive. He told the people to wait three days and then he would give his answer.

Rehoboam consulted with some old men who had helped his father rule the kingdom. They told him to speak kindly to the people and promise to make their work easier. He was not happy with their advice, and he sent them away.

He called some of the other young princes together and asked them what to do. They told him to speak harshly to the people and threaten to make their work harder if they ever complained at all. They told him to tell the people he would do just as he pleased if they made him their king. Rehoboam liked their advice and decided to follow it.

After three days, the people returned to hear what Rehoboam would do if they made him their king. He told them he would be harsher than King Solomon, and they would fear and respect him as a stern ruler.

Rehoboam Accepts the Advice of the Young Princes

Nearly all of the people decided they did not want such a king. Only the people in the tribe of Judah decided to make him their king. Rehoboam thought the others would soon respect him as king, and he sent a tax collector to gather money from the other tribes. Instead of giving money to his tax collector, they threw stones at him. Rehoboam knew that the people in the other tribes were displeased with him, and he stayed away from the other tribes' lands.

He returned home to the tribe of Judah, and he decided to send soldiers to fight the other tribes. God sent a prophet to tell him not to do this, since God no longer wanted one ruler over all the tribes. Rehoboam listened to the prophet and kept his soldiers at home.

E-2 Two Golden Calves
1 Kings 12:25 – 13:6

The people of the ten tribes who did not choose Rehoboam to be their king met together to select their king. They chose Jeroboam, and he ruled his kingdom from the city of Shechem.

Jeroboam knew it was God who caused the people to choose him as their king. He remembered God promised to bless the people if he ruled them wisely.

However, Jeroboam did not trust in God as fully as David had done. He believed he had to help himself and that he shouldn't expect God to help him all the time.

Jeroboam had seen the temples for idols that Solomon had built and even worshiped in, and he had seen the temples to the various Egyptian gods.

One of Jeroboam's Golden Calves

He was afraid to let his people go to Jerusalem and worship in the temple. He thought they might wish to reunite as a people and he would no longer be their leader. He decided to change their religion so that they would have no reason to go to Jersusalem.

He collected much gold, and from this gold he made two golden calves. He told the people these were the gods that were responsible for their release from Egypt, and he was placing one golden calf in the northern half of the land and one in the southern half.

221

Worshiping the Golden Calf at Bethel

He made houses or temples for the golden calves, selected priests, and even had feasts and holy days on the same days as those in Jerusalem.

God was very angry that Jeroboam had not trusted in him to keep the people of Israel from reuniting and turning against him. God sent a prophet to warn Jeroboam. The prophet told him that the altar would fall apart and the ashes would fall on the ground. This would be a sign from God.

Jeroboam became angry and told his men to stop the prophet. When Jeroboam reached out to grab the man, the flesh of his hand stuck to the bone, and he could not move his hand at all. At that moment the stones of the altar at Bethel fell apart, and the ashes poured out onto the ground.

Jeroboam became very fearful. He begged the prophet to pray to God and ask for his hand to be healed. The prophet prayed, and the king's hand was made well again.

E-3 WHY A LION KILLED A PROPHET
1 KINGS 13:7-32

The prophet who spoke to Jeroboam had been warned by God not to eat or drink at that place and to return to his own home by a different road than the one he had traveled there on. The king offered to let him stay overnight and even offered him money, but the prophet remembered God's warning and said he had to return home.

Some sons of a different prophet heard what he said to the king, and they told their father what they had heard. Their father wanted to talk to him, and he prepared his animals to travel. He hurried to find him before he left.

When he saw an old man sitting under a tree, the prophet asked him if he was the prophet from Judah. "I am," he answered. He invited him to go to his home and share some bread. He told him that he could not because God had told him not to eat anything and to return home.

The old man told a lie to the prophet from Judah. He told him that an angel had appeared to him and told him to bring the prophet to his home to eat bread. The prophet believed this. While he was eating, God spoke to him and told him that he would be punished for his disobedience. The prophet left and started to hurry home.

Soon a lion appeared and killed him, but the lion did not try to eat him. The ass that the prophet had been riding on stood there, waiting for his master to arise.

Some people gathered to see what had happened. The old man who had lied about the angel heard about it, and he went to see for himself. He felt very bad, and he and his sons took the prophet's body and buried it. The old man told his sons to bury him in the same place after he died.

The Body of the Disobedient Prophet

223

E-4 WHAT THE BLIND PROPHET TOLD THE QUEEN OF ISRAEL
1 KINGS 14:1-20

King Jeroboam and his wife had a little son named Abijah. He was a good child, and they hoped that he would grow up to be a strong man. But one day he became sick, and for several days he would not leave his bed.

When weeks passed by and still the boy was very ill, Jeroboam decided to seek the advice of a prophet. He was afraid for the prophet to know who was asking for help, so he disguised his wife as a poor woman and sent her to see Ahijah, the prophet who had told him he would be the first king of Israel.

Ahijah was now an old man and blind, but he knew the woman was Jeroboam's wife because God told him so. He asked why she was trying to hide herself from him, and then he told her that he had sad news for her.

The prophet told her that her husband must be punished for turning to idol worship. He said that the little boy would die as soon as she returned to the city gates and that eventually all of Jeroboam's sons and daughters would be killed and the kingdom would be taken away from his family forever. The little boy died as soon as she returned to the city.

After Jeroboam died, his son took the throne, and a wicked man soon killed him. Then all the sons and daughters of Jeroboam were killed, and their bodies were thrown into the streets for the wild dogs and birds to eat. This was the punishment for Jeroboam's sins of turning his people away from God and making everyone worship idols.

Jeroboam's Family Is Killed

E-5 The King Who Tried to Destroy Idol-Worship
1 Kings 15:8-24; 2 Chronicles 14:1 – 16:14

During the years that Rehoboam and his son Abijah ruled the kingdom of Judah, a young prince named Asa was growing up in Jerusalem. After his father Abijah died, Asa became the new king of Judah. He was a wise ruler and tried to turn his people back to God. He had his servants tear down all the idols and all of the altars built to worship the false gods.

One day Asa learned that his own grandmother, the queen, was worshiping an idol, and he was very disappointed. He refused to allow her to be queen any longer, and he destroyed her personal idol. He wanted to make sure everyone understood that they were no longer to worship idols.

Asa Destroys the Queen's Idols

Asa grew wiser and his kingdom grew stronger. His people respected him. He had peace for ten years in his country, and then God allowed a strong army from Ethiopia to attack his kingdom. His soldiers were fighting bravely, but they were being defeated. Asa had a lot of faith in God. He prayed for God to help him, and God answered his prayer. The Ethiopian soldiers ran away in fear, leaving many valuables and animals which were brought back to Jerusalem.

God sent a prophet to speak to Asa. The prophet told him that God would protect him as long as he remained faithful, but God would no longer protect him if he turned away from God as his ancestors had done. Asa decided to always remain faithful and true to God.

Soon the people in the land of Israel began to hear that God was blessing Asa the king of Judah, and they started going there to worship at the temple and to offer sacrifices once again. They all worshiped God together, and God was pleased.

Baasha, the king of Israel, was jealous of King Asa because some of his people had left his land to live in the land of Judah. He planned to use soldiers based in a southern city to block anyone else from traveling to or from Judah.

King Asa heard about his plan and was irritated. He tried to think of a way to stop the plan, but he did not ask God for help. He sent money to the king who was to the north of King Baasha, and he asked him to cause trouble for King Baasha so that he would have to send his soldiers there. The other king agreed to help King Asa, and King Baasha diverted his soldiers to the north.

King Asa's Men Attacking King Baasha's City

While the soldiers were away, King Asa's men destroyed the city King Baasha was building, which he was planning to use as a base for his soldiers.

God sent another prophet to tell King Asa that he had done wrong by asking a different king for help instead of asking God. The prophet told him that he would have wars as long as he was alive. The king did not believe the prophet and put him in prison.

Years later, King Asa's feet became diseased, and he suffered a great deal. He would not ask God for help and trusted only in his doctors. He died after two more years of suffering. He had ruled longer than any other king of Judah before him.

E-6 WHY BIRDS FED A PROPHET
1 KINGS 16:29 – 17:24

Things were not going well in the kingdom of Israel where the people continued to worship the golden calves. All of the kings were wicked, and Ahab was the wickedest in the sight of God. He married Jezebel, a heathen princess, and she brought her religion to his land. Ahab built temples for her gods and he worshiped with her. But this wasn't enough for Jezebel. She brought many priests of Baal, her god, into the country, and she ordered that all of the prophets of God be killed. God was very unhappy and angry.

One day Ahab was surprised to see a strange-looking man standing in front of him. He was the prophet Elijah, who had been sent by God to talk to him. Before the king could say anything, Elijah told him that there would be no more dew on the ground or rain from the sky until he said so, and then he turned and walked away.

At first Ahab paid no attention to what Elijah had told him. Then he began to notice there was no rain and not even any dew on the ground. Ahab sent men to find Elijah but no one could find him. Ahab became alarmed since the crops would die and there would be no food without any rain. He asked neighboring kings to help him find the prophet.

Elijah Is Fed by Ravens

God had told Elijah where to hide from King Ahab. He drank water from a nearby stream, and birds brought bread and meat to him every day, just as God had said they would.

After many days, even the stream began to dry up because of the lack of rain. Elijah wondered what he would do. God told him to leave that place and go a city called Zarephath. God told him a widow there would care for him.

227

The Widow of Zarephath Helps Elijah

Near the gates of the city, Elijah saw a woman dressed poorly. He though she might be the widow he was searching for. He first asked her for water, and she started to go into the city to get some for him.

Then he asked her for some food. She said she had nothing to give but only a handful of meal and a little oil. She said she was planning to cook that for her son and herself before they became ill from hunger.

Elijah told her to go ahead and cook a meal for them and also for him. God would not allow her to run out of food or oil until the famine was over.

She started to cook, and she did have more than enough food and oil for all of them. Every day the same thing happened, and she never ran out of food or oil. Elijah stayed with her for many months. Elijah was grateful to the woman.

One day her son became very sick and died. She asked Elijah what she had done to deserve this. Elijah felt very bad for her. He took the body of the boy upstairs and prayed that God would restore his life. God heard his prayers and brought the boy back to life. Elijah carried him downstairs to his mother.

Elijah Raises the Widow of Zarephath's Son

She was overjoyed when she saw her son alive. She said that she knew Elijah must truly be a man of God who spoke the truth.

E-7 How God Showed His Great Power on Mount Caramel
1 Kings 18:1-40

After Elijah's visit, there was no rain in the land of Israel for over three years. No food would grow, the grass died, and most of the animals became sick and malnourished.

Ahab was convinced that there would be no rain until Elijah returned to announce it. He sent many messengers to find the prophet, but none of them were able to find Elijah.

One day Ahab called his chief servant Obadiah and told him they must find green pasture for the animals or they would all die. The king and the servant set off in opposite directions, each trying to find green pasture.

Obadiah had not gone far when he saw Elijah, and he knew at once who he was. The prophet told him to return to Ahab and tell him that he had arrived. Obadiah told him that he was afraid to leave him alone because the king would surely kill him if he could not find Elijah immediately. Elijah promised to visit the king that same day, and Obadiah went to find King Ahab.

Elijah Denouncing Ahab

Ahab listened to the news, and he hurried with Obadiah to the place where he had seen the prophet. When they found Elijah there, the king was angry at first. He asked him if he was the one who had been troubling their country.

Elijah said he hadn't been the cause of the trouble, but he knew the wicked actions of the king and his ancestors were the cause. They had turned away from God, and God was punishing them. Elijah told the king to bring all the prophets of Baal to Mount Caramel, along with all the people of the kingdom. Ahab hurried to do what the prophet said.

When the people gathered together, they listened carefully to Elijah. He told the people that they must decide to follow Baal or to follow God. He said that Baal had 450 prophets, and there was only one of him, but he would show them that God was much more powerful than Baal.

He told them to prepare sacrifices, and whichever God answered by setting the sacrifice on fire would be the true God. The people prepared the sacrifices and waited to see what would happen.

Elijah allowed the prophets of Baal to choose the altar for their sacrifice, and he chose the other altar. Elijah told them to call on Baal to send fire from heaven and burn up the sacrifice they offered. It did not take long for Baal's many priests to prepare the sacrifice and pray to Baal, but nothing happened. The prophets of Baal cried aloud for many hours, but still nothing happened. They even cut themselves with knives to get Baal's attention.

When evening came, Elijah gathered twelve stones together to rebuild the altar at the temple in Jerusalem, which had been torn down. He had the people pour four barrels of water over his sacrifice, until the meat and wood were completely soaked and water ran down into the circular ditch surrounding the area.

When everything was ready, Elijah called on God, and fire came down from heaven and burnt everything up. The flames even dried up the water in the ditch. The people were amazed, and they decided that God obviously was much more powerful than Baal.

E-8 THE LITTLE CLOUD THAT BROUGHT MUCH RAIN
1 KINGS 18:40 – 19:3

Elijah knew his work was just beginning when God sent the fire that burned up his sacrifice. He commanded the people to capture the wicked priests of Baal and kill all of them.

The Prophets of Baal Are Killed

Ahab did not know what to do. He wondered how his wife would react when she learned that all of the priests of Baal had been put to death. Elijah told him not to worry and enjoy the feast. He said that soon there would be a great rain and an end to the famine.

Elijah Warns Ahab of the Coming Rain

Elijah prayed over and over for rain, a total of seven times. After the seventh time, his servant reported seeing a small cloud. Elijah told Ahab and the others to return home to Jezreel; otherwise they would be caught in the rain.

Elijah was very happy because God had shown his power in Israel that day. The wind blew and a very strong rain came, enough to cause the streams to overflow and soak all the dry ground.

Ahab knew that Elijah had also returned to Jezreel. He hurried to his palace to tell Jezebel about all that happened that day. Ahab did not want to punish Elijah, but he was afraid his wicked wife would want to.

Jezebel flew into a rage when she heard how all of the priests of Baal had been killed. She sent a message to Elijah, telling him he would be dead by that time the next day. Elijah hurried to escape, fearing the wrath of the wicked queen.

E-9 WHAT AN ANGEL FOUND UNDER A JUNIPER TREE
1 KINGS 19:3-21

One day God sent an angel into the wilderness south of Judah. There was an unhappy man all alone there, and God wanted the angel to comfort him. The angel saw a man lying on the ground under a Juniper tree. That man was Elijah, and he had run away from Queen Jezebel.

An Angel Feeds Elijah

Elijah was very unhappy, and he certainly had not expected to end up running for his life. Instead of respecting what God had done, Jezebel didn't care about anything except revenge for proving that God was more powerful than Baal. She was determined to have Elijah killed.

The angel did not awaken Elijah right away. First he made a fire and baked a cake. Then the angel awakened him. Elijah saw the food and a bottle of water. He was very hungry. He ate the food and drank the water. Then he went back to sleep.

The angel appeared a second time with more food. He urged Elijah to eat because he had a long journey ahead of him. Elijah ate the special food the angel had prepared, and he was not hungry again for forty days. He went to the mountain where God first spoke to Moses from a burning bush and he hid in a cave.

Elijah Hides in a Cave

God appeared to him and told him to leave the cave and stand on the mountain. Elijah did what God told him.

God caused a great wind to sweep across the mountain and break the rocks into pieces. God caused an earthquake to shake the mountain, and a fire burned many of the trees.

After all of this was over, Elijah heard a quiet voice, and he knew this was the voice of God. God asked him why he was hiding, and he answered that he was the only one left in the land who believed in God.

God told him that wasn't true and that there were 7,000 people who had never worshiped Baal. God sent Elijah to do the work of a prophet in the land of Israel. God told him to anoint a young man named Elisha to be the next great prophet after he should die.

Elijah was not afraid to return to Israel because he knew God was protecting him, and he knew there were 7,000 other faithful people there. He found Elisha, and he anointed him to become the next great prophet, as God had commanded. Elisha broke his plow into pieces and sacrificed his oxen to God. He left his field to become the servant of the man who heard the voice of God.

Elijah Summoning Elisha

E-10 Ahab and the Beggar King
1 Kings 20

King Ahab had an enemy named Benhadad. Benhadad ruled over the country of Syria, which is to the north of Israel. This king hated the people of Israel and wanted to make all of them his slaves.

Benhadad and thirty-two of his friends who were also kings decided to go to war against Ahab. They brought their armies down and camped near Ahab's capital city, Samaria. While they were preparing to invade, God sent a prophet to tell Ahab that God would protect him from his enemies and give him victory when they fought.

Ahab had a small army compared to the great number of soldiers from Syria, but he trusted in God, and his few men went out bravely to attack Benhadad and his soldiers. They found him and the other kings drinking wine. Soon the whole army ran away in fear, including their drunken leaders. King Ahab's army killed most of the Syrians, and only a few of the other kings returned home alive.

The Children of Israel Attack the Syrians

After this victory, God sent the prophet to talk to Ahab again and tell him the Syrians would return the next year to renew the fight. Ahab prepared his army for another attack. One year later, the Syrian army returned. They believed that the God of Israel was a god of the hills only, and they did not pitch their tents in the hills near Samaria again. Instead, they camped on the plains in the north country of Israel. They planned to fight in the valley, and they believed their gods would give them victory there, away from the hills.

Ahab gathered his soldiers and set out to meet the enemy again. Ahab was not afraid because the prophet had told him that the Syrians would be defeated since they believed that God only had power in the hills. God wanted to prove that he could help them fight on the plains or the hills.

When the battle began, the small army of Israel fought bravely and killed many of the Syrians. Other Syrians with King Benhadad ran to a nearby city called Aphek. They thought they could hide inside the city walls, but instead the city walls fell down on them once they were inside, and thousands of soldiers were killed.

King Benhadad was not hurt because he hid in a place away from the

The Second Battle Against the Syrians

crumbling walls. But he was afraid to come out of his hiding place. Some of his servants urged him to act humbly and hope that perhaps Ahab would treat him kindly and spare his life.

Some of those servants presented themselves to King Ahab and said that they would be his servants. They told him that their king had asked for his life to be spared. Ahab was glad to hear Benhadad was still alive. He told the servants to bring the king to him. Benhadad acted very humbly, and eventually King Ahab allowed him to return to Syria.

God was not pleased that Ahab allowed the wicked king to escape with no punishment. He sent a prophet to tell Ahab that he had done wrong. He told Ahab that he had allowed a bad man to escape justice, and God was going to make him pay with his own life. He realized that he had done wrong, and he returned to his palace feeling very guilty and anxious.

E-11 HOW A KINGS'S UNHAPPINESS COST A MAN'S LIFE
1 KINGS 21

Ahab built a summerhouse in the little city of Jezreel, to the north of Samaria. It had beautiful lawns and gardens of flowers and trees. He tried hard to make it very beautiful. One day the king noticed a vineyard across from his gardens. The vineyard belonged to a man named Naboth. The king wanted to pay Naboth for the vineyard or trade him other land for it.

Naboth Refuses to Sell His Land

He found Naboth and offered to pay him for the land. Naboth said the land had been in his family for many generations, and there was no way he could sell it or trade it for other land. Ahab was disappointed and still wanted the land for his own, but he returned to his home in Samaria.

His wife Jezebel could tell he was unhappy, and she asked him why. He told her about his experience at Jezreel with the man who refused to sell the vineyard that he wanted. Ahab knew that his wicked wife would find a way to get the vineyard, and she even told him that she would. Jezebel wrote letters using her husband's seal, ordering the rulers to stone Naboth to death. She told the rulers to have two men testify falsely that Naboth had spoken against God and King Ahab. The people believed the two men and put Naboth to death. A messenger reported the news to Jezebel that Naboth was now dead. She told her husband to go

Elijah Denouncing Ahab's Crime in the Vineyard

and claim the vineyard, since Naboth was no longer alive to refuse him.

When he reached the vineyard, Ahab was surprised to find Elijah between the rows of grapevines. Elijah told him that he had killed and wrongfully taken possession of this land, and he would soon die for this great evil act. Ahab trembled as he listened to the prophet.

Elijah said that all of Ahab's children would also be punished. And Jezebel would die a horrible death, worse than the others, because she had caused Ahab to do so much evil in the land of Israel.

Ahab was very sorry. He dressed himself in sackcloth and refused to eat. God could tell that he truly was sorry, and God decided that Ahab's children and wife wouldn't die until after he did.

An arrow wounded King Ahab as he was watching his army fight a battle. He asked to be taken away from the battlefield, and eventually he was slain by enemy soldiers.

The Death of Ahab

E-12 WHEN FIRE FELL FROM THE SKY
2 KINGS 1

After King Ahab died, one of his sons, Ahaziah, became the new king. He was wicked and worshiped Baal, the idol his mother Jezebel worshiped. And he hated the people who tried to please God.

But Ahaziah did not rule for very long. One day he had an accident and badly injured himself by falling down. He lay in bed for many days. Finally he called some of his men and told them to go to the land of the Philistines and ask their god whether he would ever be healed of his injuries.

God knew what Ahaziah was doing, and he sent an angel to tell Elijah to find the messengers Ahazhiah had sent to the land of the Philistines. The angel told Elijah to tell them that Ahaziah would never be cured of his disease.

Elijah found the men, and he asked if there was no God in Israel, or why they had to go to the god of the Philistines for an answer. He told them that the Lord God had said that the king would never again be up to get up out of his bed.

Elijah left, and the men decided to return to their king at once and tell him what they had heard. The king wondered why they had returned so soon. They told him about the strange man they had met and what he had told them.

The king knew it must have been Elijah who spoke to the messengers. He was displeased with Elijah, and he sent a group of men to find him and take him to Samaria. They found him on top of a hill, but Elijah refused to come down because he knew they planned to do him harm.

Elijah said that if he were a man of God, fire would come down from the sky and destroy all of them. Fire fell from the sky and burned up the captain and his men. When the first group of men did not return, the king sent a second group. They were killed by fire, just as the first group had been.

Finally the king sent a third group of men to capture Elijah. This captain knew what had happened to the other men, and he was afraid of Elijah and his God. Instead of demanding that he leave the hill, the captain climbed the hill, fell down before Elijah, and begged for mercy. The angel of God who often spoke to Elijah told him not to be afraid but to go with the men to Samaria to see the king.

Elijah went to the palace to see the sick king. He was not afraid of him, and he told Ahaziah the same words he had told the messengers – that he would never leave his bed. Not long after, Ahaziah died and his brother Jehoram ruled Israel.

The Messengers of Ahaziah Destroyed By Fire

Elijah the prophet was now an old man. He had worked hard to stop the worship of Baal in the land of Israel, and he tried to get the people to return to worshiping the true God.

Elijah knew he wouldn't live much longer, and he planned to have the younger prophet Elisha take over his work. Elijah visited the schools where the young prophets learned about God, and perhaps he told them that he would die soon. He wanted Elisha to stay with them, but Elisha did not want to leave Elijah alone since he knew he was going to die soon.

Elisha stayed with the old prophet, and the younger prophets followed far behind them. When they came to the Jordan River, the old prophet took off his robe and struck the waters of the river with it. The waters parted at once, and a dry path appeared between the waters. The two prophets walked across to the other side.

Elijah Divides the Waters of the Jordan River

Elisha asked that when Elijah went to heaven, God should bless him with a double portion of Elijah's spirit. Elijah told him that if he saw God take him away then he would know that God would bless him this way.

The two men walked on. Suddenly a chariot of fire and horses of fire pushed between them and separated them. Then there was a great whirlwind,

Elijah Ascends to Heaven

and Elisha saw his old friend taken up into heaven in the whirlwind.

The chariot, horses, and Elijah disappeared into the clouds. Lying on the ground was Elijah's robe. Elisha picked it up and started to return to the land of Israel.

The young prophets stood waiting by the river, long after they had lost sight of the two men. When Elisha came back alone, they saw him. They saw him strike the waters with Elijah's robe as Elijah had done before, and the waters parted once again. The young prophets knew that the spirit and powers of Elijah were now with Elisha. They hurried to meet him and bowed at his feet.

Some of the young prophets wanted to find the body of Elijah and bury him on one of the mountains. Elisha knew the body was nowhere to be found, but he let the young prophets search anyway after they pleaded with him. They searched for three days. When they returned, Elisha told them they should have listened to him the first time. Elisha stayed there for a while and taught the young men at the school of the prophets in Jericho.

245

E-14 Why Two Hungry Bears Killed Some Children
2 Kings 2:19-25

Bethel was a city in the land of Israel where Jeroboam had set up one of the two golden calves for his citizens to worship. The people there worshiped the calf and had turned away from God.

Other people living near Bethel still loved God. They wanted to see their religion become more popular, and they had started a school in Bethel called a "school of the prophets," like the one in Jericho. Elijah and Elisha used to visit the school.

After Elijah went up to heaven in a great whirlwind, Elisha took over his work, including visiting the schools of the prophets and teaching the people of Israel to worship only God. He also carried messages from God to different kings in the land, as Elijah had done.

Elisha stayed in Jericho for a while after Elijah was taken from him. One day the men of the city went to him and said that the water from the spring was making people sick and even killing them. Elisha told the men to bring him a new bottle with some salt in it. He took the salt and threw it into the spring, and he told them that the water would no longer make anyone ill because God had healed the waters.

Then Elisha started on his journey to visit the school of the prophets at Bethel. As he approached the city, he met a large group of children. Their

The Children Mock Elisha

246

parents were idol worshipers, and they did not respect the prophets of God. They had heard that Elijah went up to heaven in a whirlwind but they did not believe it.

The children began to make fun of Elisha. They danced around him and mocked him by telling him to go up to heaven as Elijah had done. Elisha knew these children would never grow up to be good men and women; they would grow up to worship idols and only harm others. He prayed for God to punish them for their wrongdoing.

Soon two hungry bears came out of the woods and killed forty-two of the children. Some of the children got away, and they learned that it was wrong to make fun of people who worship God the way they had done to Elisha. After Elisha's visit at Bethel he went to Mount Caramel and then back to Samaria, the capital of Israel.

Bears Kill the Children

E-15 Elisha's Miracle that Saved Two Boys From Becoming Slaves
2 Kings 4:1-7

Elisha the prophet visited the poor people in the land of Israel as well as the rich. He listened to the troubles of the poor people. They loved him very much and always made him feel like a welcome guest.

Two little boys lived in one of the homes Elisha often visited. They were brothers, and their father was one of the young prophets. They lived happy lives even though they were poor. One day their father became very sick and died, leaving them with only their poor mother.

Later, a rich man stopped at their home. He said he was there to collect the money that their father had borrowed before he became sick and died. The mother told him she had no money. He said he would take the boys to be his slaves if she couldn't pay the money, but he would give her more time to pay before doing this.

The mother didn't know what to do. She decided to ask Elisha for help. Elisha felt sorry for her. He asked her what she had in her house. She told him she had nothing except a pot of oil. The prophet knew this would be enough for God to help her. He told her to go home and borrow empty jars, bowls, and pots from her neighbors. He told her that after she had many containers, she was to close the door to her home and begin filling the containers with oil, one by one.

The boys wondered what was going on, and she told them what the prophet had told her. They helped her fill the containers with oil. Never before had they seen so much oil in one place. They knew that God was causing the amount of oil to increase. Finally they had filled all the containers. The widow hurried to find Elisha and ask him what to do.

Elisha knew the widow would be back and he was waiting for her. He told her to go home and sell all the oil she had. There would be enough money to pay the debt her dead husband owed and still have money left over for her and her children.

The mother was very grateful. She made sure the boys understood that God had saved them, and she tried to teach them to always serve and love God.

Elisha Teaching in Shunem

E-16 A Little Boy Who Died and Became Alive Again
2 Kings 4:8-37

Elisha went from one place to another, always teaching the people to love and serve the true God. One day he came to the city of Shunem, where a rich woman and her husband lived. The woman invited Elisha and his servant to stay with her because she believed that he was a true prophet of God.

Every time he returned to Shunem, he stayed with the woman and her husband. Eventually the couple built a room with a bed, chair, table, and candlestick so that Elisha would have his own room whenever he stayed with them.

Soon Elisha returned, and he was pleased to see the room they had built for him. Elisha and his servant wanted to repay their kindness, and they asked the woman what she needed. She told them she didn't need anything at all, and she didn't need any favors.

Elisha realized that the couple had no children. He told the woman that because she had been so kind, God would give her a son. She thought it sounded too good to be true, but soon she had a baby boy.

A few years passed, and the child grew old enough to walk and follow his father around. One day he was in the fields while his father worked, and suddenly the child's head became very sore and he started to cry. A servant carried the child home.

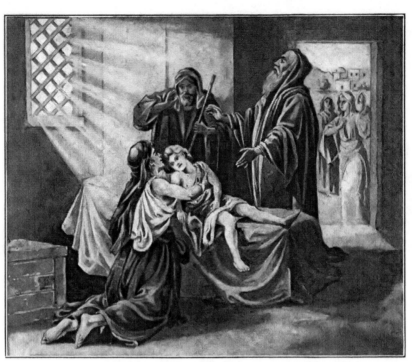

Elisha Brings Life to the Boy in Shunem

The mother was very alarmed to see her son so ill. She picked held him and help him in her arms, but he died soon after. She took the child's body and laid him on Elisha's bed. Then she hurried to find Elisha. It was a long ride to Mount Caramel where Elisha was teaching, but she didn't care about the distance. She hoped that Elisha could somehow help her son.

Elisha saw the woman coming far down the road, and he sent his servant to greet her. She ran past Elisha's servant and hurried on until she reached Elisha. When she reached him she fell down at his feet, crying. Elisha figured out that something was wrong with her little boy. He told his servant to hurry to her home and place Elisha's staff across the face of the child. The servant did this, and still the child was dead. The servant went back to meet with the mother and Elisha.

Elisha knew that he had to help the child himself. He went into the room with the child's body and closed the door. He prayed very hard for God to make the child alive again. He placed his face on the child's face and his hands on the child's hands. The child's body became warm, and soon he was walking around again.

He called to the woman and told her to take her son. She saw that her child was alive again, and she bowed at Elisha's feet to show her gratitude. He told her it was God's power that had saved her boy.

The Boy Goes Outside With His Mother

E-17 ELISHA'S KINDNESS TO THE POOR
2 KINGS 4:38-44; 6:1-7

There was a time when food was scarce in the land of Israel, and the poor people had little to eat. Elisha went to visit the young prophets who lived at Gilgal during this time. One of the young men went to pick some vegetables, and he accidentally mixed a poisonous gourd in with the other food.

When the young men began to eat, they discovered that the food was poisoned. Some of the men were very upset. Elisha told them everything would turn out fine and not to worry. He threw some flour into the poisoned container of food and mixed everything together. Then he commanded the young men to feed the food to the hungry people. The poor people ate, and they did not become sick from the poisonous gourd.

While Elisha was staying with the poor people, a man brought him a present of twenty loaves of barley bread and some ears of grain. Elisha knew everyone was hungry, and he told a servant to prepare the food for all of the prophets. The servant did not believe this was possible because there

251

was not nearly enough food for 100 men. Elisha told his servant that God would bless the food and that it would be enough for everyone. God increased the amount of food until there was plenty for all of them.

A different day, a group of young prophets went down the Jordan River to build new homes for themselves. Elisha was with them again. They were cutting down the trees along the river's bank to use as wood for their new homes. While they were cutting the trees down, one man's axe blade fell into a muddy part of the river and he could not find it. He was worried because he had borrowed the axe and didn't have the money to buy a new one. He told Elisha what had happened.

Elisha threw a stick into the water where the man had lost the axe blade. As the men were watching, the axe blade floated to the surface like a piece of wood. Elisha told the men to take it from the water before it floated away. The men who watched were reminded of the power of God.

Elisha Saves the Man's Axe Blade From the River

E-18 How a Slave Girl Helped a Man Find God
2 Kings 5:1-27

The Syrians lived just to the north of Israel. They did not know about the God of Israel. They worshipped a god called Rimmon, and they had temples for worshiping him in their cities.

The Syrians would often come down and steal things from the Israelites. Sometimes they even stole children to be sold as slaves to rich people in their own land.

One time a band of robbers stole a little girl away from her mother's home. They sold the child to a rich captain in the Syrian army named Naaman. Naaman brought the child to his wife to become her servant.

Naaman's wife was kind to her, and after a while the child began to like her new home. She still missed her old home, but she had grown to love Naaman's wife.

When the slave-girl had been living in Naaman's home for a while, she learned that he had a terrible disease called leprosy. Leprosy causes all parts of the body to drop off as it spreads, and eventually the person suffering with the disease always dies.

One day the little girl was talking to Naaman's wife, and she said that the prophet in Samaria could cure him of the disease. The girl knew about some of the miracles Elisha had performed.

Naaman's wife told him what the little girl had said, and Naaman told the king. The king liked Naaman and wanted him to be cured of leprosy. The king told Naaman he would write a letter for him to the king of Israel and ask him to cure the disease. Of course Naaman would have to go to Samaria.

The king of Syria sent gold and fine clothes as a gift to the king of Israel. He believed that the king of Israel would simply command the prophet to heal Naaman. When they arrived at the palace in Samaria, a messenger delivered the letter and gifts to the king of Israel while Naaman and his servants waited outside.

The letter troubled the king of Israel. He thought the king of Syria was looking for an excuse to start a war. Elisha spoke to the king and told him to send the man with leprosy to him. The king was glad Elisha had offered to help, and he sent Naaman and his servants to Elisha's house.

Elisha sent his servant down to speak to Naaman, and to tell him to go to the Jordan River and dip himself in the water seven times. Then he would be

Naaman Is Cured of Leprosy

cured of the disease. Naaman was offended that Elisha would not speak with
him directly instead of sending his servant to speak with him.

He refused to bathe in the water of the Jordan River, and he stated that
it was too dirty. He said that he would bathe in his own river at home. His
servants knew that he should obey Elisha's words if he wished to be cured
of his leprosy. They told him that he should just do what Elisha had said and
bathe seven times in the Jordan River.

He realized that he should listen to his servants and that he was wrong.
He headed for the Jordan River. He went into the water and dipped his body
seven times. The leprosy disappeared immediately.

He was very happy and he wanted to thank Elisha. He hurried back to his
house. This time Elisha came out and spoke with him. Naaman said he knew
the God of Israel had healed him and that no other god was more powerful.
Naaman offered him gifts but Elisha refused. He wanted him to understand
that God's miracles cannot be bought with money.

Naaman Offers Presents to Elisha

Naaman wanted to bring some soil from Israel to build an altar to God. He promised not to worship idols anymore, and he started the journey back to Syria.

Elisha's servant was unhappy that Elisha refused to accept the gifts that Naaman offered. After Elisha went back inside, the servant decided to go outside and try to get some of the gifts. Naaman saw him there and stopped his chariot.

The servant lied and told him that Elisha had sent him to get some silver and clothes to give to the poor people. Naaman gave the servant what he asked for and even gave him more. Instead of giving these gifts to Elisha, the servant hid them with the intention of keeping them for himself.

When he returned to Elisha's house, Elisha told him that he knew what he had done. Elisha told him that because of his sin, Naaman's leprosy would afflict him, and the servant developed the fatal disease himself.

The Boy Joash Is Made King

Joash was only seven years old when he became the king of Judah. As a little prince, he was never allowed to play like a normal child. He had to be protected from his wicked grandmother, Queen Athaliah. She had already killed his brothers and sisters so that only she could rule. For six years she had ruled as queen, but her people hated her. She did not worship God, and she was not a descendant of David.

When Joash was old enough, the high priest anointed him as king in the temple at Jerusalem. Many people guarded him carefully during the ceremony.

The wicked queen did not know about the plan to make him king, but she heard people shouting in the temple and went to investigate. She was shocked to see little Joash standing there with a crown on his head.

The high priest saw her, and he commanded the men to catch her and carry her away. They took her outside the city and killed her. Her friends the idol worshipers became afraid and did not try to do anything else to Joash or those who believed in God.

Queen Athaliah Is Captured

Joash's uncle, the high priest, ruled the people until the boy was mature enough to become king. Joash learned much by watching his uncle make important decisions. After Joash became king, his uncle continued to advise and help him.

Joash Raising Money to Repair the Temple

The wicked queen had destroyed much of the temple, and she had taken parts from it to decorate the temple of Baal. Joash wanted to repair the temple and restore it to the way Solomon had built it originally. To raise money to pay for the construction costs, he placed a large collection box at the door of the temple. People left money by dropping it through the hole in the top of the box. This plan worked well, and there was plenty of money to repair the temple.

While Joash's uncle the high priest was alive, Joash ruled wisely. After he died, however, the idol worshipers persuaded Joash to make wrong decisions. In his last days, Joash had forgotten about God and did many things that displeased God. He even commanded wicked men to kill Zechariah, a prophet of God.

After this happened, God allowed the Syrians to come to Judah and kill many of the idol worshipers. Joash became sick with diseases. While he lay sleeping, some of his servants went into his bedroom and killed him.

King Joash Tells the People to Stone Zechariah

E-20 How Elisha Led His Enemies into a Trap
2 Kings 6:8-23

The king of Syria began to look at Israel with the eyes of a greedy man. He wanted to attack the cities of Israel one by one and cause King Jehoram to lose control of his country. He started by attacking the first city. The Syrian soldiers were surprised to find the city strongly guarded. They returned to their king, and he sent them to attack a different city.

Again they found the city strongly guarded. Each time they tried a different city, they found that King Jehoram had it strongly protected.

The king of Syria believed that there must be a spy among his men telling King Jehoram where he planned to attack next. He wanted to catch the spy and punish him. One of the soldiers told the king of Syria that the prophet Elisha was helping King Jehoram know the battle plans ahead of time, so that he could plan his defenses.

The king knew that he would have to eliminate Elisha if he was ever going to be successful at attacking the cities of Israel. He sent men to find out where Elisha was living, and he planned to take him by force back to Syria. The men reported that Elisha was living in Dothan, and the king of Syria prepared chariots, horses and many men to go after him.

One morning a few days later, Elisha's servant was frightened to see soldiers when he went outside. He ran into the house and warned Elisha, but Elisha was not frightened at all. Elisha told him that they had more protectors than the Syrians. The servant didn't understand. Elisha said a prayer, and suddenly the servant could see thousands of chariots of fire in the mountains. He was no longer afraid.

When the Syrians came closer, Elisha asked God to make all of them go blind, and God answered his prayer. Then Elisha went out to them and told them he would lead them to the prophet they were searching for. He led them to Samaria. Elisha prayed for God to remove the blindness. They could see that they were inside the city walls where King Jerhoram lived, and they were very afraid.

At first King Jehoram thought Elisha wanted him to have the Syrians killed. Elisha said he was only to offer them bread and water, and then send them on their way. King Jehoram did as Elisha had asked. After the Syrians left, they never tried to bother Elisha again.

E-21 WHERE FOUR LEPERS FOUND FOOD FOR A STARVING CITY
2 KINGS 6:24 – 7:20

Benhadad, the king of Syria, led his army into Israel and camped around the walls of Samaria, where King Jehoram was living. He waited day after day for the people to open the gates to the city, but they did not open them at all.

Benhadad knew that sooner or later they would have to open the gates to get food; otherwise they would starve. Eventually the people inside the walls became so hungry they were forced to eat their own horses and donkeys.

The Famine in Samaria

One day, King Jehoram learned that some people were even eating their own children. He became very sad. He decided that Elisha was to blame for their troubles, and he decided to kill Elisha.

Elisha knew that Jehoram was sending a man to take him and cut off his head. He told his friends to stop the man at the door and wait until the king himself arrived. Soon Jehoram arrived, as Elisha had predicted. Elisha boldly told him that food would be sold very cheaply at the city gates the very next day, but Jehoram's soldier did not believe him. Elisha told the soldier that he would get to see the food but would never eat of it. The king decided to let Elisha live long enough to find out whether food would be available the next day.

Lepers Outside the City

That evening, four people with the disease of leprosy came to the city gates and sat down. They were tired and hungry. They knew there was no food inside the city, and they had decided to give themselves up as prisoners to the Syrian soldiers. When they approached the camp, they saw that every tent was empty. They began to gather all the food and valuables they could find.

They decided they must tell the people inside the walls of Samaria what they had found. They hurried to the gate and told the gatekeeper the news. Soon the good news traveled around the city.

The reason the tents were empty was because God had caused the Syrians to hear a strange noise, like the sound of a very large army approaching. They feared Jehoram had sent for help from other cities and kings. They did not want to be defeated and they had run away. As they were running, they had dropped most of their possessions.

As soon as King Jehoram heard what happened, he sent men to search for the army, believing they were probably hiding nearby, waiting for the people to go outside the city and search for food. But the king's men could not find the Syrian army at all. They told the king how the road was littered with their possessions including their valuables, as though they had dropped them while they were running.

The next day, the people gathered much food from the tents and brought it to the gate to be sold. The soldier who had not believed Elisha's words was standing at the gate, trying to allow only a few people outside at a time. The people were so excited that they pushed him down and trampled over him, killing him. Elisha's prediction came true: the soldier saw the food, but he never got to eat any of it.

Jezebel's Servants Throw Her From a Window

Jehu was anointed king by one of Elisha's servants following God's command. A servant killed Jehoram because God did not want anyone from the house of Ahab to stay alive. Jehu confronted Jezebel and urged her servants to throw her out a window.

The Remains of Jezebel

Jezebel's servants threw her from the window, and that is how she was killed. Dogs ate her body, as Elisha had predicted. Eventually, when he was very old, Elisha became ill and died.

E-22 THE PROPHET WHO TRIED TO RUN AWAY FROM GOD
JONAH 1 – 4

During the years that Elisha was a prophet in Israel, the Syrians often tried to attack the Israelites. After Elisha died, the Syrian nation grew weaker, and they were not nearly as much of a threat.

Then a new enemy arose to the east: the king of Assyria. He conquered many nearby countries, and the Israelites were beginning to fear him as he advanced closer and closer.

Nineveh was the capital of Assyria and where their king lived. It was a very large and very old city; many thousands of people lived within its walls. The people there worshiped idols and did not serve God. Year after year they became more wicked until God wanted to destroy all of them. But God knew that the people inside the city were ignorant and never had a chance to learn about him. God decided to send a prophet to tell them that their city would be destroyed because of their sins.

Jonah was the prophet God chose to send to Nineveh. However, Jonah did not want to go someplace so far away. He thought it would be better if God simply destroyed the city. Jonah decided to disobey God and sail away to a different city instead of sailing to Nineveh as he was told to do.

Jonah found a ship headed to Tarshish, which was to the west instead of the east. He went down into the hull of the ship and fell asleep. God knew what Jonah was doing, and he was not willing to have Jonah disobey him. God sent a terrible storm that threatened to wreck the ship. The sailors prayed to their gods and idols, but the storm only grew worse. Finally the captain went to the lower part of the ship and found Jonah sleeping.

The captain awakened Jonah and told him to ask his God for help. Jonah knew God was angry with him already, and he did not dare to ask God for help. The sailors decided one of them aboard the ship must be the cause of the trouble. They figured it must be Jonah after they cast lots and he lost.

They asked Jonah what he was doing there, and he explained that he was from Israel and that he worshiped the God who made both the sea and the land. The sailors were frightened, since they had never heard of such a God before. Jonah told them how he was running from God, and the sailors thought surely God must be punishing Jonah with the storm.

Jonah told the men to throw him overboard and the storm would stop. The soldiers did not want to harm him, but they threw him overboard, and soon the winds and the rains stopped.

Jonah Thrown Into the Sea by the Sailors

When Jonah was in the water a very large fish swallowed him. He was in the belly of the fish for three days and nights before the fish threw him up onto land. By that time, Jonah was more than willing to go to Nineveh and preach God's message. He knew that God's way was the only way for him.

Jonah Cast Forth by the Fish

Jonah went into the city and shouted that Nineveh would be destroyed in forty days. He went from corner to corner, shouting this over and over. The people were interested in what he had to say and they listened to him. Some of the people told the king what Jonah had said and the king was frightened. The king took off his royal robes and dressed in sackcloth and ashes. He was very sorry for his sins. He commanded all the people in the city to do as he was doing and pray to God for forgiveness.

Jonah Preaching in Nineveh

After Jonah finished preaching, he went outside the great walls and waited to see fire fall from the sky and burn up the city. But no fire fell. God had decided to spare the people because they had repented and changed their ways. Jonah thought the people would call him a false prophet, and he was afraid to go back to his own land.

Jonah Under a Vine Shelter

God taught Jonah a lesson by causing a vine to grow up out of the ground in one night and make a shelter from the sun for him. Then God caused a worm to destroy the vine, and Jonah became very unhappy. God spoke to Jonah and told him that just as Jonah was sorry to see the plant die, God would be sorry to see the people die. Jonah learned that God looks on all people as precious, even those who do not know how to worship him.

E-23 THE SAD ENDING OF THE KINGDOM OF ISRAEL
2 KINGS 17

The people of Nineveh believed God's prophet and asked God to forgive them. They repented and were not destroyed, but the people of Israel had not believed the prophets that God had sent to them. Some of the people believed, but most did not. Their kings refused to worship God in the right way, and they continued worshiping the golden calves.

Many years passed, and God saw that the Israelites would never worship him again as they had when David and Solomon led them. Nineteen kings had ruled in the land of Israel, and many times God had helped these kings out of trouble. Still they had not led their people to worship God.

At last God allowed an enemy to carry them all away to a strange land. Hoshea was king of Israel when the great Assyrian army came and took over his land. For a while Hoshea and his people paid a large sum of money each year to the Assyrian nation, and they were allowed to stay on their lands.

The King of Assyria Demands Money

The People Carried Away to Become Slaves in Assyria

Hoshea asked the king of Egypt for help, and he refused to pay more money to the Assyrians. The king of Assyria sent his army once again. The army took Hoshea and all his people away from their homes and brought them to heathen cities where they lived as slaves. This was their punishment for idol worship, and they were never allowed to return home again.

The Assyrian king now ruled the country where the ten tribes of Israel had lived. He brought his own people to live in the cities, including Samaria. They worked the fields and vineyards, and they paid the Assyrian king part of what they earned.

The new inhabitants of Israel were idol worshipers. They did not know at all about the true God. After they had lived there for a while, they became afraid of the God of Israel when many lions came out of the woods and killed their people working in the fields. They believed that the God of Israel was angry because they did not know how to worship him. They sent messengers back to Nineveh to tell the king about their troubles. They asked him to send an Israelite priest to teach them the proper way to worship God.

The king sent an Israelite priest to live in Bethel. He taught the people how to worship God, but they also continued to worship their own gods. Their religion became a mixture of right and wrong.

The Israelite Priest Teaches in Bethel

E-24 The Good King Hezekiah
2 Kings 18 –20; 2 Chronicles 29 – 32

After the Assyrians took the people of Israel away to be slaves, only the tribe of Judah remained. Hezekiah was the king of Judah at that time. When Hezekiah took over as ruler, the kingdom of Judah was very weak. For many years men who did not serve the true God had ruled, and they had even closed down the temple.

Hezekiah's Servants Report the Message From the King of Assyria

Hezekiah began at once to restore the true religion. He called for the priests and the Levites to come to Jerusalem and clean the temple. When everything was ready, he sent invitations to the people of Judah and all of Israel, and he commanded them to once again begin keeping the Feast of the Passover, which they had forgotten about for many years.

Some of the people laughed when they received the king's invitation to attend the Feast of the Passover. They had worshiped idols for so long that they had forgotten about the true God. But many people from the land of Judah did go to the feast.

Hezekiah destroyed the idols in his land, and he tried to teach his people to do right. He went to Jerusalem and found the brass serpent that Moses made in the wilderness. He saw the people worshiping it as if it was an idol and he threw it into a fire. He tore down the altars that had been used to worship false gods, and he did much work to strengthen his kingdom.

The king of Assyria had been in power since before Hezekiah became king of Judah. Every year the people of Judah paid money to the Assyrians.

But King Hezekiah didn't want to pay the money any longer. He built up the walls of Jerusalem, and he prepared a strong army to fight the Assyrians.

Hezekiah's army was very small compared to the Assyrian army. They came into the land of Judah and took over the cities, one by one. When they approached Jerusalem, the king knew his army would be no match for them. He realized that he had made a mistake by refusing to pay the money. He sent a message to the King of Assyria, promising to pay whatever was necessary to avoid more fighting.

The King of Assyria thought that would be his chance to destroy the country of Judah. He demanded a very high tax. King Hezekiah had to use gold and silver from the temple to pay it.

Then the King of Assyria sent a messenger, saying he was going to invade the city and take the people of Jerusalem to become slaves, just as he had done to the people in the land of Israel. Hezekiah was afraid when he heard the message. He knew his army was not strong enough to defend against such a powerful enemy.

He took the threatening letter into the temple and placed it before the altar. He asked God to help him and his people. Then he sent some of his princes to visit the prophet Isaiah and ask him what God wanted to happen. Isaiah answered that the city would not be invaded. Instead the king of Assyria would go back to his own country the way that he came, and he would be killed there with a sword.

King Hezekiah Prays for Help With the Letter

The Angel Visits the Assyrian Army Camp

That same night, an angel visited the camp of the Assyrian soldiers and caused everyone to become very sick. Many of them were dead by the morning. All of the leaders of the army were among the dead, and the king hurried back to his own land. He never tried to fight against King Hezekiah again. Eventually the king of Assyria was killed by two of his own sons while worshiping in the temple of his god in Nineveh.

Isaiah Tells Hezekiah He Must Die

Years later, Hezekiah became ill, and Isaiah told him that he must prepare to die. Hezekiah did not want to leave his people alone, and he prayed that God might allow him to rule for a while longer, since he had always tried to be faithful to God.

God told Isaiah that he would add fifteen years to King Hezekiah's life, and after three days he would be well enough to worship at the temple. Hezekiah was glad to hear the news but he asked for a sign to prove that it was true. Isaiah said he could either make the sundial go forward or backward ten degrees. Hezekiah said that he would like to see the sundial go backward. Isaiah prayed, and the shadow on the sundial moved backward ten degrees.

Hezekiah was healed of his disease, and he lived for fifteen years longer. During that time, he built up his kingdom and became very rich. He grew proud of his riches and God reminded him to be humble. Everyone grieved when he died, since he had been the best of all the kings of Judah.

King Hezekiah Showing Off His Riches

E-25 THE STORY ABOUT A FORGOTTEN BOOK
2 CHRONICLES 34, 35

It was time to renovate the temple of God in Jerusalem. Many years had passed since Joash had repaired it. It was in disrepair, and one king had even placed an altar for Baal inside of it. That king was dead, and his grandson Josiah was the new king. Josiah believed in God, and he wanted to do the right thing and repair the temple so that the people could worship there.

Many skilled workmen were hired to help repair the temple. The altars to Baal and other idols were torn out and burned. The high priest took charge and told everyone where to put everything in each room. Hidden away under some trash, the high priest found a strange book.

This was the book Moses had written before he died: the Book of the Law. It had all of God's commandments, and Moses had ordered that it should be read aloud to all of the Israelites every seven years. Many years had passed since anyone had read it, and it had been forgotten about

Shaphan Reading the Book of the Law for King Josiah

completely by nearly everyone.

The high priest called a servant and asked him to take the book to King Josiah. Josiah had never heard the laws before, and he asked his servant to read the book aloud to him. The servant, Shaphan, read everything, including that God would continue to bless the people as long as they served him faithfully. He also read about God's promise to punish the people if they turned away from him and worshiped idols.

Josiah was alarmed since he knew that the people had disobeyed God's law, and he feared the awful punishments they deserved. He tore his clothes and cried because he was so sad. He sent his servants to ask Huldah, a prophetess or female prophet, about God's plan to punish the people.

Levites Reading the Law to the People

Huldah said that God would punish the people if they turned away from him and worshiped idols, but because Josiah was trying to do the right thing and be a good leader, God would not punish the people while he was king.

Josiah tried to remember all of the laws, and he wanted the people to hear them, too. He called all of the people together and read from the book. He promised God to keep the law and serve only him, and he commanded the people to keep the law. The people liked Josiah and did as he told them.

Josiah prepared to keep the annual Passover Feast. He provided many lambs from his own flocks, and the people had the greatest Passover Feast since the time of Samuel.

Josiah ruled the people for thirty-one years. He began to rule when he was a child, only eight years old. Of course he had help when he was very young, but he soon learned to make wise decisions and rule wisely with God's help.

At the end of Josiah's reign, the king of Egypt went to fight against the king of Assyria, and he marched through Judah. Josiah was not pleased that the Egyptian soldiers were marching though his land, and he prepared to fight against them. The king of Egypt told him there was no need for them to fight, but Josiah didn't listen.

The Death of Josiah

Josiah dressed like a soldier and went to fight with his army against the Egyptian army. An arrow wounded him, and his soldiers brought him back to Jerusalem in a chariot. He died soon after, and he was buried among the great kings of Judah. The prophet Jeremiah wept for him because he knew Josiah was the last king who would try to keep the commandments found in Moses's Book of the Law.

E-26 THE WEEPING PROPHET
JEREMIAH 1 – 52

While Josiah was the king in Judah, God called a young man named Jeremiah to be a prophet. At first he feared the responsibility of being a prophet, and he told God that he could not do it because he was too young. God told him he wasn't too young and that God would lead him in his actions. Jeremiah was no longer afraid, but he knew that he might have to suffer persecution as the other prophets before him had.

Jeremiah

Jeremiah was treated well while Josiah was the king. But after Josiah died and one of Josiah's sons became king, the people quickly returned to worshiping idols again. They no longer cared about God and they refused to listen to Jeremiah. The king of Egypt captured and took away the king of Judah, and he forced the people to pay large sums of money every year. Then another of Josiah's sons took the throne in Judah.

Josiah's sons were not good men like their father had been. They forgot

Baruch Writing Jeremiah's Prophecies

about God and allowed idols to be set up throughout their land. They even treated the prophets unkindly because they warned people that God would punish them for their bad behavior.

One day Jeremiah told his dear friend Baruch the words that God spoke to him, and Baruch wrote the words in a book. Then he took the book out to the people and read it to them. Soon the princes of Judah heard about it, and they asked Baruch to read it to them. They were frightened when they heard

Jehoiakim Burning the Book Page by Page

that their land would soon be taken away from them. They asked to borrow the book in order to read it to the king. The princes warned Baruch that both he and Jeremiah should hide themselves in case the king became angry.

Jehoiakim, Josiah's son, was the king at the time. He listened while the princes read the book to him. After each page was read, the king cut it out with a knife and threw it into a fire. He did not believe the words of God, and he wanted to punish Jeremiah and his friend but he could not find them.

The princes sent word to Jeremiah and Baruch, telling them that the king was angry and the book had been destroyed. Once again the prophet and his

Jeremiah Is Lowered Into a Dungeon

friend wrote down the words of God. Not long after, a king and his army from Chaldea, east of Judah, came and took some of the people away to Babylon. Jehoiakim was placed in a prison and kept there for many years.

Jehoiachin, son of Jehoiakim, ruled Judah for three months. Then Zedekiah, another of Jehoiakim's sons, took over, and he was even more wicked than his father had been. He put Jeremiah in prison because he spoke the words of God. He was put into a dungeon, below the main part of the prison, and he was kept there for a long time. It was dark and dirty, and Jeremiah had only bread and water to eat and drink.

The people of Jerusalem were also having difficult times. The king of Babylon had come with a strong army that was camped around the city walls. No one could enter or leave the city, and the food supply was running low.

The king of Judah was afraid of the army outside the city, and he called for Jeremiah to help him with advice. Jeremiah was brought out of the dungeon. He told the king that God was going to allow the army to capture Jerusalem and even the temple would be destroyed. He said that God would

Jeremiah Visits the King

not allow the people to be killed if they would offer themselves to become the prisoners of the Chaldean king, Nebuchadnezzar. Then they would not all starve inside the city walls.

Jeremiah asked the king not to send him back into the dark dungeon again. He was kept in the court of the prison and treated more kindly. Still he did not have his freedom.

The people of Jerusalem were not willing to become prisoners of the enemy army as Jeremiah had told them to do. Months passed, and the people grew weaker and weaker from lack of food. The king decided to try to sneak out in the middle of the night, hoping that he would not be seen.

King Zedekiah did not get far before the enemy army captured him. They tied chains around his hands and feet. They poked out his eyes and led him away to Babylon. Many of his people were taken with him. Nebuchadnezzar and his army broke down the walls of Jerusalem and set fire to the temple. First they removed all the gold and silver, which they brought to their own land.

Jeremiah was allowed to remain in the land of Judah, along with many of the poor people. He lived to be an old man. As long as he lived, he continued to warn the people, as God had told him to do. Because he lived in such a time of trouble, he was a sad man. He was sad because of the suffering of the people and also because they had sinned so much against God. For this reason, he was called "the weeping prophet."

Jeremiah Lives in the Court of the Prison

King Zedekiah Is Blinded and Taken Prisoner

285

Ezekiel Prophesying

Part F: Stories About the Jews
Daniel, Nehemiah, Haggai, Ezra, Esther, Malachi

F-1 When the People of Judah Lived in a Strange Land
2 Chronicles 36:14-21

After Jerusalem was destroyed, the Chaldean army started the journey back to Babylon. They took Zedekiah, the king of Judah, and many of his people along with them.

The prisoners were both men and women, and their ages ranged from very young to very old. Day after day they marched on, stopping only at night to camp. They were called "Jews," which means the people of Judah. The Jews today are descendants of those people.

The Chaldean Army With Prisoners From the Tribe of Judah

When the journey was over, the Jews found that their new ruler did not treat them badly at all. They were given fields and houses, and they were permitted to work for themselves as they had done in their own country. The Chaldean king even trained some of them to be nobles and rulers.

God had not forgotten his people. He sent messages to them through the prophet Jeremiah. God promised to return them to their own country if they would try to please him. The people rejoiced when they heard Jeremiah's letters. They wanted to return home as quickly as possible.

The Jews refused to worship idols in the land of Babylon, and they were trying hard to please God. They often met together in groups to talk about the land of Judah and the temple that had been destroyed.

Ezekiel's Vision of the Valley of Dry Bones

288

Sometimes the Chaldeans asked the Jews to sing and play music for them, but the Jews always refused. They said that their music did not belong in a foreign land.

The Jews were careful to teach their children about the true God. They remembered the laws of Moses and did not forget their hope of returning to their homeland of Judah.

In the land of Babylon, another man began to receive messages from God. His name was Ezekiel. He had been among the first captives when Jehoiachin was taken to Babylon. Afterward, he warned the other people in Judah about God's punishment for their disobedience.

Ezekiel saw visions from God, and he encouraged the people to believe that eventually they would return to their own land. He told the people to stop sinning and do as God wanted them to. God would restore life to the country of Israel, just as he had restored life to the many bones in one of Ezekiel's visions – if only the people would trust and believe in him.

F-2 FOUR BRAVE BOYS
DANIEL 1

The Four Boys

In the king's palace at Babylon, a group of young boys were being educated. They had lived in the palace in Jerusalem before being taken to Babylon. Among them were four boys who seemed to be more thoughtful than their friends.

These boys were Daniel, Hannaniah, Mishael, and Azariah. They had been princes in Judah during the rule of King Jehoiakim, and they served the true God.

King Nebuchadnezzar had ordered the chief officer of the palace to teach these young boys the ways of the Chaldeans. He wanted them to be able to help rule in Babylon once they were grown men. The king made sure that they were given the best food, to help them grow into strong and intelligent young men.

Daniel and his three friends wanted to keep the laws that God had given to the people of Israel, and those laws said that certain foods should not be eaten. But the Chaldeans prepared those forbidden foods anyway. They also cooked their food in ways prohibited by the laws of God. Daniel and his friends decided to refuse the Chaldean food unless it was prepared the way that they thought it should be.

The chief officer liked Daniel and his friends. Daniel told the chief officer that he and his friends could not eat the food from the king's table. The officer told the boys that the king would blame him and kill him if the boys were not looking strong and healthy as a result of not eating properly.

Daniel and His Three Friends Refuse the King's Food

Daniel asked that they be allowed to eat the kinds of food that they wanted for the next ten days. Because the officer liked the boys, he agreed to do as Daniel asked. For ten days he fed them vegetable food and bread instead of the meat and wine from the king's table.

At the end of the ten days, the officer saw that Daniel and his friends looked even healthier than the other boys in the palace. He continued to give them their special diet. God blessed the boys with much intelligence, and they quickly learned the language and knowledge of the Chaldeans.

When three years had passed, the king asked that all the boys be brought before him. He asked them difficult questions, and he saw that Daniel and his friends were wiser than any of the other boys and even the wisest men in Babylon. Nebuchadnezzar was very pleased with the four Jewish boys, and he gave them places of honor in his kingdom.

F-3 HOW DANIEL BECAME A GREAT MAN IN BABYLON
DANIEL 2

After Daniel and his three friends were considered wise men, the king had a strange dream. The dream troubled him greatly, and he could not go back to sleep again. He believed the dream must have a meaning, and he decided to ask the wise men in his kingdom.

In the morning, Nebuchadnezzar could no longer recall the details of the dream. He called for the wise men and asked them to help him. The wise men were puzzled, since they did not know what the king had forgotten about his dream. He told them he had forgotten it, but if they truly were wise men they should be able to tell him. The wise men said no one could do that. The king became angry and threatened to kill them all if they did not tell him about the dream, but still they did not know what the king had forgotten.

The king ordered the captain of his guard to kill all the wise men. When he came to Daniel's house, Daniel and his friends knew nothing about what had happened with the king's dream. Daniel begged the captain to let him speak with the king.

He told the king he would figure out the answer to his dream if the king would give him a little time. The king agreed. Daniel knew that no person could do what the king wanted, but he also knew that God had the power to give him the answer. Daniel and his three friends prayed to God for help.

That night, God showed Daniel in a vision what the king's dream had been and what it meant. Daniel was very grateful to God. He prayed a prayer of thanks. Then he went to the captain of the king's guard. He told him that he had the answer and asked him not to kill the wise men yet.

Daniel told the king that the power to know his dream came from God. He told the king that when he went to sleep, he had been wondering about what would happen in future years. In his dream, God had showed him what would happen in the future.

291

King Nebuchadnezzar's Dream

Daniel told him the dream: he saw a great and bright image standing before him. The head of the image was gold, the chest and arms were silver, the waist and hips were made of brass, the legs were iron, and the feet were part iron and part clay. Then he saw a stone rolling toward the feet. The stone broke the feet, causing the whole image to fall down and break into pieces. It became like dust and the wind blew it away. Then the stone grew until it became a great mountain that filled the whole earth.

Nebuchadnezzar listened intently. Daniel told him that he would explain the meaning of the dream and that God intended he should learn something from it. The great image represented four great kingdoms of Earth. His kingdom was the first, and the head of gold represented his kingdom. After him would come another king that was not as great, represented by the chest and arms made of silver. The parts of brass showed the third kingdom. The iron legs and the feet showed the fourth kingdom. Daniel told him the fourth kingdom would be very strong at first, but afterwards it would become weaker, represented by the feet made of both iron and clay.

Daniel told him God was planning to set up a kingdom greater than all the others, represented by the stone. God's kingdom would increase in size until it filled the earth, and it would destroy all the others. He told the king

292

Daniel

that was the meaning of his dream.

Nebuchadnezzar was amazed at the wisdom of young Daniel. He fell down to worship him. But Daniel told him God was the one who had given him the answer. Nebuchadnezzar gave many gifts to Daniel and made him the ruler of all the province of Babylon. He was also made the chief of all the wise men. At Daniel's request, his three friends were given important positions. Daniel's three friends became known to the king as Shadrach, Meshach, and Abednego.

King Nebuchadnezzar grew in power until he became the greatest living king in the world at that time. Year after year he added new countries to his kingdom, and in every country the people feared him greatly. All of this caused him to become very proud and to think himself very great.

Nebuchadnezzar decided to make a god and force the people of every country to worship it. He built a large image, ninety feet high, and he covered it with gold. The image was set up on the plain of Dura, near Babylon, and it could be seen from far away.

The king sent a command to the princes, rulers, and officers of every nation to come to the plain of Dura where there was to be a large gathering. They were afraid to disobey. Daniel's three friends came, but for some reason Daniel himself was not there.

King Nebuchadnezzar was pleased to see such a vast number of men on the plain before the golden image. He had one of his servants make an announcement: When music played, everyone was to bow down and worship the golden image, or else they would be thrown into a fiery furnace.

Daniel's Three Friends Do Not Bow to the Idol

Soon the music began to play, and the people fell to their knees, afraid to disobey the king. Everyone except Daniel's three friends bowed and worshiped the image.

Some people were jealous of Shadrach, Meshach, and Abednego because the king had given them positions of power in the kingdom. When they saw that they had not kneeled as they were ordered to, they hurried to tell the king.

The king was surprised to hear this news. He liked the three men and thought that they were good at their jobs. So, he decided to give them another chance to listen to his order. They told the king they did not want another chance, and the only god they would worship was the true God in heaven. They told him their God was so powerful that he would save them from the fiery furnace, and they were not worried even one bit.

Nebuchadnezzar could not understand why these Jews were refusing to worship his god and he became angry. He thought they were simply stubborn and disobedient. He commanded his servants to add more fuel to the fire and make it seven times hotter than it had been. He told the strongest men in his army to bind Shadrach, Meshach, and Abednego with cords and throw them into the fire.

The Fiery Furnace

Daniel's three friends were not afraid. They did not cry out as they were tied up and thrown into the furnace. The flames were so hot that they killed the soldiers who threw them in.

The king was watching, and he saw his own soldiers killed by the flames. Then he saw the three men walking aroud inside the furnace after their cords had been burned off. He saw a fourth person in the flames with them, and he thought the fourth person looked like a god.

At first the king did not believe his eyes. He asked his servants if they had thrown three or four persons into the fire, and the servants told him there should only be three. The king ran to the door of the furnace and called to the three men, telling them to come to him at once. He addressed them as the servants of the highest God.

The princes and nobles watched in amazement as the three men walked out of the fire and approached the king. They saw that the fire had not harmed them at all, and they did not even smell like smoke. But the cords that they were tied with had been burnt to ashes.

The king was no longer angry with Shadrach, Meshach, and Abednego. He believed they were great men and wished to honor them. He knew they served a great God, and he blessed the God of the Jews. He commanded everyone never to speak against God. Afterward, the three Jews were given even more important positions in his kingdom.

F-5 HOW GOD HUMBLED KING NEBUCHADNEZZAR'S PROUD HEART
DANIEL 4

One night while King Nebuchadnezzar lay sleeping in his palace, God caused him to have another strange dream. This time he remembered the

dream and he wondered what it meant. Once again he sent for the wise men and told them about the dream. The wise men were relieved he could remember the dream that time, but still they did not understand its meaning.

The king sent them away and called for Daniel. He believed Daniel received help from God and that Daniel was the wisest of the wise men because of the God's help.

Daniel listened as the king told him about the dream. God caused Daniel to understand what the

Daniel Before Nebuchadnezzar

dream meant. At first he was afraid to tell the king what the dream meant, but Nebuchadnezzar told Daniel to tell him anyway and not to worry.

In his dream, Nebuchadnezzar had seen a tree grow up out of the ground and become so great that the top reached the sky. All the animals found shelter underneath its branches, and birds made their nests in the tree. All the people of the Earth came to eat its fruit. Nebuchadnezzar had seen God tell him to cut the tree down, cut off the branches, remove the leaves, and scatter the fruit. The animals would have to leave it, and dew from heaven would come upon it for seven years. The stump and the roots were to be left in the ground for seven years so that everyone would know there was a God in heaven that rules over the earth.

Daniel knew the dream was a warning from God to the proud king. He knew Nebuchadnezzar did not believe in God. Daniel spoke bravely and told the king that the tree represented him, a great king known in every part of the land. As the tree was cut down for seven years, the king would lose his kingdom for seven years, and he would live with regular men and their animals. But when the king humbled himself and began to worship God, he would be returned to power.

Nebuchadnezzar Loses His Mind

297

Daniel knew that God was merciful, and he believed that God would save the king from such severe punishment if he would begin to do the right thing. He urged Nebuchadnezzar to change his ways and begin to worship God. Then Daniel went home.

One year passed by and nothing unusual happened. Nebuchadnezzar did not do anything differently, and perhaps he forgot about the strange dream. He grew even more proud as he reflected on everything he had done and built. One day as he walked around in his palace, feeling very proud, God spoke to him and told him that his kingdom was taken away from him.

The king lost his mind and began to act like a wild animal. The people were afraid of him, and they drove him out of the city. He lived in the fields and ate grass like the oxen. His hair and nails grew very long. For seven years he lived like an animal. Then God allowed his mind to return to normal. Nebuchadnezzar praised God for his greatness and thanked him for his mercy.

When the people saw that their king was in his right mind again, they welcomed him back. They honored him as their king, just as they had done before. Nebuchadnezzar did not forget the lesson God had taught him, and he no longer believed his greatness and glory came from his own strength.

F-6 STRANGE HANDWRITING ON THE WALL OF THE PALACE
DANIEL 5

A great feast was being held in the palace at Babylon. The new king, Belshazzar, had invited a thousand princes and nobles to enjoy the feast with him and his many wives. While they were drinking wine together, the king remembered the beautiful cups of gold that Nebuchadnezzar had brought from the temple in Jerusalem. He told his servant to bring the gold cups into the palace. They were filled with wine and passed around to the guests. As they drank, they praised their false gods of gold, silver, wood, and stone.

Belshazzar's heart was happy, and he felt very secure with his guests in his palace. He joined them in praising the false gods. Then he turned pale and the gladness left his heart. A great fear swept over him and caused his knees to tremble. On the wall over the palace, near the candlestick, he saw the fingers of a man's hand writing strange words he could not read.

Everything grew quiet in the banquet hall. No one could understand the strange words being written on the wall, and everyone became afraid. The king commanded that the wise men be brought in to help understand the meaning of the words. He promised to give a reward to whoever understood, but no one did.

Belshazzar's Banquet Is Interrupted

News of the strange handwriting spread through the palace, and soon the queen mother heard about it. And she heard that the wise men did not understand the words. She came into the banquet hall, and she told the king that he should contact a very wise man whom everyone had forgotten about. She thought he would understand the words.

Daniel had grown old. For a long time he had lived quietly in Babylon, since the kings who followed Nebuchadnezzar had not given him any important position. The queen mother remembered how he had interpreted Nebuchadnezzar's dreams and she knew that he was very wise.

Belshazzar sent for Daniel to come quickly. He promised to dress Daniel in royal garments and make him the third ruler in the kingdom if he could help him understand the meaning of the strange words. Daniel did not care to be a ruler or to have fancy clothes, but he told the king that he would read the writing and tell him the meaning.

Daniel Interprets the Writing

First Daniel reminded Belshazzar of the great punishment that God had placed upon Nebuchadnezzar because of his wickedness and pride. Belshazzar had known about this, but still he dared to be proud and to mock God. He and his guests had drunk wine out of the cups from the temple while praising false gods.

Daniel told him that God had written the words because of his behavior. The words were Mene, Tekel, Upharsin, and they mean:

Mene: God has numbered your kingdom and already finished it.

Tekel: you are weighed in the balance and found to be lacking.

Upharsin: your kingdom is divided and is given to the Medes and Persians.

Belshazzar commanded his servants to bring a royal garment and put it on Daniel. Then he put a gold chain around Daniel's neck and proclaimed that he was the third ruler in the kingdom. But that very night the Medes and the Persians invaded the kingdom. They killed Belshazzar and placed the Median king, Darius, on the throne.

F-7 DANIEL IN THE LION'S DEN
DANIEL 6

King Darius, the new ruler, chose 120 princes to help him govern the people of his new kingdom. He appointed three presidents to rule over these princes. Because he found Daniel to be so wise, he appointed him to be the first president. Daniel ruled over all the princes and the other two presidents.

The other princes and presidents were jealous of Daniel and they grew to hate him. They watched him carefully, hoping to find fault with his actions. They learned only that he was faithful to God and loyal to the king. Finally they decided that they would have to find a different way to rob Daniel of his power.

Daniel Praying Beside a Window

Darius was surprised to see all of his princes assembled before him. He did not notice that Daniel was absent. They told him they wished to have him pass a law that anyone who asked a request of any man or god except for King Darius would be thrown into a den of lions. The law would remain in effect for thirty days. The king had no idea that they were plotting against

Daniel, and he agreed to the law.

Daniel heard about the new law, but he continued to pray three times every day near an open window as he always had done. The men saw him, and they told King Darius what they had seen. They told the king that Daniel must be punished since the law was to apply to everyone.

Then the king figured out what the men had planned by passing the law. He figured out that the princes had not wanted to honor him but just wanted to get rid of Daniel. Darius was very sorry that he had listened to their

Daniel in the Lions' Den

words. He tried to find some way to avoid enforcing the law on Daniel but he could not. As the sun was setting, the princes and other presidents came to him and told him that the law must be enforced. He could not delay any longer, and he ordered that Daniel be thrown into the lions' den.

The king told Daniel how sorry he was to have to punish him. He told him that he knew his God would protect him from the lions. Then Daniel was put in with the lions, and a stone was put in front of the door to keep him from leaving. The king put his seal on the stone so that no one would dare move it. Then, sadly, the king went back home to his palace.

Darius could not sleep at all that night. He was too troubled to enjoy any entertainment, and all he could think about was his loyal servant being attacked by the lions. At the break of dawn, he hurried to the lions' den. He called to Daniel, asking him if his God had saved him from the lions.

The king was greatly relieved to hear Daniel answer him. Daniel said that his God had sent an angel to shut the mouths of the lions. God knew that he did not deserve to be punished in such a way for praying.

Darius called for his servants to remove Daniel from the den. Then he ordered that the wicked men who conspired against Daniel be thrown in with the lions. The lions immediately tore them to pieces.

Darius wrote letters to the people of every nation, telling them how God had protected Daniel from the lions. And he made a law that all of his people should fear and respect the God of the Jews.

F-8 DANIEL'S ANGEL VISITOR
DANIEL 8 – 12

Daniel had lived for many years in the capital cities of the eastern kings. He had helped the kings rule their countries. During those many years, he had never forgotten his home city of Jerusalem and the temple that had been destroyed by Nebuchadnezzar.

Daniel had read the letters the prophet Jeremiah had written to the Jews who were prisoners in Babylon, and he knew that the Jews could return to their own land after seventy years. He knew the seventy years were almost over, and he wished for his people to return home and rebuild their temple in Jerusalem.

Instead of praying three times every day as he had always done, Daniel often prayed all day long. Sometimes he didn't even stop praying to eat. He dressed in sackcloth and ashes while he prayed, to show that he was very sorry for his sins and the sins of his people.

Daniel's prayers were heard. One evening while he was praying, an angel

An Angel Touches Daniel While He Prays

came to talk to him. This angel had appeared once before to Daniel when God had caused him to see a vision. This time the angel appeared to comfort Daniel. The angel told him that someday God would send a Savior who would suffer and die for the sins of all people.

Daniel continued to work for the king. When Darius died, the new king, Cyrus, took Daniel to his capital city in Persia, and Daniel worked for King Cyrus there. He continued to pray, even while working for the king.

One day during the rule of King Cyrus, Daniel and several of his companions were praying by a riverside, and Daniel saw a heavenly visitor standing in front of him. The heavenly visitor's face shone like lightning and his eyes were bright like fire. Even his arms and feet were shiny like polished brass. Daniel could not look directly at him, and he fell to the ground. The men who were with Daniel could not see the heavenly visitor, but they felt the earth tremble and they ran away in fear.

As Daniel lay on the ground, the angel touched him. Daniel rose up on his knees, and the angel spoke. His voice sounded like many voices. At first Daniel could not speak, but the angel touched his lips and caused strength to return to Daniel's body. Daniel talked for a long time with the heavenly visitor, and he wrote down what was said in a book.

Daniel was one of the greatest prophets as well as a great man in the country where he lived. Through his courage and faith in God, he caused several heathen kings to respect the religion of the Jews, and he lived to see the time when King Cyrus allowed the Jews to return again to Judah.

F-9 THE HOMECOMING OF THE JEWS
EZRA 1:1 – 3:7

A large number of people had gathered in the valley along the Euphrates River, preparing to set out on a long journey. They were both old and young, but all of the people were Jews preparing to return to the land of their fathers – the land of Judah. King Cyrus had sent a message to all the Jews in his land, telling them that God had said it was time to rebuild the temple in Jerusalem and that the Jews were to do this.

Daniel was too old to return to Jerusalem, and perhaps the king did not want him to go. But there were many others who were eager to go and rebuild the temple. One of those who were ready to return was Zerubbabel, a brave young man from the family of David. He became the leader of the people who were returning to Jerusalem, ruling as a prince under the command of King Cyrus.

When the long journey began, the people moved slowly up the road they had traveled many years earlier when they left Judah. Some rode horses, camels, and donkeys while others walked. They carried musical instruments which they planned to play in the new temple, once it was finished.

Cyrus had given them the gold and silver objects that Nebuchadnezzar had taken from the temple before it was set on fire. And they had additional gold and silver donated by King Cyrus's other subjects.

Cyrus Returns the Gold and Silver Objects for the Temple

Not all of the Jews returned to Judah. Many had successful lives in their new homes and did not care to leave. They wanted to assist, and they sent gifts of money and materials to help with the construction of the new temple. They were happy that the temple was going to be rebuilt, and they looked forward to visiting Jerusalem for feasts and other occasions.

Some People Mourn Over the Ruins of Jerusalem

When they were nearing the end of the journey, the travelers could see the crumbled walls of Jerusalem. Some of the people were very sad because they remembered how beautiful and prosperous the city had looked before it was destroyed. Many of the younger Jews had never seen Jerusalem before, and they were just glad to be returning to the land Nebuchadnezzar had taken from them.

Offering Sacrifices as the Temple Is Rebuilt

Among the ruins, the people located the place where the temple had stood. They found the rock where the altar had been built. The priests and Levites cleared the ground and began to build a new altar. Then they began to offer sacrifices to God each morning and evening as the Law of Moses commanded them to.

F-10 How the New Temple Was Built in Jerusalem
Ezra 3:7 – 6:22; Haggai 1, 2

When Zerubbabel and those who traveled with him first reached Jerusalem, winter was approaching, and they had to build homes for themselves before beginning work on the temple. As soon as winter was over and it was springtime, they set to work on the great job of rebuilding the temple.

Every man aged twenty and older was given a job. Zerubbabel and Jeshua, the high priest, hired carpenters and masons to construct the new building. They obtained wood from the Lebanon Mountains after receiving permission from King Cyrus.

When everything was ready, the workers laid the foundation of the new temple. Everyone sang together and played their musical instruments, giving praise to God. Most of the people were glad, but there were some

Rebuilding the Temple

who remembered how beautiful the temple built by King Solomon had been, and they were not as happy.

Some people from the country asked for jobs, but they were refused because they were not Jews. They were Samaritans, people who came to live in Israel after the northern tribes were carried away into captivity. They had a mixed religion – a mixture of the true religion and idol-worship.

Presenting Letters of Complaint to the King of Persia

When Zerubbabel and Jeshua refused to let them help build the temple, they grew angry and tried to hinder the work. They sent letters to the king of Persia, accusing the Jews of treating them unfairly and building a rebel city.

After several letters, the king stopped work on the temple. Several years passed, and still the Jews were not allowed to finish their temple. They built comfortable homes for themselves and worked in the fields near Jerusalem.

The King's Men Stop Work on the Temple

Finally, God caused the new king of Persia to become friendly toward them. However, the Jews never asked him for permission to finish the temple. God sent a prophet named Haggai to urge them to begin work on the temple again. And God sent another prophet named Zechariah, who said that Zerubbabel had begun rebuilding the temple and it should be finished.

Once again Zerubbabel and Jeshua began to work on the temple. The Samaritans saw what they were doing and asked who gave them the orders to rebuild the temple. They answered that King Cyrus had told them to do so. They wrote a letter to the King of Persia, the new King Darius, telling him what was going on. He checked the records and found out that indeed King Cyrus had told the Jews to rebuild the temple.

The king sent a letter back to the Samaritans, telling them not to hinder

311

the Jews anymore, but instead to give them money to help with their work. The letter also said they would have their houses torn down and be killed if they refused to help. The Samaritans were afraid from that time and no longer tried to hinder the Jews.

When the temple was finally complete, the Jews held a great feast and offered many sacrifices to God. They were happy that the new king of Persia was their friend and that they no longer had to worry about their interfering neighbors, the Samaritans.

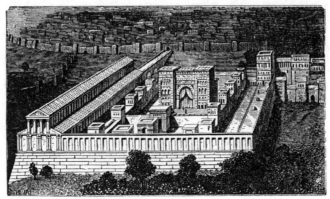

TEMPLE REBUILT

F-11 A BEAUTIFUL GIRL WHO BECAME A QUEEN
ESTHER 1, 2

Esther, a Jew, was only a little girl when both her parents died. She went to live in the home of one of her cousins, Mordecai. Her new home was in the city of Shushan, where the king of Persia lived. Her cousin Mordecai had a job in the king's household. He was very kind to Esther, and he loved her as his own child.

After Esther had grown up to be a young woman, the king of Persia, Ahasuerus, had a great feast in his palace. He invited all the nobles and rulers of his kingdom. Then, at the end of the feast, he invited all the men of Shushan to share in the festivities.

The queen, Vashti, gave a feast for all the women while the king's feast was going on. On the last day of the feast, the king grew careless because he had drunk so much wine. He wished for everyone to see how beautiful his wife was. He sent some of his servants to bring her into his part of the palace, where all the guests could behold her beauty.

The queen refused to appear in front of all the men of Shushan. She told the king's servants that she would not go. She believed the king's request was unwise because it was against the customs of her people. Normally,

Queen Vashti Refusing to Obey King Ahasuerus

women wore veils and only a woman's husband was allowed to see her face.

King Ahasuerus was angry when the servants returned alone and told him that Vashti would not go with them. He called his wise men and asked them what should be done with his disobedient wife. One wise man told him that he should select another woman to be his queen; otherwise all the women of the kingdom would believe it was acceptable to disobey their husbands. The

Publishing the King's Decree

king liked this advice, and he never allowed Vashti to come into his presence again. He refused to let her be his queen any longer, and he decided to choose another beautiful young woman.

He sent a decree or commandment throughout his kingdom that the most

Esther Is Made Queen

beautiful young women should all be brought before him. He would choose one to be the new queen.

Mordecai knew that Esther was beautiful and young, and he believed that she would make an excellent queen. So, he sent her to the palace. She learned how to behave politely, and Mordecai told her never to tell anyone that her people were Jews.

After living in the palace for some time, Esther was brought before the king. She pleased him so much that he chose her to be the new queen. He placed the royal crown on her head, and she was given many servants and rooms in the palace. He had a great feast, called Esther's feast, and announced that Esther was the queen.

314

Mordecai at the King's Gate

Mordecai could no longer see the young woman he had cared for as tenderly as his own daughter. But every day he passed by the palace where she lived, and she could see him from her window. Her servants relayed messages to and from Mordecai for her. Then Mordecai would return to his job as a watchman at the king's gate.

While sitting at the gate, Mordecai saw two servants of the king who were whispering about some secret matter. He watched closely and listened carefully. He learned that they were angry with the king and were planning to kill him. He sent a message to the king through Queen Esther, and she told the king the message came from Mordecai.

The king investigated the matter. He found that the men were guilty and put them to death. The king forgot about how Mordecai had helped him, and Mordecai was never rewarded. He had no idea that Mordecai, a Jew, was related to his new wife, Queen Esther.

F-12 THE MAN WHO PLANNED TO DESTROY ALL THE JEWS
ESTHER 3:1 – 4:3

Haman was a proud prince at the royal palace of Shushan. He was very rich and clever, and he knew how to flatter the king when he appeared before him. The king honored Haman above all the other princes, and he ordered his servants to pay respect to him.

Mordecai Will Not Bow to Haman

Mordecai was one of the king's servants, and he kept watch at the king's gate. Whenever Haman passed through the gate, the king's servants were supposed to bow down before him with their faces in the dust. They all did so except Mordecai. He said that he would not bow down to any man but only to God.

The king's servants were not pleased when they saw that Mordecai refused to bow down to Haman. They asked him why he was disobeying the king's orders. Mordecai told them that he was a Jew and that he would not bow down to anyone except the God of the Jews. The servants hurried to tell Haman about Mordecai's unwillingness to bow down before him.

Haman's pride was deeply wounded when he heard that Mordecai the Jew refused to honor him. He became very angry and decided to punish Mordecai. He thought it would look petty to punish only one Jew. Instead, he decided to kill all of the Jews. He did not know that Queen Esther was also a Jew.

Haman helped to rule the kingdom of Persia, and he often appeared before the king. He thought it would be easy to get the king's consent to kill all of the Jews, although he did not want the king to know the reason for his anger toward the Jewish people. He told the king that there was a group of people in the land who did not obey the king's laws, that they were unprofitable in the kingdom, and that he wanted to pass a law to have them destroyed. Haman offered to pay the money to hire the soldiers to kill them.

King Ahasuerus did not know much about the Jews or their strange religion. He did not know that his beautiful queen was Jewish. The king told Haman to write letters to the rulers in every part of the kingdom, telling them that on a certain day they should destroy all of the Jews in their country, including every man, woman, and child.

After the letters were written, Haman gave them to postmen who carried them to every part of the kingdom. He believed he had done a great deed that would bring him much honor, and he went to the palace to dine with the king. He felt like the most important person in Persia aside from the king.

Soon, news of the letter reached the ears of the Jews in every part of Persia. They wondered why their king had suddenly become so displeased with them. They had always been good citizens and never caused any trouble. Many had become very successful and productive. Now they were to be killed and their riches seized. Everywhere they cried, dressed in sackcloth and ashes, and prayed while fasting.

Mordecai was among the first of the Jews to hear about the cruel law. He knew at once that Haman had made the law. He knew that even Esther would have to be killed if the law was to be carried out. He dressed in sackcloth and was very sad. He did not enter the king's gate since no one was allowed to enter while dressed in sackcloth. He could not even send a message to Esther. He hoped that Esther would hear about him and send a messenger to find out why he was so troubled. Then he could tell her about the cruel law, and hopefully she would think of a way to save their lives.

F-13 HOW QUEEN ESTHER SAVED THE LIVES OF HER PEOPLE
ESTHER 4:4 – 10:3

Esther was happy in her beautiful palace. She was kind to her servants, and they enjoyed working for her. But she did not forget about Mordecai and the help he had given her when she was younger. She watched him pass by her window every day, and she was always eager to read the messages he sent.

One day Mordecai did not pass by as usual, and Esther thought he might be sick. Soon after, her servants told her he was walking through the streets of the city dressed in sackcloth and crying loudly. Queen Esther wondered what was going on. She gathered some new clothes to send to him. She watched from her window, and she saw her servant returning with the new clothes. Mordecai refused to take them, and she knew that something must be very wrong. She sent another servant to find out the cause of his troubles.

Mordecai told the servant how Haman was planning to give money to the king to have all the Jews killed. He gave the servant a copy of the letter that Haman had written, and the servant brought it to Esther. The servant told Esther that Mordecai wanted her to tell the king that she was a Jew and that Haman had planned to kill her along with all her people.

At first Esther was afraid to go to the king. She knew that anyone approaching the king without first being summoned would be killed unless the king held out his golden scepter. She knew the king was busy, and she was afraid to disturb him. She sent the servant back to tell Mordecai that she could not yet tell the king, not until he should call for her.

Mordecai told the servant to tell Esther that she would eventually be killed anyway and that she must take the risk. Esther was still afraid. She told Mordecai to have all the Jews in Shuman fast and pray for three days, asking God to make the king receptive to seeing her. After the three days were over, Esther dressed in her finest clothes and went in to see the king.

Esther Goes to See the King

318

The king was surprised to see Esther standing timidly before his throne. He knew that there must have been a good reason for this, and he held out his golden scepter. He told her to tell him what she wanted and he would grant her wish. She did not immediately tell him what was bothering her, but she asked to dine with Haman and the king.

Haman felt honored because he was the only guest invited to dine with the king and queen. While they were eating, the king again asked Esther to tell him what she wanted. She said that she would tell him the next day if she could once again dine with Haman and the king. The king agreed.

As he was leaving the gate, Haman was once again troubled when Mordecai did not bow before him. He wanted to have Mordecai hanged.

Reading the Book of Records

That night the king could not sleep. As he tossed and turned, he commanded his servants to bring the book of records, which contained the history of everything that happened since he became king. The king heard his servant read about how Mordecai had saved him from the two people who planned to kill him. The king asked if anything had been done to reward Mordecai, and he was told that nothing had been done.

Haman went to the palace the next morning, intending to ask for

319

permission to hang Mordecai. Before he could speak, the king asked him what should be done to reward someone the king wanted to honor.

Believing the king wanted to honor him, Haman said that the person the king wanted to honor should be dressed in the king's royal garments and placed on the king's horse wearing the king's crown; he should ride through the city for everyone to see, accompanied by the most noble prince.

The king was pleased with Haman's answer. He told Haman that since he was the noblest prince, he should take the royal garments, horse, and crown to Mordecai. Then do everything just as he had said.

The Triumph of Mordecai

Haman was afraid to disobey the king. He dressed Mordecai in the royal garments and crown and led him through the streets on horseback, proclaiming that the king wanted to honor him. Then he returned with Mordecai to the palace and returned the royal garments and crown to the king. Afterward, he ran home, covering his head in shame.

Haman had forgotten about the invitation to dine with the king and queen, so the king sent a messenger to bring him to the palace. For the third time the king asked Esther what she wanted, and again he promised to grant her anything, even to give her half the kingdom if she wanted that.

Esther Accuses Haman

Haman's Sentence Is Decided

Esther told him that she wished for her life and her people's lives to be spared; otherwise they would all be killed. The king asked her who would do such a wicked thing, and she pointed to Haman. Haman was frightened.

He did not know that Esther was a Jew, and he had no idea that Mordecai had raised her. Haman was speechless, and he fell down and begged for mercy from Esther after the king angrily left the room.

The king walked in his garden, deciding how to punish Haman. One of his servants showed him the gallows that Haman had prepared to hang Mordecai. The king ordered that Haman be hanged on his own gallows.

The Feast of Purim

After Haman's death, Mordecai was given a position of high honor in the kingdom. He sent letters to the Jews in every part of the land, telling them to fight for their lives on the day Haman ordered that they should be killed.

No harm came to the Jews, and they celebrated this victory with a festival called the Feast of Purim. Even today the Jews keep this traditional feast, and they always tell the story of Esther, the beautiful queen who saved the lives of her people.

F-14 How Ezra Taught God's Law to the Jews
Ezra 7 – 10; Nehemiah 8

After many years, there was a new ruler in Persia. Artaxerxes sat on the throne in Shushan and governed many lands, including Judah. The king wished to know what was happening in Judah, and he sent a messenger to Jerusalem to find out. The messenger was a priest named Ezra. He was a strong-hearted, courageous man like Daniel had been. And he was a scribe, or someone who wrote books.

Artaxerxes Allows the Jews to Go to Judah

Ezra wanted to teach Jews everywhere about the Law of God, which had been given by Moses to the Israelites. With the permission of the king, he organized other Jews in his own land who wanted to go to Judah and help the poor Jews who lived there.

Ezra had told his king much about God and his great power and willingness to help those who serve him. The king was very interested. He believed the God of the Jews must be very powerful. The king didn't want to

Ezra Prays

displease such a great God, and he gave Ezra much gold and silver for him
to take to the temple in Jerusalem.

When Ezra and the other Jews were ready to begin their journey, they
fasted and prayed for God to bless them and protect them from the many
dangers along their way. They were in danger from both wild animals and
people that lived in the desert who often robbed travelers. Then they started
out on the long journey.

After about four months of travel, they reached Judah in safety and with all their possessions. They were very happy to reach the city where the temple was. After resting for three days, they brought their gifts of silver and gold to the priests who were in charge of the temple.

Ezra soon learned that things were not going well in Judah. The poor Jews were discouraged, and many of them had made friends with their heathen neighbors. They had allowed their sons and daughters to marry heathen people, and they were not teaching their children to keep the Law of God. They had never rebuilt the city of Jerusalem and its walls were in ruins, just as Nebuchadnezzar and his army had left them years before.

Ezra was deeply troubled by what he saw. He knew they had sinned by marrying heathen people, and he knew God would not bless them while they were not obeying his law. He prayed that God would forgive them, and he called them all to Jerusalem to warn them about the wrong they had done.

Ezra Reading the Law

The people were glad to have Ezra teach them. They needed a teacher from God and they listened to him attentively. For a long time they had been without God's law, and when they heard it they quit their wrongdoing.

Ezra stayed with the people and he continued to teach them. He read from the scrolls he had written, and they never grew tired of listening. Ezra read to them from the books of Moses, Samuel, David, and the other prophets, since they had very few books of their own.

F-15 THE KING'S CUPBEARER AND HIS STORY
NEHEMIAH 1:1 – 2:18

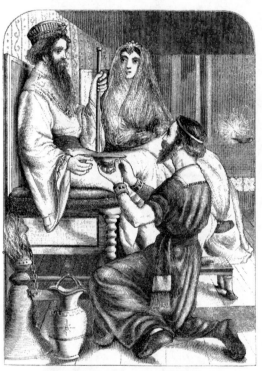

The King's Servant Nehemiah

In the palace of King Artaxerxes lived a young Jewish servant named Nehemiah. He was humble even though he was rich and the servant the king favored most.

He was working in the palace during King Artaxerxes's twelfth year as king. His brother Hanni and other men arrived from the land of Judah, and he asked them what was going on in Jerusalem and with the Jews who had gone there to rebuild the temple.

His brothers sadly shook their heads and told him that things were not going well there. The walls that had been torn down decades earlier had never been repaired, and the place looked very desolate and poor. The Jews who lived there were poor people who were oppressed by their enemies around them.

Nehemiah sat down and cried when he heard this news. He wanted to try to help them, but he knew that he needed the king's permission. He fasted and prayed to God for the king to allow him to go to Jerusalem and rebuild the walls and the city. One day when he was pouring wine for the king, first Nehemiah prayed. And then he asked the king to allow him to go to Jerusalem to help rebuild the city, as his people were living in a city with broken walls and being oppressed by their enemies. The king and his wife talked, and they realized that Nehemiah would be gone for many days.

The king and his wife agreed that their servant could leave, and the king gave Nehemiah letters to show to other rulers so that special favor would be shown to him in those lands. And the king arranged for Nehemiah to have all the wood he needed from his own forest, to be used for rebuilding the gates of the city walls.

Even though the other rulers did not want Nehemiah to help the poor Jews in Jerusalem, they were afraid not to help Nehemiah after they saw the letters from the king of Persia.

Nehemiah Rides Toward Jerusalem

Nehemiah Inspects the Walls of Jerusalem

After a few days, Nehemiah reached Jerusalem and inspected the walls. He found them to be in heaps and ruins, and nothing was left of what used to be a wall around the entire city. He talked to the priests and rulers and told them why he was there. He told them that Jerusalem was in a sad state and that God himself must be displeased. And he told them how he had prayed to be allowed to go and how the king had given him permission. After listening to him and seeing the letters from the king, they all decided to help him build the wall around the city and restore the city to its former state.

Rebuilding the Walls of Jerusalem

News of Nehemiah's arrival and the plan to rebuild the city walls spread rapidly in Jerusalem, and the people were thankful that he was there. Almost everyone helped to rebuild the broken walls, and some rich women hired workers to work on certain parts of the wall.

The high priest agreed to rebuild the gate that was used by the sheep and their shepherds. There were other gates to be rebuilt, and others agreed to do those jobs. Soon many gates were standing, and sections of wall were being built between them. Many people rebuilt the parts of the wall closest to their homes, and others did even more. Throwing away debris from the old wall and bringing all the stones for the new wall were also major jobs. Nehemiah rode around on his horse and supervised everything.

When two enemies of Jerusalem who lived nearby heard about the new wall, they became very angry. These men, Sanballat and Tobiah, feared the Jews would no longer allow them to come into their city and rob them. At first they made fun of the wall, saying that even a fox could knock it down. Nehemiah and his workers paid no attention to the jokes from their enemies. They just kept working.

Nehemiah Reads the Letter From Sanballat and Tobiah

Then Sanballat and Tobiah wrote a letter to Nehemiah, accusing him of wanting to take control of Jerusalem and no longer respecting the king of Persia. Nehemiah told them that was not true at all.

The enemies were angry. They planned to attack Jerusalem and kill the men building the walls. Nehemiah heard about their plan, and he armed the men with swords and spears. They stood spread out along the wall, waiting for an attack. The enemies heard about this, and they decided not to attack at that time.

The walls were almost done except for finishing the doors on the gates. The enemies tried to lure Nehemiah away from Jerusalem by asking him to go on a business trip when they really planned to kill him. He told them that he couldn't go because his work was too important.

After fifty-two days, the entire wall was finished. The people were very grateful that Nehemiah had come to encourage them to fix the wall of their ruined city. The people trusted Nehemiah, and they told him why they were so poor and so discouraged. Nehemiah contacted some of the other rulers and made them promise to help support Jerusalem.

For twelve years Nehemiah stayed in Jerusalem and acted as its governor. He knew Artaxerxes, the king, would be expecting him back in Shushan because he had promised to return at that time. He made his brother Hanni and another man rulers of the city while he was absent. When he saw the king, the king allowed him to return to Jerusalem and continue to be its ruler. During his next visit, he spent more time teaching the people about the commandments and laws of God.

Because of the efforts of Nehemiah and Ezra the priest, many people began to respect the teachings of God's law. They began to marry people who believed only as they did, they stopped worshiping idols, and they even wrote down books of law and traditions. God was not pleased with these books of laws as he had not commanded them, but God saw that they were trying to do better.

Malachi, the last of the prophets, spoke God's words to the people while Nehemiah was still alive. He told the people about the coming of the Savior, and he wrote his words down in a book. His book, Malachi, is the last book of the Old Testament.

Between The Old and New Testaments

More than 400 years passed between the time of the Old Testament and the time of the New Testament. During those years, many changes and events took place in the history of the Jews.

Although the Jews were allowed to return from Babylon to Judah, God did not permit them to become a separate kingdom as they had been before. Kings of other lands ruled them.

Once, the Jews did choose their own ruler, a son of a priest. But soon they were conquered by the Roman army and under the rule of Rome. Because the capital of Rome was very far from Judah, the Roman leaders appointed King Herod to rule over the Jews. Herod did many wicked things and was not liked by the Jews.

HEROD'S TEMPLE

After eighteen years as king, Herod was tired of having so many enemies and people who didn't like him. He decided to tear down the old temple and build a new, more beautiful temple in its place. It took years and thousands of men to build Herod's new temple. When it was finished, the Jews were very proud of it, and the priests continued to offer sacrifices to God there each morning and evening.

Stories of

The New Testament

In Two Parts

The Angel Appears to Zacharias at the Altar

Part G: Stories About Jesus
Matthew, Mark, Luke, John, Acts 1:1-15

G-1 The Parents of John the Baptist
Luke 1: 1-23

Zacharias was a very old priest who was a descendant of Aaron, the brother of Moses. His wife Elizabeth was also from the family of priests. Zacharias and his wife loved God, and they always tried to do their best to please him. They knew God had promised to send a Savior for all men from the family of David, and they looked forward to the time when the Savior would arrive.

Zacharias and Elizabeth had been married for a long time but they didn't have any children. They had prayed many times, asking to be blessed with a son or a daughter, but God had never answered their prayers. They continued to love and serve God, knowing that God always does what is best.

Zacharias did not work in the temple every day. There were many priests and they all took turns working. When it was his turn, Zacharias left his home in Judah and went to Jerusalem. His job was to burn incense on the golden altar, where only the priests could enter. Twice each day, at the time of the morning and evening sacrifices, he made sure the incense was fresh and burning properly.

One day when Zacharias was offering incense on the golden altar as usual, he was surprised to see an angel standing on the right side of the altar, watching him. At first Zacharias was afraid, and the angel told him that there was nothing to fear. The angel told him that he and Elizabeth would be blessed with a son, and they should name him John. John would be great in the eyes of God. He would never drink wine or alcohol, and he would have the power of God's spirit within him, as Elijah had. He would have the power to turn people away from their sins and get them to serve God.

Zacharias asked the angel for a sign. The angel told him he was Gabriel, the angel who stands in the presence of God. Because Zacharias had not believed him, the angel said, Zacharias would not be able to speak until the child was born. That would be his sign. Then the angel disappeared.

When Zacharias came out of the temple, he could not speak, but he used his hands to tell the people that he had seen a vision from God. Soon it was time for Zacharias to return to his home in the country of Judah. He knew that the time would come when he would be able to speak again.

Mary was a Jewish woman. She had grown up in Nazareth, a city of Galilee. She was expecting to marry an honorable man named Joseph. Both Mary and Joseph were descendants of King David, but they were poor people. Joseph was a carpenter. He worked with his hands and tools to earn money and to build a home for himself and Mary.

One day God sent an angel to talk to Mary because God had chosen her to be the mother of the Savior he was going to send into the world. Mary was surprised when she saw the angel, and she was even more surprised when she heard his words. The angel told her that God would protect and bless her because she was the mother of the Son of God. He told her that Jesus, her son, would be a king and that he would rule forever.

The Angel Appears to Mary

Mary Visits Elizabeth

The angel told Mary how God was giving Zacharias and Elizabeth a child even though they were very old. The angel said nothing was too hard for God to do. Mary believed the angel's words, and the angel left and went back to heaven.

Elizabeth, the old lady mentioned by the angel, was Mary's cousin. Mary knew that she had wanted a child, and she was very happy to hear she would have one. Mary decided to visit her cousin Elizabeth.

As soon as Mary arrived, God caused Elizabeth to know that Mary would be the mother of the Son of God, and they were both very happy for each other. The two women spent several days together, and then Mary returned to Bethlehem.

God spoke to Joseph the carpenter in a dream and told him about Jesus's birth. Joseph was glad, and he took Mary into his home and waited for the angel's promise to come true.

G-3 John the Baptist as a Young Man
Luke 1:57-80

Everyone who knew them rejoiced when the angel promised a child to Elizabeth and Zacharias. When it was time to give him a name, many of the friends and relatives who were there suggested that his name should be Zacharias, like his father.

Elizabeth told them that his name was John. The others questioned this decision, and they asked Zacharias what his name should be. Zacharias still could not speak, but he wrote, "His name is John."

Zacharias Writes John's Name

The others thought this was strange, but they understood the parents' wishes. Then Zacharias began to speak normally, as he had before seeing the angel. He praised God for giving him a wonderful baby.

News of the story of John's birth spread throughout the land, and the people believed that surely he would grow up to be a great man. Zacharias received wisdom from God, and he told his son that one day he would grow up to be a prophet of the highest power and that he would give the people knowledge of the way to salvation from their sins.

Zacharias spoke many other words that had been told to him by God. He raised his son and continued to care for him. He saw that God was blessing young John and causing him to grow both strong and brave.

Zacharias and Elizabeth probably did not live to see the day when John began his work, which was after he was thirty years old. Until that time he lived quietly in the desert and studied the writings of all the prophets of God. He listened to the voice of God and began to understand what God wanted him to do.

On the streets of Nazareth, the people were very excited. The emperor of Rome had commanded that everyone in his empire must put their names on lists because he wished to have the names of all of his people. The people were afraid to disobey the command.

Soon people everywhere were headed to their hometowns to write their names. Joseph and Mary headed to Bethlehem since they were from the family of David. When they arrived, they saw that the city was very busy with people from many different places who had returned to add their names to the list. All of the hotels and lodging places were full, and Joseph and Mary did not know where they would stay.

Mary needed a place to rest, and after learning that no hotel rooms were available, finally they ended up staying in the stable at the inn. One night soon after they arrived in Bethlehem, Mary gave birth to Jesus. She wrapped him in soft cloths and laid him in a manger where the cattle fed, since she had no better place.

Shepherds were watching their flocks that night in a field near Bethlehem. They knew about God's promise of a Savior. An angel appeared to them, and at first they were afraid. The angel told them not to be afraid, and that he had news of great joy for all people: That day a Savior had been born, and they would find him in swaddling clothes, or soft clothes, and lying in a manger, or box that holds food for animals.

The First Angel Appears to the Shepherds

Then a multitude of angels joined the first angel, and they all began to sing a wonderful song. When the song was over, the angels went back to heaven and the darkness of the night returned. The shepherds decided to go to Bethlehem at once to see what God had told them about.

The Shepherds Visit Baby Jesus

They found Mary and Joseph in the stable with the baby Savior lying in the manger. The shepherds told Joseph and Mary about the song the angels had sung. They knelt before the baby, and then the shepherds went out into the streets to tell everyone about the angels they had seen and the Son of God who had been born that night.

Baby Jesus at the Temple

When the baby was eight days old, Joseph and Mary gave him the name told to them by the angel. That name, Jesus, means "salvation."

There was a law among the Jews that an offering would be made to God for the first-born male child in each family. A rich family was to sacrifice a lamb, but God would be happy with two pigeons from a poor family.

When Jesus was forty days old, Joseph and Mary took him to the temple at Jerusalem to give their offering. Since they were poor, they brought two pigeons.

An old man named Simeon was at the temple that day. He had served God for many years, and he wanted to see the Savior that God had promised to send into the world. God caused Simeon to know that baby Jesus was the Savior. He came over to see the baby and Mary. He was very happy to see Jesus since he had been waiting for such a long time.

Anna, an older woman who sometimes acted as a prophet, was also in the temple. She too gave thanks to God when she saw Jesus.

Mary never forgot the words of these dear old people. And she remembered the story of the shepherds and what the angel had told her. She didn't know how it would happen, but she trusted in God that someday her son would be the King and Savior of the world.

G-5 THE WISE MEN WHO FOLLOWED A STAR
MATTHEW 2

In the country to the east of Judah lived some wise men who studied the stars in the sky. One night they discovered a new star, one that they had never seen before. God caused them to know by the sign of this star that Christ, the King of the Jews, had been born.

These wise men wanted to see the child that God had sent into the world. They thought that the Jews must be very happy to have their long-awaited King. The wise men were very rich, and they decided to go at once to see the Savior and bring him precious gifts.

For many days they traveled across the desert, and finally they came to the land of the Jews. They hurried to Jerusalem, expecting that the child would be living in the most beautiful place in the land.

Herod, the man who ruled the land of Judah as part of the Roman Empire, met the strangers on horseback in Jerusalem. They told him they were looking for the child who was born King of the Jews. Herod was puzzled because he had heard nothing about such a child. He was even more puzzled when the Jews he asked didn't know either.

Herod called all of the priests and scribes and asked them where the Savior was to be born. After studying the scrolls containing the writings of the prophets, they said the city of Bethlehem was where the child would be born. Herod told the wise men to look for the child in Bethlehem.

Herod did not believe that the Jewish people should have their own king, and he wanted to find a way to stop this from happening. He told the wise men to send a message to him as soon as they had found the child, and he would join them in worshiping him. Herod told the wise men to leave for Bethlehem at once.

The wise men once again rode on their camels to the south. Night was beginning to fall, but they decided to journey on anyway. When they left the city gates, the star that they had seen in the east appeared before them and seemed to lead their way.

The Wise Men Guided by the Star

When the star reached Bethlehem, it stopped over the place where Mary and Joseph were living. The wise men saw the child, and they knew that they had found the right place. They knelt before him and gave him the rich treasures they had brought from their homeland.

The Wise Men Give Gifts to Jesus

God spoke to the wise men in a dream and warned them not to tell Herod that they had found the baby. They returned to their own country on a different road, and they never saw Herod again.

An angel spoke to Joseph in a dream and warned him to take his wife and child and flee at once to Egypt because Herod was going to try to kill baby

An Angel Tells Joseph to Go to Egypt

The Flight Into Egypt

Jesus. The angel told Joseph that they should stay in Egypt until the angel appeared again and told them to leave.

Joseph got up out of bed and left while it was still dark. He took Mary and the baby and hurried out of Bethlehem. For many days they traveled to the southwest until they reached the land of Egypt.

Herod's Soldiers Kill the Babies

Herod became angry when the wise men did not send any news to him. He thought that they suspected he would harm Jesus, and he blamed himself for appearing too eager to find him.

Herod sent soldiers to kill every baby in and around Bethlehem, two years of age and younger. All the babies were killed, and Herod thought he must have killed the future King of the Jews.

Jesus was no longer a baby and was starting to grow up in Egypt when the angel appeared to Joseph again, telling him that Herod was dead. The angel told them to return to their own land.

On the way back to Bethlehem, Joseph heard that Herod's son was the new ruler, and he feared that he might be like his dad. So, Joseph decided to live in Nazareth in the country of Galilee, where he and Mary had lived before Jesus was born. Joseph thought this would be safer for his son than returning to Bethlehem.

G-6 WHEN JESUS WAS A BOY
LUKE 2:40-52

Nazareth was nearly seventy miles from Jerusalem. The Jews who lived there could not travel to Jerusalem every week to worship God, so they built a house of worship, called a synagogue, in their own town. They attended religious services there and listened to readings of the books written by Moses and the other prophets.

When Jesus was old enough, Mary and Joseph sent him to school at the synagogue, where Jewish children were taught how to read and write. Jesus learned to read the books of Moses and the prophets, and he probably memorized much of what he read, since he didn't have his own books.

One spring morning when he was twelve years old, Jesus and his family started on a journey to Jerusalem to attend the Passover Feast. He was very interested to see the temple and hear the words of the priests and scribes. When the feast was over and it was time to leave, everyone from Nazareth left as a group, and no one noticed that Jesus was not with the others.

Soon someone noticed that Jesus was missing, and his family searched for three days until they found him at the temple. He was asking questions that the wise teachers couldn't answer. Mary was surprised to find him there. Jesus told her that she should have known where to find him, since he was learning the business of God. The wise men asked Jesus many difficult questions that he was able to answer.

Jesus was an obedient child, and he left with his parents and returned to Nazareth. Jesus learned much at the temple, and he also watched his father at work until he could do the work of a carpenter himself. By his kind, thoughtful ways, Jesus won many friends. Jesus lived in his humble home in Nazareth until he was about thirty years old.

Young Jesus With the Teachers

G-7 The Strange Preacher in the Wilderness
Matthew 3; Mark 1:2-11; Luke 3:1-23; John 1:15-34

While Jesus was growing up in Nazareth, Zacharias's son John was growing up in the desert country of Judea. John stayed in the desert country, listening to God's voice.

John the Baptist Preaching in the Wilderness

When he became a man, John left the desert and began to tell God's words to the people. John did not go into the cities to preach God's message. Instead he stayed in the wilderness of Judea near the Jordan River.

People came from far away to hear him speak. The last prophet had been Malachi 400 years earlier; the people believed that John was a prophet, and they came in great numbers to see and hear him.

John told the people to turn away from sin and do the right thing because God's kingdom was close at hand. He said that the King the Jews had been seeking would soon be with them. In the Jordan River, he baptized those who confessed their sins. They called him "John the Baptist" because he did this.

All types of people were baptized. When some religious rulers called Pharisees and Sadducees went to be baptized, God told John the Baptist to tell them to turn away from their sins before they could enter the kingdom of God.

John tried to teach everyone to get along and help each other. He taught people not to be greedy and to help the poor. News of John the Baptist spread throughout the land. Some people wondered if he was Elijah returned to Earth again.

He wore unconventional clothes and ate dried locusts and honey from the wilderness. He was bold, like Elijah had been, and he was unafraid to speak the truth to anyone.

John told the people that he was not great at all, but the King who would be following him would be great. John said he was baptizing people with water, and the King would baptize them with the Holy Spirit, sent down from heaven.

One day Jesus went to see John the Baptist. Jesus asked to be baptized, and John was surprised. He told Jesus that he should be baptizing him since Jesus was so much greater. Jesus told him that he must be baptized because it was part of God's plan. John took Jesus into the Jordan River and baptized him there.

When they were coming up out of the water, a dove landed on Jesus's head. This was the spirit of God. A voice from heaven said, "This is my beloved Son, in whom I am well pleased."

John continued to preach after Jesus was baptized. Sometimes Herod heard him. Herod was troubled because John told him about his sins, and Herod's wife disliked John so much that she wanted her husband to kill him. To please his wife, Herod had John thrown into prison.

The Baptism of Jesus

354

G-8 The Temptation of Jesus
Matthew 4:1-11; Mark 1:12,13; Luke 4:1-14

God sent Jesus into the world to save people from their sins. The first sin was when Eve ate the forbidden fruit in the Garden of Eden. Since that time, all men had sinned against God in some way. Satan knew of God's plan to save men from their sins through Jesus. Satan wanted to make Jesus want to sin, just as he had done to Eve.

After Jesus was baptized and the voice from heaven was heard, Jesus lived in the wilderness for forty days with the wild animals. God protected him and did not allow him to be harmed.

Satan found Jesus all alone in the wilderness. He tried many different ways to get Jesus to sin. But Jesus would not listen.

Satan Tempts Jesus in the Wilderness

355

After the forty days were over, Jesus was very weak from not eating for so long. Satan suggested that Jesus should turn three stones into bread, if he was hungry and truly the Son of God.

Instead of trying to prove anything to Satan, Jesus told him, "Man shall not live by bread alone but by every word of God." Although he was hungry and weak, Jesus chose to trust in God to take care of him.

Satan told Jesus that he must show the people a sign by jumping down from the top of the temple, and God would keep his bones from breaking. Satan tried to trick Jesus with religious writings but Jesus knew better. Jesus knew that no one should tempt God and expect angels to protect him.

Then Satan caused Jesus to see all the kingdoms of the world. Satan told Jesus that he was the ruler of these kingdoms, and he would give them all to him if he would fall down and worship him. Jesus knew that Satan was a liar. He told him to get away and that God said he was the only one who should be worshiped.

Satan left Jesus alone when he realized he could find no way at all to make him sin. When he left, angels came and took care of Jesus's needs. Jesus learned to resist all forms of temptation; this helped him to better understand and help the men and women he was there to save.

G-9 Five Men Who Met Jesus
John 1:35-51

Many people who heard John the Baptist preach by the riverside believed his words, and they began to look for the coming of the King from heaven. They believed he would set up a kingdom in Judea, like David had done. And they believed the Jews would be his favored people.

One day after Jesus had returned from the wilderness, John the Baptist saw him walking along the road near the river. John cried out, "Behold the Lamb of God who bears the sin of the world!"

Two young men from Galilee were with John that day and they heard him speak. These young men had been disciples or learners of John, and they were interested in the teachings of God. They had heard John speak about Jesus, and they turned at once to follow him.

Jesus took them to his home and talked with them all day. They believed he was the King or Messiah after they listened to him, and they were very glad that they had found him.

One of the young men was Andrew. He went to get his brother Simon, because he knew he would want to see Jesus also. Simon was listening to John speak in the wilderness, as they all did most every day. Andrew told

Jesus Talks to Nathaniel and Phillip

Simon that he had found the Messiah.

When Jesus saw Simon, he told him that his new name would be Peter. After he listened to Jesus, Peter believed that he was the King of the Jews. Both Andrew and Peter decided to follow Jesus. The next day Jesus began his journey back to Galilee, and these men went with him.

They met a man named Phillip along the way. Jesus asked Phillip to follow him along with the others, and Phillip agreed. He listened to Jesus speak, and soon he believed Jesus was the Messiah and King.

Phillip had a neighbor named Nathaniel who had often talked to him about the time when the Messiah would come. Phillip ran to tell him that they had found the Messiah, and he was Jesus of Nazareth. Nathaniel knew the Scriptures and believed the Messiah would come from Bethlehem, but he did not yet know where Jesus was born.

When they approached Jesus, Nathaniel and Phillip were surprised that he knew so much about them and what they had been doing. Nathaniel soon believed that he was the Messiah and the Son of God.

G-10 THE WEDDING WHERE JESUS SHOWED HIS POWER
JOHN 2:1-11

Jesus's mother and some friends of his family lived in a little town in Galilee called Cana. One day these friends invited Jesus, his followers, and his mother to attend a wedding in their home. Many others were also attending the wedding. Before long, the wine was running out.

Mary, the mother of Jesus, told Jesus that the wine was all gone, and she hoped that somehow he could help. She told the servants to do whatever Jesus said.

The Wedding in Cana

Jesus told the servants to fill all of the water-pots with water. After they had done this, Jesus told them to fill the wine containers with what was in the water-pots. They were surprised to see that wine flowed out of the water-pots instead of water.

The person in charge of the feast always tasted the food and wine before it was served. The wine was given to him for tasting, and he said that he was surprised the best wine was being served last instead of first, as was usually the custom.

Turning water into wine was the first public miracle that Jesus performed, and it showed that he was willing to help people. When his followers saw this miracle, it made them believe in him even more strongly.

G-11 THE GREAT TEACHER IN JERUSALEM
JOHN 2:13-3:21

It was time for another yearly Passover Feast in Jerusalem, and people came from all over to attend. Jesus and his four disciples - Andrew, Simon, Phillip, and Nathaniel - were all there.

Jesus Drives Out the Moneychangers and Animal Sellers

359

Only the priests were allowed to enter the rooms of the temple, and the people who went to worship stayed outside in the courts while the priests offered sacrifices. When Jesus went into the court, he was surprised to see people selling animals for sacrifices and others exchanging different types of currency, or changing money. The people needed to convert their currency into half-shekels before they could donate money to the priests and temple, and others were profiting by charging them for this service.

Jesus knew that the people could not pray in the court with all this noise and commotion. He made a whip by tying cords together, and then he drove out all the animals and the men who were selling them. He turned over the tables used by the moneychangers, and he told them that the temple was a place of prayer and not a marketplace.

Most of the people were pleased by what Jesus did, but some questioned his authority to do it. They asked to see a sign to prove his power. He told them, "Destroy this temple, and in three days I will raise it." They thought he was talking about Herod's temple, but he was really talking about his own body, meaning he would rise up from being dead after three days.

At the Passover Feast, Jesus began to teach and to perform miracles. Many people believed what he said, especially after seeing what he could do. One man who believed him was Nicodemus, a Pharisee, or ruler among the Jews. Nicodemus was a very rich man. Most of the other Pharisees did not believe in Jesus or John the Baptist as Nicodemus did.

One night Nicodemus went to the place where Jesus was staying, and he asked to have a talk with him. Jesus was glad to talk to Nicodemus. Jesus told him that no man could enter the kingdom of God unless he was first born again. Nicodemus didn't understand, and Jesus explained that he was talking about a spiritual rebirth, or change of heart. God loved mankind enough to send his only Son to die for the sins of all men and women, and anyone who believes in him and accepts the gift of salvation would have everlasting life.

Then Jesus reminded Nicodemus of the story of Moses in the wilderness, when the people had been disobedient and God sent fiery snakes into the camp. Jesus told him that the people who were about to die from the snakebites found relief by looking to the brass snake that Moses had put up on a pole, and people who have sin in their hearts could find relief by looking to the Son of man, who would be raised up also.

Nicodemus did not understand that Jesus was talking about the way he would be put on a cross and killed to save all people from their sins. But he believed that Jesus was a great teacher sent down from heaven.

Jesus Talks With Nicodemus

G-12 THE TIRED STRANGER WHO RESTED BY A WELL
JOHN 4:1-43

Samaria was a little country between Judea and Galilee. The people there worshiped God, but they did so at their own temple and not in Jerusalem. They considered the Jews their enemies, and the Jews would not take the road through Samaria when traveling to and from Galilee, even though it was shorter.

Although Jesus was a Jew, he did not consider the Samaritans to be his enemies, and he knew that God loved all people. He did not mind walking through their land, and he hoped to teach them about the kingdom of heaven. His disciples went with him on the way back to Nazareth, and they had gone as far as a little city called Sychar.

Near the city was a well called Jacob's well, dug by Jacob, who was a grandson of Abraham. Jesus stopped to rest at the well, and his disciples went to find food.

361

Jacob's Well, Near Sychar

A woman from Sychar came to the well to draw water. She saw Jesus sitting there, and she knew he was a Jew. She didn't speak to him because the Jews and the Samaritans didn't speak to each other. After she got her water from the well, Jesus asked her for a drink. She told him that Jews and Samaritans normally didn't help each other.

Jesus told her that if she knew who he was, she would give him a drink, and he would give her living water to drink. She was interested in what he said, and she knew he must not be like the other Jews she had met and heard about. She told him that he had no rope to draw water; therefore he couldn't give her any water to drink.

Jesus told her that the living water he spoke of does not come from any well. It flows within a person, and the person never becomes thirsty again.

The woman did not know Jesus was talking about the gift of salvation, and she told him that she wanted some of the living water so that she would not need to return to the well again. Jesus began to tell the woman about many of the wrong things she had done. She was very surprised that Jesus knew so much about her sins, and she said he must be a prophet.

She asked Jesus whether she should worship God in Jerusalem or at the temple in Samaria. Jesus said God had brought salvation through the Jews,

362

Jesus and the Woman From Samaria

but the time had come when believers could pray to God from anywhere and not just Jerusalem. He told her that God is a spirit, and he is everywhere.

The woman said that she knew the Messiah would be coming, and Jesus told her that he was the Messiah. The woman looked at him with joy and wonder. At that moment the disciples returned with food, and the woman ran to tell her friends about the remarkable stranger she had met, leaving her

363

water jug behind.

The disciples wondered why Jesus would talk to a Samaritan, but they didn't say anything. They tried to get Jesus to eat, and he said that he had already had food. They asked him what he meant, and he said that his food was to do the will of his Father, who had sent him into the world.

The woman told her friends that Jesus knew everything she had ever done and that he must be the Messiah. The people wanted to meet him themselves, and they went to Jacob's well. Jesus talked with the Samaritans about God, and they invited him to stay in their city and teach them more. He spent two days in Sychar. Then he went on to Nazareth, leaving behind some new believers in Samaria.

G-13 A Man Who Had Great Faith in Jesus's Power
John 4:45-54

Many people who lived in the country of Galilee were eager to see Jesus. They had heard about him turning water into wine, and they heard about his teachings and miracles at the Passover Feast. When he left Sychar and returned with his disciples, news spread rapidly from one city to another. The Galilean people hoped that he would come to their cities and perform miracles among them, too.

One man did not want to wait for Jesus to come to his city. He lived in Capernaum, and he was a ruler in that city. He had compassion for the poor, which was unusual among the rulers.

This nobleman's son had been stricken with a fever, and the doctors could not make him well. Hearing of Jesus, he decided to go to Cana where he was and beg him to come to Capernaum to heal his child. He found Jesus and told him about his very sick son that he thought would die without his help. Jesus told the man that he would not believe God sent him unless he saw signs and wonders.

The man begged him to go at once or the little boy would die. Jesus told him not to worry but to return home without him and his son would be fine.

The man believed Jesus and returned home. When he arrived, the servants told him that his son was no longer sick. The man asked the servants when he began to get better. They told him it was at the seventh hour of the previous day, and the man knew that was when he had met with Jesus. Not only the man but also his entire household believed Jesus had saved the boy when they heard what had happened.

G-14 The Angry Mob on the Hilltop of Nazareth
Luke 4:16-32

In the city of Nazareth, Jesus attended the Sabbath day service as he had always done when he was there. Jesus had just returned after being away. Many people had heard about his teachings and miracles, and they were eager to learn more about him. Jesus stood up and read from the book of Isaiah about the coming of the Messiah. After reading from Isaiah, Jesus sat down. The people waited for him to explain the meaning of the Scriptures.

Jesus in the Synagogue

Some of the people there were proud men who had known Jesus for a long time, and they refused to believe he was the King of the Jews, even after hearing about his miracles. They considered him only a poor man. But the proud men were surprised when Jesus spoke so well. When Jesus explained that he was the Messiah promised by Isaiah, the men didn't know what to think.

Jesus told them that no prophet had ever been honored by his own people. He reminded them of Elijah's troubles and how God had blessed the poor widow who helped him to hide. God had also blessed Naman because he obeyed Elisha's words.

The proud men objected to Jesus's suggestion that God blessed people other than the Jews. Many of them left before the service was over, and this caused a disruption.

Some men grabbed Jesus and took him outside, and an angry mob of people followed, wanting to punish Jesus for what he had said. The mob took Jesus to a high hill, intending to throw him onto the rocks below. But it was not yet time for Jesus to die, and he was able to walk away quietly.

Preparing to Throw Jesus off a Cliff

He went away to live in Capernaum, a city by the Sea of Galilee. The men who drove Jesus away from Nazareth did not know what they had done. Because they refused to believe in Jesus as the one promised by Isaiah, they never received the gift of salvation.

G-15 Four Men Who Quit Fishing to Follow Jesus
Matthew 4:18-22; Mark 1:16-34; Luke 4:33 – 5:11

Jesus's disciples had not gone with him to Nazareth. They had returned to their homes in Capernaum. After the men of Nazareth tried to kill him and Jesus went to Capernaum, he was reunited with his disciples.

Jesus taught in the synagogue, and the people of Capernaum were glad to listen to him. His words were different from the usual Jewish teachers who always repeated the same lessons.

One morning Andrew and Simon were busy at work in their fishing boats on the Sea of Galilee when they saw Jesus walking on the shore. He called to them, and they left their boats and followed him. Soon they saw two other fishermen in a ship fixing their torn nets. These men were brothers, and their names were James and John. They were partners in the fishing business with Simon and Andrew. When they saw their partners with Jesus they stopped their work, wondering where Simon and Andrew were going. Jesus called to them also, and they left their ship.

With the four fishermen accompanying him, Jesus returned to the city. On the next Sabbath day, they all went with him to the synagogue where many people had gathered to hear his words.

Satan caused one man in the crowd at the synagogue to have an evil spirit in him. The spirit caused the man to yell and scream at Jesus. Jesus commanded the spirit of Satan to come out of the man. The man fell onto the floor, and the evil spirit came out of him, since Jesus had the power to cast out evil spirits that went into the bodies of people.

News of Jesus casting out the evil spirit spread throughout the city, and everybody became interested in the great teacher who was living among them. They were glad he was there, and they wanted him to help their sick friends and loved ones.

Jesus had gone to the home of Simon and Andrew to help Simon's sick mother-in-law. They told Jesus about her fever and brought him to her bedside. Jesus held her hand, and at once her fever subsided and she regained her strength. She rose up from her bed and helped to prepare food for the disciples and Jesus.

Jesus Casts Out Evil Spirits

Soon many people were heading toward Simon's house, bringing their friends who were crippled, blind, and suffering from other problems. All of them asked Jesus to help cure their illnesses. Jesus was glad to help. He touched them one by one and made them well, and he cast out more spirits.

Finally everyone left, and Jesus lay down to sleep in Simon's house. He was very tired, but he slept for only a few hours. Then he got up and left the city. He wanted a place to talk privately with his heavenly Father.

Jesus Preaches From the Boat on the Sea of Galilee

The next day, people began returning to Simon's house in search of Jesus, but Jesus was no longer there. Simon and his friends began to search for Jesus, and they found him at his place of prayer. They told him about the people who wanted to see him, and he said that he had to preach about the kingdom of God in other cities also. The disciples went with him to other cities in Galilee. Jesus taught in those synagogues and cast out more evil spirits. Many people believed in him.

After a while he returned to Capernaum, and his disciples went back to the work of fishing. Jesus continued to teach the people who came to hear him. One day Jesus went to the seashore where the disciples were working, and many people followed him there. Jesus asked for permission to speak to the people from aboard Simon's ship.

When Jesus finished speaking, he told Simon to row out into the deep water and lower his nets. Simon told him they had caught nothing all night, but they would do as he said. This time a great number of fish filled the nets as soon as they were lowered into the water. It took all four disciples to raise the nets because they were so heavy with fish. They had never seen so many fish in one net before. Soon both ships were so full of fish that they began to sink.

The Nets Are Filled With Fish

The fishermen knew that Jesus had performed a miracle by causing so many fish to become caught in the nets. Simon told Jesus that he wasn't worthy of all he had been given. Jesus told him from that time on he would catch men instead of fish. Simon understood that he must leave the fishing business and follow Jesus everywhere he went. The fishermen left their ships and walked with Jesus from one city to another, helping him and learning more about the kingdom of God.

G-16 How Matthew Became a Disciple of Jesus
Matthew 9:9-13; Mark 2:14-17; Luke 5:27-32

All the Jews despised the tax collectors who worked for the Roman government. The Jews wanted to have their own Jewish ruler and be free of the Roman state. For this reason, they were eagerly awaiting the time when the kingdom of God would come. They believed God would send them a strong King who would free them from the rule of other nations. They did not understand that their greatest enemy was Satan and that they needed to be freed from their sins.

The Jews who worked for the Roman government were called "publicans." Some of them were tax collectors who took tax money from the other Jews, and often they took too much. Because they stole from the people, they became rich themselves and the people hated them. Not all of the publicans were thieves, but the people believed they were and called all of them sinners.

One day while Jesus was passing along a street in Capernaum, he saw a man named Matthew sitting at a publican's table, taking money from the people. Although Matthew was a publican, Jesus knew he had a good heart and would make a worthy disciple. Jesus asked Matthew to follow him, and Matthew gladly obeyed.

Matthew was also called Levi, as the Jews often had two names. He thought many of his old friends would be glad to listen to Jesus. Matthew prepared a great feast and called many of his friends and associates together, including other publicans. Jesus and the other disciples came to the feast.

The scribes and Pharisees also came to Matthew's house, even though they had not been invited to the feast. They stood around, watching and talking to each other about what they saw. This was not considered rude, and Matthew was not surprised that they were there.

These onlookers didn't approve of Jesus and the disciples sitting with Matthew and the other publicans. They called Jesus's disciples aside and asked them why Jesus was socializing with sinners.

Jesus heard their question, and he told them that healthy people do not need a doctor, but sick people do. Jesus said he was there to help sinners to repent. He knew that the scribes and Pharisees believed themselves to be righteous and not in need of repentance. But he knew that the publicans and sinners realized that they were not pleasing God, and they would listen to his words. Many of them were willing to change their ways and follow Jesus.

Jesus and Matthew

Matthew became a very useful man for God. He wrote the book called "The Gospel According to Matthew" in the New Testament. His book gives us more words of Jesus than any of the other Gospel books.

G-17 How Jesus Healed a Crippled Man and a Withered Hand
Matthew 12:1-15; Mark 2:23 – 3:6; Luke 6:1-12; John 5:1-18

Not far from the temple in Jerusalem was a pool called Bethesda. Sometimes the water in the pool bubbled, and people believed they would be healed of their illnesses if they went into the bubbling water. Sick, blind, and crippled people waited beside the pool on its many nearby porches.

One Sabbath day while Jesus was in Jerusalem, he walked through the porches beside the pool. He saw the afflicted people who hoped to be healed in the waters. He saw a crippled man lying on a mat who hadn't walked in nearly forty years. He asked the man if he wanted to be made well.

The Pool of Bethesda

373

The Disciples Picking Corn on the Sabbath

The man told him that he had no one to help him into the water when it started bubbling, and someone else always stepped in first. Jesus told him, "Rise up, take your bed, and walk!" The man felt strength entering his weak body and he sprang to his feet. Then he rolled up his mat and started walking home.

Some religious Jews saw the man carrying his mat on the Sabbath day, and they believed it was wrong to carry any burdens on the Sabbath. They asked him why he was carrying the bed, and he told them how he had been healed and told to walk away with his bed.

The religious Jews demanded to know who had told him to break the rules of the Sabbath. But the old man didn't know who Jesus was, and he couldn't tell them his name.

Soon after, Jesus found the man in the temple, worshiping God. Jesus warned the man not to sin or something worse than lameness would afflict him. Then the man knew who Jesus was, and he ran out to tell the people that it was Jesus who had made him well.

The Jews were angry because Jesus had healed him on the Sabbath day. They did not care about the poor man as much as they wanted to appear righteous. Jesus told them that he worked on the Sabbath, just like his Father, God. They were even angrier because he said that God was his Father, and they wanted to kill him.

After this time, the Pharisees became enemies of Jesus. They often followed him, trying to find fault. One Sabbath day while he was walking through a field of corn, his disciples picked off some kernels to eat because they were hungry. The Pharisees were watching, and they told Jesus his disciples were breaking the law by gathering food on the Sabbath. Jesus reminded the Pharisees how the priests work every Sabbath offering

Jesus Heals the Man's Withered Hand

sacrifices, and he told them that God was not pleased with their regard for the Sabbath laws, since they would not even allow a person to do right.

When Jesus returned to Galilee, there were Pharisees in the temple watching him on the Sabbath day. Jesus saw a man with a withered hand who wanted to be healed. He saw the Pharisees and he asked them if it was lawful to do good works on the Sabbath. He told them that if they had a sheep that fell into a pit on the Sabbath, they would try to save it, and a man is more important than a sheep.

Then he turned to the man standing before him and told him to stretch out his withered hand. The man obeyed, and immediately the hand was healed. The Pharisees went out of the synagogue in an angry mood, wanting to kill Jesus. The man who had been healed went home feeling very happy.

Jesus and His Disciples

In addition to the fishermen, Philip, Nathaniel, Matthew, and many other people wanted to learn about the teachings of Jesus. They decided to follow him from one place to another. The time came when Jesus decided to choose twelve men he could prepare to help with his great work. He wanted to send these men into different lands to preach the message of the kingdom of God.

Jesus could see the hearts of all men, but he wanted help from God to decide which twelve helpers to pick. One night he went away quietly and climbed up the slope of a mountain. He knelt down and prayed for God to give him the help, strength, and wisdom to do his work.

When morning came, Jesus was ready to choose his helpers. He left his place of prayer and joined the disciples who were waiting for him. He chose Simon whom he called Peter, and Andrew, his brother. Then he chose James and John, the fishermen who had been partners with Simon and Andrew.

He chose Matthew, the publican, and Philip and Nathaniel of Capernaum.

Christ Sends the Apostles Forth

He picked Thomas, and another James, and another Simon, then Judas the brother of James, and last of all he chose Judas Iscariot.

Jesus gave these twelve men the power to cure diseases and cast out demons. He also appointed them to preach the kingdom of God. He called them his "apostles," which means those who are sent out.

G-19 THE SERMON ON THE MOUNTAINSIDE
MATTHEW 5 – 7; LUKE 6:17-49

After Jesus had chosen his twelve apostles, who were also still called disciples, he met with them on the side of the mountain to teach them how to do his great work. Other people followed and listened to him also.

Jesus began his sermon by saying, "Blessed are the poor in spirit, for theirs is the kingdom of heaven." He meant that proud people like the Pharisees and scribes would never enter the kingdom of heaven, but people who were humble and knew they needed God's help would be able to.

Next Jesus said, "Blessed are they that mourn, for they shall be comforted." He meant that God loves to comfort the sad and troubled.

"Blessed are the meek, for they shall inherit the earth," Jesus said next. He meant that gentle people who do not lose their tempers receive blessings from God.

The Sermon on the Mount

Jesus continued, "Blessed are those who hunger and thirst after righteousness, for they shall be filled." He meant that only those who know they are not righteous without God's help would receive God's help.

"Blessed are they who show mercy to others," said Jesus, "for mercy shall be shown to them. And blessed are those with pure hearts, for they shall see God. And blessed are the peacemakers, for they shall be called the children of God." The disciples understood that God would bless those who

378

are merciful toward others, those who do not allow sin to enter their hearts, and those who try to make peace where trouble exists.

Then Jesus said, "Blessed are those who are persecuted for the sake of righteousness, for theirs is the kingdom of heaven." He meant that in the kingdom of heaven God would eventually bless those who had been hurt or killed for their beliefs on Earth. Jesus said those who had been persecuted should be glad because they would have a reward for them in heaven.

Jesus taught the people how Christians should live, including how to pray and how to treat their friends. He told them that enemies should be loved and prayed for. And he told them about God's love for all of them.

At the end of the sermon, Jesus said to them, "Those who hear my words and do them are like the man who builds his house on a foundation of rock. When the winds blow and the rains fall, that foundation of rock will stand firm, and the house will not fall. But those who hear my words and do not obey them are like the man who builds his house on a foundation of sand. When the winds blow and the rains fall, the foundation will be washed away, and the house will fall."

Jesus meant those people who hear and obey his words would be saved, and they would be safe from harm when God judges them. But those who do not obey would not be safe from God's wrath. When the sermon was over, the people thought Jesus's words were more powerful than any previous books of Moses or any of the other prophets.

G-20 How Jesus Healed a Leper
Matthew 8:1-4; Mark 1:40-45; Luke 5:12-16

When Jesus and his twelve disciples came down from the mountain, many people followed them. These people were from various cities and different parts of the country.

One man there had heard about Jesus's power to perform miracles, and he needed help because he had the terrible flesh-eating disease of leprosy. The man ran to Jesus when he saw him and asked to be healed. Jesus felt very sorry for the dying man.

Most people were afraid to even be near a leper, or person with leprosy, but Jesus was not. Jesus reached out and touched the man, and immediately he was healed. The man sprang to his feet and was very grateful. Jesus told the man to go the temple and make an offering to God, as was the law for anyone who had been healed of leprosy. Jesus also told the man not to tell anyone who had healed him.

Jesus Heals a Leper

But soon news of the miracle had spread, and everyone was talking about how the man with leprosy had been healed. The poor man had been so glad that he told his friends about it, and they told more people who also told more people. Many left their homes to find the wonderful healer who could cure leprosy with only the touch of his hand.

G-21 How a Roman Captain Showed His Faith
Matthew 8:5-13; Luke 7:1-10

After healing the leper, Jesus returned with his disciples to Capernaum. News that he would be going there had spread, and many people had gathered to see him. One of the people was a Roman captain who commanded 100 soldiers. This captain, or centurion, was friendly toward the Jews although he was not Jewish himself. The Jews respected him because he had helped to build their synagogue, and he had always acted kindly.

One day, one of the centurion's servants became very sick. The next day he grew worse, and soon it seemed that he would not live much longer. The centurion loved the servant and was very sad that he was so ill. The

380

centurion knew of Jesus's power to heal the sick, but he was afraid to ask Jesus himself because he was not Jewish. So, the centurion asked the teachers in the synagogue to go and ask Jesus for him. They were glad to help him.

They told Jesus about the centurion and how he had helped to build the synagogue. They explained that his servant was very sick and needed help. Jesus went with them.

As they were nearing the centurion's home, they saw some men coming toward them. They were friends of the centurion, and they told Jesus the centurion did not feel he was worthy to have Jesus enter his house. He asked if Jesus would please heal the servant from outside the house.

Jesus was impressed that this man had such faith in his abilities to heal. He told the others that the faith of this Gentile, or non-Jew, was stronger than the faith of any Jewish person he had ever met. He told the centurion's friends that his servant would be made well.

When they went inside the house, they found that the servant had been healed. Everyone there realized that Jesus's power was so great that he did not even need to be near someone to heal him.

G-22 WHY FOUR MEN DAMAGED THE ROOF OF A HOUSE
MATTHEW 9:2-8; MARK 2:1-12; LUKE 5:18-26

Crowds followed Jesus wherever he went. Many were his friends; others wanted to listen to him speak and watch him perform miracles; and still others followed him hoping to find fault with his actions.

One day, Jesus was in a house in Capernaum, and so many people followed him into the house that there was no more room for anyone else to enter. The faultfinders were there, along with Jesus's friends and the others.

Jesus healed all the sick people who were brought before him in the crowded house. Suddenly, everyone heard a noise overhead, and they were surprised to see a bed being lowered from the ceiling. On the bed was a crippled man.

The man's four friends had tried to enter the house with him on his bed, but the house was too crowded. Determined to have him healed, they removed some tiles from the roof and lowered him down. No one knew what Jesus would do, but he told the man, "Be cheerful, because your sins are forgiven."

The look of pain on the man's face was replaced with a happy smile. The faultfinders were watching Jesus. They couldn't believe he told the man his sins were forgiven, which they believed only God had the power to do.

The Man's Friends Lower Him From the Roof

Jesus knew what the men were thinking, and he told them that he did have the power to heal and to forgive sins. He told the crippled man to rise up and carry his own bed to his house.

Immediately all the stiffness left the man's body and his strength returned. He rose up, rolled up his bed, and carried it on his shoulders. The surprised people made a path for him, and he walked out into the street to join his happy friends.

Great respect for God and Jesus came over the people in the house. They believed that they had seen something truly amazing that day.

G-23 When a Sorrowful Widow Became Joyful
Luke 7:11-18

A widow with only one child lived in the city of Nain, near Galilee. One day her young son became sick. This was a sad time for the widow. Every day he grew sicker and finally he died. The widow was very unhappy, now that both her husband and son were dead.

Her friends and neighbors helped her prepare the boy's body for burial. They wrapped the body in linens and placed it on a bier, or frame for carrying it. They started to walk outside the city gates. Then they saw Jesus and his twelve disciples approaching.

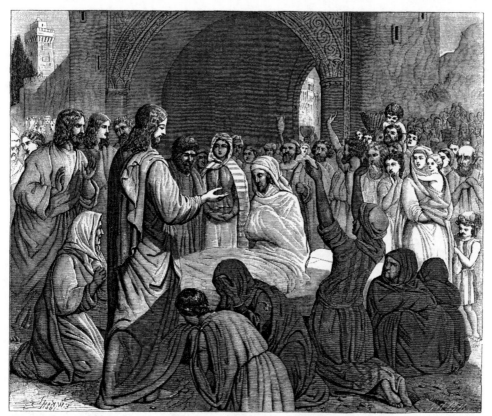

Jesus Tells the Boy to Arise

Jesus saw the widow whose son had just died, and he felt very sorry for her. Jesus told her not to weep. He went up to the lifeless body and spoke, "Young man, I tell you to arise!" They saw the lifeless body rise up to a sitting position, and they heard the boy's voice. They quickly unwrapped the linens, and Jesus took him to his mother.

Everyone was silent. They couldn't believe what they had seen. Soon they were convinced that Jesus had raised the boy from the dead and they began to rejoice. Some said Jesus was a great prophet, and others said God had acted through Jesus, as only God could bring someone back to life.

News of this event spread throughout the land. Even John the Baptist heard about it while in Herod's prison. John wanted to know if Jesus was really the Savior, and he asked two of Jesus's disciples to bring back more information for him when they came to visit him the next time. The two men returned to Jesus and saw many people being healed: deaf, blind, crippled, lepers, and even those possessed by evil spirits were healed.

Jesus turned to the two men who had come from visiting John the Baptist,

John the Baptist Beheaded

and he told them to return and tell John all that they had seen. The men went back to John and told him everything.

Not long after, Herod commanded that John should be killed to please his wicked stepdaughter who wanted John's head. John the Baptist's friends helped bury his body, and they told Jesus how John had died.

G-24 A Pharisee, A Sinful Woman, and Jesus
Luke 7:36-50

In one of the cities of Galilee where Jesus was teaching, a Pharisee named Simon came to hear him. Like many of the other Pharisees, Simon tried to find fault with Jesus. Because he didn't find anything wrong with what Jesus was doing, he asked Jesus to have dinner with him at his house. He planned to watch him closely and possibly find something wrong then.

Jesus went to Simon the Pharisee's house along with many other people. Those who were invited sat on couches near the table, and the uninvited who attended had to stand. While they were eating, a woman named Mary entered the room, and she saw Jesus. At once she knelt at his feet. She wept tears for her sins, and her tears fell on Jesus's feet. She dried his feet with her hair and kissed them. She poured expensive perfume on his feet.

Simon the Pharisee knew the woman, and he knew that she was a great sinner. He had heard many things about her that were not good. He was surprised that Jesus allowed her to come near him, and he didn't think Jesus would allow this if he really were a prophet.

Jesus knew about the woman's past, and he also knew what Simon was thinking. He told Simon he was going to tell him a story: There was a rich man who had loaned money to two poor men. The first he loaned a large sum of money, and the second man he loaned only a small amount. When the time came to repay the loan, neither could pay back the money they borrowed. They both came to the rich man, and he freely forgave them both.

Jesus asked Simon which of the two men loved the rich man the most. Simon said it was the one who owed the larger debt. Jesus said he was correct. Jesus told Simon that he had not given him water to wash his feet, but the woman had done so with her tears and her hair. Simon had not given him a kiss of welcome, but the woman had kissed his feet. Simon had not anointed his head with oil, as he did for his true friends, but the woman had poured costly perfume on his feet. Her sins were much, and she was forgiven for much. Those who sins are little are forgiven little.

Jesus told the woman that her sins were forgiven because of her faith and that she should go home in peace. The woman was sorry because she had done wrong, and Jesus forgave all the wrong that she had ever done. But Simon, the proud Pharisee, believed that he was too good to need forgiveness, and Jesus did not forgive him. Only those who are sorry for their sins can know the forgiveness of Jesus, the Savior.

Mary Anoints the Feet of Jesus

Jesus Teaches by the Seaside

One day Jesus went to Capernaum with his disciples and he walked by the seaside. Many people followed him, wishing to go with him if he left the city again. Jesus stepped onto a boat at the water's edge and sat down to begin teaching while the people stood listening on the shore.

Jesus began to teach by parables, or short stories with messages. While he sat in the boat, he told them four parables. The first was about a man who went out to scatter seeds in his field. Jesus called him a sewer. This is the first story:

"One day a sewer went out to the field with a bag of grain and began to scatter the seeds on the ground. The breeze caught each handful and helped to scatter them. Some of the seeds fell by the roadside, and birds ate those. Other seeds fell in stony places where the roots could not grow well, and soon they withered and died. Still other seeds fell where thorns were growing, and the thorns soon choked out the seeds and the seedlings died."

"Not all of the seed was wasted. Some of it fell on good ground, and it sprouted there and sent its roots deep down into the rich soil. The plants grew into large stalks of grain that produced many more seeds than the sewer had originally scattered."

The disciples wondered what this story meant. They asked Jesus why he was trying to teach people with stories. He told them that only those who really cared about understanding would figure out the meanings and understand, while those who didn't truly wish to know never would know.

Then Jesus explained to his disciples what he meant: "The sewer is like one who speaks the truths of God, and the different kinds are soil are the different conditions of the hearts of people who hear his words."

"Those who hear the words but do not seek to understand are like the roadside where the seeds fell. Those who understand the word of God but do not continue to obey are like the stony places where the roots could not grow deep enough."

"Those who hear and receive the word of God into their hearts but later allow riches and pleasures to crowd out the truths are like soil where thorns sprang up. But those who hear and obey the words of God are like the good ground, where some of the seeds fell and sprouted and grew into stalks that produced much grain."

Jesus told another story to the people: "The kingdom of heaven is like a man who sewed good seeds in his field, but while he and his men slept an

The Enemy Scatters Tares

enemy came and scattered bad seeds all over the field. These bad seeds are called tares. Both the good seeds and bad seeds began to grow. Soon stalks of grain were growing alongside the tares. The man's servant came to him and asked him if he had sewn good seeds or tares. The man told him an enemy had planted the tares. The servant wanted to know if he should rip up the tares. The man told him to wait until the harvest; otherwise he would damage the stalks of grain while ripping up the tares. At harvest time, they would separate the two, burn the tares in a fire, and put the wheat into the barn.

The third story was about a grain of mustard seed. Jesus said the kingdom of heaven is like a tiny grain which soon grows into a bush so large that birds could sit in its branches.

Then he said the kingdom of heaven is also like yeast, which is put into dough when mixing bread. The yeast worked through the dough and caused it to rise, making good bread. Something that seems small is very powerful.

When Jesus finished all his stories he sent the people away, and then he left the boat and returned to the city. The disciples asked him to explain the story about the tares.

Jesus told them the good seed was like the people of God, and the man who sewed the good seed was the Son of man (or Jesus.) The bad seeds or tares were the wicked people, and the enemy was Satan. The harvest will be at the end of the world, and the reapers are angels. The wicked people would be separated from the good and thrown into the fire, and the good people would enter heaven.

G-26 THE FLOODED SHIP THAT DID NOT SINK
MATTHEW 8:23-34; MARK 4:35 – 5:20; LUKE 8:22-40

One stormy night, a little ship was being tossed about by waves and wind on the Sea of Galilee. It had sailed far from the shore when the storm began, and the sailors feared for their lives. The ship began to be filled with water as the waves splashed, and they became even more afraid. The sailors were disciples of Jesus, and they were taking him across the Sea. Jesus had fallen asleep, and he did not know about the dangerous storm.

They awakened Jesus, telling him that they were in fear for their lives. He told them that they should have faith. He spoke to the wind, telling it to be still, and the storm stopped at once. The disciples were surprised to see that Jesus had power even over the winds and waves.

The sailors brought their ship to the land of the Gadarenes, on the other side of the Sea from Capernaum. When they stepped onto the shore, a man

Jesus Quiets the Storm

came running to meet them. He was wild and crazy because evil spirits or demons possessed him. Other people who knew him were afraid of him. People tried to keep him in chains but he always broke free. The man fell down in front of Jesus, wanting to worship him.

Jesus knew evil spirits troubled the man, and he commanded them to leave the man. The spirits begged Jesus to leave them alone. Jesus asked, "What is your name?" and the sprits replied, "Legion, for we are many."

The Possessed Man Breaks His Chains

The man was deeply troubled because he had many evil spirits inside him.

There was a herd of 2,000 hogs on the mountainside nearby. The Jews did not eat hogs, but the people of this land did. Jesus allowed the evil spirits to enter the hogs. At once the hogs ran into the Sea and were drowned.

The keepers of the hogs were frightened, and they ran to tell others what had happened. Soon a crowd gathered and saw the man at Jesus's feet, acting normal and no longer crazy. He even had a look of peace on his face.

The people were surprised to hear what Jesus had done for the man they

391

all feared. But they were not pleased, having lost all of their hogs. They did not want Jesus to stay any longer, even though he might heal others. They were selfish and cared more about money and their hogs. So Jesus left.

The man that Jesus helped followed Jesus and begged to be allowed to go with him. Jesus told him to return home and tell his friends what great things the Lord had done for him. The man gladly obeyed, going from city to city, telling everyone about the unbelievable power of Jesus.

Jesus in Galilee

G-27 The Little Girl Who Came Back to Life
Matthew 9:18-10:42; Mark 5:22-43; Luke 8:41-9:6

When Jesus and his disciples returned from the land of the Gadarenes, they saw a crowd standing on the shore, eager to welcome them back to Capernaum. Again Jesus taught them and healed many sick people.

A man came running up to Jesus, and he told him that his little daughter was very sick at home. He asked Jesus to touch her and heal her. The man was a ruler of the synagogue in Capernaum and his name was Jairus. Jesus, the disciples, and others from the crowd followed.

In the crowd was a woman who had been ill for twelve years. She had spent all her money on doctors, yet they could not cure her. Now she had no more money and still was very sick. She hoped Jesus could make her well again. The crowd was very dense, and she slowly made her way to Jesus. She decided not to bother him but only to touch his garment, believing that she would then be healed. She touched his clothes, and she felt the healing power go through her body. Then she stepped back into the crowd.

Jesus knew what the woman had done. He knew about her desire to be healed and her other thoughts. He turned around and asked the crowd who had touched him to be healed.

The woman fell before Jesus, telling him her sad story. He told her that her faith had made her well, and to go in peace.

Jairus stood by waiting impatiently. He was afraid his little daughter might die before Jesus would arrive. Soon one of his servants came out to meet them and told them that his daughter was already dead. Jesus saw how upset Jairus was, and he told him to have faith and the little girl would be made well.

When they arrived at the house, many people were grieving. Jesus told them that she was not dead but merely sleeping. Jesus sent everyone out of the room except for the mother, father, and three disciples: Simon Peter, James and John. While holding her hand, he told the little girl to rise up. She opened her eyes, got up, and walked around the room. He told her parents to get some food for her and asked them to tell no one what he had done, since he already had so many people following him everywhere.

When they left the home of Jairus, two blind men followed them, asking Jesus to be healed. He asked if they had faith in his abilities to heal them, and they said they did. He touched their eyes and they began to see. Jesus asked them to tell no one, but they went everywhere, telling people about this miracle.

Raising the Daughter of Jairus

A mute (or dumb) man who had an evil spirit within him was brought to Jesus. Jesus cast the spirit out and caused the man to be able to speak. Many onlookers were amazed. Some of the Pharisees suggested that Jesus's power came from Satan and not from God. They were jealous of him and said terrible things.

The Dumb Man Possessed

So many people wanted to hear Jesus that he could not teach them all. He sent his twelve disciples to go into other cities. He gave them the power to heal the sick and cast out evil spirits, and even to raise the dead. The amount of work was too much for Jesus to do alone. The twelve apostles went into other towns and villages, as Jesus had commanded.

G-28 A Miracle from a Boy's Lunch Basket
Matthew 14:13-23; Mark 6:31-46; Luke 9:7-17;
John 6:1-15

The apostles that Jesus had sent out to teach and perform miracles in the towns and cities of Galilee had returned. They told their master about their success in healing the sick and casting out evil spirits. So many people were coming to hear about Jesus and have their loved ones healed that he barely had time to rest or even eat. Jesus called his twelve disciples aside and told them that they needed to find a quiet place and rest for a while.

Taking a ship, they sailed to the other side of the Sea of Galilee and went into a desert place near a mountain. They did not find much time to rest there because more people started to arrive there, too. Jesus said the people were like sheep with no shepherd.

There were 5,000 men from different parts of Galilee. Some had brought their wives and children, and other women had come too. Many of them had nothing to eat. One boy had brought a lunch basket, and inside were five little loaves of barley bread and two small fishes.

Jesus continued to heal the sick and taught the people many things about the kingdom of heaven. As the day progressed, many people realized that they could find no food in the desert where they were. The disciples suggested sending the people away, but Jesus knew that he could find a way to feed all of them. The boy with the lunch basket heard them talking, and he offered his small amount of food to Jesus.

Jesus told the disciples to seat the people in groups of 50 or 100 and tell them to wait for their evening meal. While they waited, he took the little loaves and fishes and broke them into small pieces and blessed them. He filled a basket for each of the twelve disciples to pass out food to the hungry people. The disciples returned, and again he filled the baskets. When everyone had eaten, there were twelve baskets full of scraps left over. Everyone had eaten enough to satisfy his or her hunger.

This miracle caused much excitement among the people. They wanted Jesus to become their king instead of letting the Roman government rule them any longer. They believed Jesus could set them free of their Roman rulers. They thought it would be great to have a king who could perform miracles.

Christ Feeding the Multitude

Jesus would not allow the people to make him their king. He was a heavenly king, but he had not come to Earth to rule an earthly kingdom. He commanded his disciples to enter their ship and return to the other side of the Sea of Galilee. Jesus told the multitude of people to go home, and he went up a nearby mountain to pray by himself.

G-29 THE MAN WHO TRIED TO WALK ON WATER
MATTHEW 14:23-36; MARK 6:46-56; JOHN 6:16-29

While Jesus was alone on the mountain, the disciples were in their ship rowing toward Capernaum. The many people were returning home, walking along the northern shore of the Sea of Galilee.

A strong wind began to blow across the Sea, pushing against the little ship. The disciples were rowing hard but they could not overpower the wind. They grew tired after many hours, and they wished for some help.

Jesus had been praying on the mountain. He had not forgotten his disciples, and he knew that they needed help with the wind. He walked out across the water as easily as walking on land, and he walked closer and closer to the ship and its tired sailors.

The disciples saw Jesus approaching them, but they were frightened because they believed he must be a spirit. They did not think he could walk on water because no one had ever done that before.

Jesus Walks on Water

Jesus Tells the Disciples Not to Fear

Jesus stopped when he heard them crying in fear, and he told them who he was and not to be afraid. Simon Peter asked Jesus to let him come out and meet him by walking on water. Jesus told him to come out. Simon Peter jumped over the side of the ship and into the water. But Simon Peter started to sink, and the other disciples heard him crying out. Simon Peter had taken his eyes off Jesus and started to look at the waves, and he was sinking.

Jesus Grabs Simon Peter's Hand

Jesus grabbed his hand and caught him, saying, "Oh man of little faith, why did you doubt?" When the two reached the ship, the other disciples welcomed them, and the wind suddenly stopped. They had no doubt that Jesus definitely was the Son of God.

G-30 HOW JESUS ANSWERED A MOTHER'S PRAYER
MATTHEW 15:21-29; MARK 7:24-30

Near the land of Galilee was a small country called Phoenicia. The people who lived there were non-Jews, or Gentiles, and many of them worshiped idols. Because they lived so close to the Jews, most of them knew of the Jewish religion which taught belief in one true God.

Jesus knew he would soon die and rise again, and he wanted to meet with his disciples to teach them more before this happened. He took them on a walk one day, and they entered the neighboring country of Phoenicia.

They went into a house, believing no one would disturb them there. But the news of Jesus had reached the people of Phoenicia, and they were eager to see him. He saw that he could not hide himself, even in a strange land.

Living in that neighborhood was a woman whose heart was very sad. She had a little girl who was tormented by a wicked spirit. She had heard of Jesus's ability to cast out spirits, and she wished that he would help her. She

400

Asking Jesus to Help Her Daughter

quickly left her work and ran to the house where Jesus was staying.

She began to tell him about the condition of her daughter, but he seemed to pay no attention to her at all. The disciples urged Jesus to send her away because she was a Gentile. Fearing that he might do this, she fell down at his feet and cried, "Lord, help me!"

He pitied the poor woman. He knew that she had faith in his ability to heal, but he wanted to test her faith. He told her that he was sent to help the lost children of Israel, not the Gentiles. She asked for just a crumb of bread, if Jesus's powers were like bread.

Jesus told her that he knew her faith in him was great. He told her that she would receive what she wanted and to go home – because the evil spirit had already left her daughter. The woman sprang to her feet and obeyed Jesus's words. She went home and found the little girl resting quietly, no longer troubled by the wicked spirit.

G-31 What a Multitude Learned About Jesus
Matthew 15:29-39; Mark 7:31 – 8:10

The Sea of Galilee

Leaving Phoenicia, Jesus and his twelve disciples journeyed to the country on the eastern side of the Sea of Galilee. In this same country, Jesus had healed the man who had a legion of spirits inside him. Jesus had sent the spirits into the many hogs that drowned, and many of the people had not wanted him to stay there after that happened.

The man who had been healed told many people about it, and then other people became interested in Jesus. They saw how this man had changed for the better, and they felt sorry that Jesus had been driven away.

People Gather to See Jesus

When Jesus went there the second time with his twelve disciples, a large group of people gathered to see him. They followed him into the country and listened to him speak for three days. He also healed many sick people.

There was one man who could neither hear nor speak plainly. Jesus put his fingers into the man's ears, touched his tongue, looked up to heaven, and said, "Be opened!" Immediately the man began to hear and speak normally. The crowd was very impressed.

Jesus Heals the Sick

The crowd was running out of food and becoming hungry by the evening of the third day. Jesus asked his disciples what food they had, and they said they only had seven loaves of bread and a few little fishes. Jesus commanded all the people to sit down. Then he blessed the food, just as he had done when he fed the 5,000 people from the little boy's lunch basket. Once again

The Miracle of the Loaves and Fishes

the loaves and fishes increased until there was enough food to feed everyone. More than 4,000 people were fed, and seven baskets of food were left over.

Jesus dismissed the crowd, and they returned home with their sick friends who had been made well. They were very glad Jesus had returned to their land after they had asked him to leave the first time. Jesus went with his disciples by ship to the country on the north side of the Sea of Galilee.

405

Jesus Cures a Blind Man

A blind man lived near Bethsaida, a town by the Sea of Galilee. He had heard about Jesus, and he wished to be healed of his blindness. One day he heard that Jesus was coming to visit Bethsaida. His friends led him to a place where Jesus and the disciples would be stopping.

Jesus did not want to attract great crowds any longer. He wished to have time alone with his disciples. He took the blind man's hand and lead him out of town. Jesus touched his eyes once and asked him if he could see. He said he could see some, but his vision was very fuzzy. Then Jesus touched his eyes again, and the man could see very clearly. He told the man not to tell anyone about this miracle because he did not want many people to flock to him at that time.

Jesus and his disciples journeyed north to a city called Caesarea Philippi, not far from Mount Hermon. On the way, Jesus asked the disciples some questions. He asked them who they thought he was. The disciples answered,

Jesus and His Disciples Journeying

"Some say you are Elijah, the prophet, come back to Earth; others say you are John the Baptist risen from the dead; others believe you are Jeremiah."

Jesus asked them again who they thought he was. Simon Peter answered boldly, "We believe you are Christ, the promised Messiah and King, the Son of the living God." Jesus asked the disciples to tell this to no one, since it wasn't yet the right time for everyone else to know this.

Jesus began to talk to the disciples about the sorrows that would come upon them at Jerusalem, when he would be taken from them and put to death by enemies among their own people. The disciples did not understand what he was talking about. They believed Jesus would soon take his place as King, and they did not want to hear him talk about dying and coming back to life after three days.

Simon Peter, who often spoke for all twelve, told him that these things would never happen. Jesus told the disciples that Satan would like for them to believe that, but not God. The disciples could not understand.

Afterward, Jesus called other people to him, and when they had gathered he began to teach them what it would mean to be one of his followers. He told them that following him would mean not pleasing themselves. He told them they must not try to save their own lives or they would lose their lives. It would not profit a man to gain the whole world and lose his eternal soul.

These statements caused the people to think about his teachings. Then Jesus said, "The Son of man shall come in the glory of his Father, with his angels; and then he shall reward every man according to his works."

G-33 THE GLORIFIED MASTER ON THE MOUNTAINSIDE
MATTHEW 17:1-13; MARK 9:2-13; LUKE 9:28-36

Jesus, Moses, and Elijah

It was difficult for Simon Peter, James, and John to climb up the rough slope of the great mountain near Caesarea Philippi, and they were very tired when they found a resting place high above the quiet valley. They were not used to climbing mountains, but Jesus had asked them to go with him to a place of prayer and they obeyed. They were so tired that they fell asleep and Jesus prayed alone.

While the three disciples were sleeping, a great change came over their master. His face began to shine brightly, and his clothing sparkled white like snow. Two men from heaven came to talk to him: Moses, who wrote down the laws of God, and Elijah the great prophet who did not die but was taken up directly into heaven from the Earth.

Moses and Elijah Disappear

While the two heavenly visitors were talking with Jesus, the disciples awoke from their sleep. They were very surprised to see Jesus's face and clothes shining brightly and Jesus talking to Moses and Elijah. As the two visitors began to disappear, Simon Peter asked Jesus for permission to build three tabernacles: for Jesus, Elijah, and Moses.

A bright cloud descended over them, and a heavenly voice spoke, "This is my Son, in whom I am well pleased; hear him." The disciples fell to the ground in fear. Then the cloud lifted.

Jesus touched the disciples and told them not to be afraid. The two visitors were gone. Simon Peter, James, and John believed even more strongly that Jesus was definitely the Son of God, after what they had witnessed there.

The next day when they all came down from the mountain, Jesus told them not to repeat what they had seen and heard there - until after he should rise from the dead. They did as he told them and didn't tell anyone.

G-34 A Suffering Child and an Anxious Father
Matthew 17:14-21; Mark 9:14-29; Luke 9:37-45

Jesus Heals the Possessed Child

Jesus and the three disciples who went to the mountain with him returned to where the other nine disciples were waiting. Jesus found them surrounded by many people.

A man came running up to Jesus and begged him to help his son. His son was crazed from being possessed by an evil spirit, and he often jumped into fire or water. He said that the disciples had tried to help him but could not. Jesus was sad because people did not have more faith. He told the man to bring the child to him.

When the father returned with the boy, the evil spirit seized him again and threw him violently to the ground. He was lying in the dust, wallowing and foaming at the mouth, and the people were astonished at what they saw. His father said that he had been like that since he was a small child.

Jesus told the man that he did not have enough faith in his ability to heal the boy and that all things are possible with faith. The man cried out saying that he did believe, and he asked for Jesus to remove any doubt he had.

Jesus commanded the evil spirit to come out of the boy and torment him no longer. The spirit gave a loud cry and came out of the child, leaving him unconscious on the ground. The people thought he was dead, but Jesus held his hand and lifted him up. The boy rose up, and Jesus took him to his father.

Jesus led his disciples away from the people and they entered into a house alone. They asked their master why they couldn't cast out the evil spirit themselves. Jesus told them it was because they did not have faith and that they should have fasted and prayed. Jesus talked more to his disciples about the need to have faith in God.

G-35 Jesus and His Disciples in Capernaum
Matthew 17:22–18:14; Mark 9:30-43; Luke 9:43-50

Jesus and his disciples journeyed back to Capernaum. Jesus talked with them again about the suffering he would soon face. He told them that he would be killed and rise again on the third day. They did not understand what he meant.

The disciples argued with each other about which of them would be the greatest in the kingdom of heaven. They believed the kingdom of heaven would be on Earth, and they thought they would all hold important offices. But they didn't say anything to Jesus about this.

Jesus did not want to attract more big crowds. He went with his disciples to a house that very few people knew about. While they were in Capernaum, a tax collector asked Simon Peter if his master had paid his taxes. Peter replied that Jesus had. When Jesus heard about this, he told Peter to catch

The Example of a Humble Child

a fish at the seashore, and he would find a piece of money inside the fish's mouth to pay their taxes. Peter found the money inside the fish's mouth and paid their taxes to the tax collector.

When all the disciples were together in the house, Jesus asked them what they had been arguing about. They were ashamed to tell him, but Jesus already knew their thoughts and what they had said to each other. Jesus found a little child and held him in his arms. He told them that no one would be able to enter the kingdom of heaven unless he was humble like a little child. And whoever was the most humble would be the greatest.

Jesus told the disciples not to hate little children because angels were protecting them. And he warned them not to cause any children to lose faith in him.

The disciple John told Jesus that they had seen a man who was not a follower casting out evil spirits in Jesus's name. John said they told him to stop. Jesus told him that this was a mistake and that anyone who performed miracles in his name was helping him, even if he was not a disciple.

G-36 JESUS TEACHES PETER ABOUT FORGIVENESS
MATTHEW 18:21-35

One day Simon Peter went to Jesus and asked him how many times he should forgive his brother if he had sinned against him and asked for forgiveness. Peter asked if seven times would be enough. Jesus told him that he should forgive his brother not only seven times but seventy times seven, or nearly 500 times.

Jesus told Peter about a king whose servant owed him a great amount of money. The king summoned him and asked him to repay the money. The king told him that he would command that the servant, his wife, their children, and all of their property be sold to repay the debt if he didn't have the money.

The servant began crying when he heard this, and he asked the king to be patient with him and he would repay every penny. The king had a kind heart and felt sorry for the man. He told him to go home; the debt would be forgiven and did not ever need to be repaid to the king.

Grabbing Poor Man's Throat

Later, the servant met a very poor man who had borrowed only a few dollars from him. He asked for the money, but the poor man did not have the money to repay him.

The servant grabbed him by the throat and threatened to throw him into the prison until he paid the money back. The poor man begged the servant to have patience with him, but the servant would not listen. He threw him into the prison. Other servants of the king were watching and they saw how unkindly he treated the poor man.

413

The King Tells His Servant He Is Wicked

They knew that the king had forgiven his debt, and they decided to tell the king what had happened. The king was surprised at the behavior of the servant after his own debt had been forgiven. The king told him that he was wicked and that he would be put into the prison until he repaid all the money he had originally owed the king, before his own debt was forgiven.

Jesus told Peter that God had forgiven his sins, but he would only do so if he forgave those who had sinned against him. God is willing to forgive our sins, but we must be willing to forgive others.

G-37 THE UNFRIENDLY SAMARITANS; THE TEN LEPERS
LUKE 9:51-62; LUKE 17:11-19

One day Jesus and his disciples left Capernaum. They took the south road leading through Samaria on their way to Jerusalem. They came to a village in Samaria where Jesus wanted to stay the night. He sent messengers to find a place for him and the disciples to rest. The people in the village knew Jesus and the disciples were Jews. The Samaritans did not usually get along with the Jews, and they did not want them to stay in their village.

414

James and his brother John were very annoyed at their unfriendly attitude. They felt they had been mistreated, and they wished to see the villagers punished. They remembered how Elijah had called fire down from heaven to destroy some wicked people, and they asked Jesus for permission to do this to the villagers. Jesus told them that he was there to save men's lives and not to destroy them. Then they all went to a different village.

Ten men with the disease of leprosy saw Jesus passing by and they called to him. They asked for mercy. Jesus heard their cries and healed them. He told them to go and show themselves to the priest, as Moses had commanded every leper who was healed to do. They understood what he meant, and as they were traveling to the priest every bit of leprosy left their bodies.

One of the ten lepers turned back to thank Jesus as soon as he realized that he was made well. He fell down before Jesus and thanked him for the miracle. This man was a Samaritan. Jesus asked the disciples where the other nine men were. He pointed out that the one man who was there at his feet thanking him for saving him was a Samaritan. He told the Samaritan, "Rise up and go on your way, for your faith has made you well."

Jesus and the Lepers

415

Jesus Teaches at the Annual Feast

G-38 Jesus at the Great Feast in Jerusalem
John 7:2-53

Summer had passed, and the cooler days of autumn had arrived again. Many huts stood in groups on the green hillsides around Jerusalem, sheltering the people who had come to attend the annual Feast of Tabernacles. The temple was crowded with visitors from many faraway places.

The first day after the feast began, people were talking about Jesus, whom they called the Teacher of Galilee. They discussed his miracles, and they wondered if he would come to Jerusalem to teach. Some of them wanted him to come, and others hated him and wanted to kill him.

Jesus did arrive, and he went into the temple to teach the people there. His enemies wanted to catch him doing something wrong. They sent men to listen to his words and find some fault, with the intention of telling the rulers about any mistakes he made.

Day after day passed and Jesus remained in the temple. No one tried to drive him away or hurt him. Many of the Jews who lived in Jerusalem knew that their leaders hated him, and they wondered why they had not put Jesus

416

in prison. They wondered whether the rulers had begun to believe that he truly was the Christ or King.

The rulers did not believe this at all. They were jealous of Jesus since he was taking a lot of attention away from them. They disliked his teachings because he accused them of only pretending to be righteous. Eventually they sent officers to take him away.

Even the officers were pleased to hear Jesus's teachings. They listened carefully to his words, and they decided that he did not deserve to be punished. They returned to the rulers without him. The chief priests and the Pharisees were very angry when the officers returned without Jesus. They asked why they had not brought him. The officers said no one had ever spoken like Jesus did and they refused to harm him.

The men who sent the officers were excited. They asked the officers if they were allowing themselves to be deceived by him. They wanted to know if any of the rulers believed in Jesus's teachings

Nicodemus, the Pharisee who had visited Jesus, was among the rulers. He loved Jesus and believed in him, but he was afraid to let the other Pharisees know for fear that they would hate him.

Nicodemus asked if the law permitted any man to be judged before hearing him and knowing what he was doing. His angry friends asked Nicodemus if he did not know that Jesus was from Galilee, and if he did not know that no prophet ever comes from Galilee. Then they dismissed the meeting and returned to their homes.

G-39 HOW JESUS ANSWERED HIS ENEMIES' QUESTION
JOHN 8

Early the next morning after the officers had refused to take Jesus away from the temple and arrest him, the Pharisees and scribes had planned another way to capture him. They would go themselves and ask a question about the teachings of the Law of Moses. They thought Jesus would answer in a way that they could find fault with.

Jesus was in the temple when his enemies approached him with a very wicked woman. The Law of Moses commanded that she should be put to death for her actions. They told Jesus the law said she should be stoned to death, and they wanted to know what he thought should be done with her.

Jesus knew that they were tempting him, and at first he paid no attention. He leaned down and wrote with his finger in the dust on the ground. But his enemies did not want to give up so easily. They believed that they had caught him in a trap. They kept asking until finally he looked up and said,

417

Jesus and the Condemned Woman

"Let the man among you who is without sin throw the first stone at her."
Then he continued writing in the dust.

The men were very surprised at his reply to their question. They looked at
each other, then at the woman, and they thought about their own sins. They
were afraid that God might punish them by killing all of them if they started
to stone the woman. The older men left first, and then the younger men left
the temple.

When only the woman was left with Jesus, he asked the woman if anyone was left to condemn her. She told him no. Then he said, "Neither do I condemn you; go, and do not commit sin any more." She turned and went away.

Many people had gathered in the temple, and Jesus began to teach them again. He began by saying, "I am the light of the world: the man who follows me shall not walk in darkness, but shall have the light of life." The Pharisees who heard him accused him of speaking too much of himself.

Jesus said he was speaking of himself, but his words were true. Jesus said his Father would agree with what he said. They asked him where his father was. Jesus answered, "If you knew me, you would know my Father. But you know neither me nor my Father."

Jesus taught in the temple all that day, telling the Jews about their sins. His enemies became more and more restless until they didn't want to listen any longer. Jesus said anyone who obeyed his words would never see death. Jesus meant that they would never die without their sins forgiven and lose their chance of everlasting life. His enemies did not understand, and they asked him why Abraham and all the prophets had died.

Jesus said that he did not honor himself but his Father, God, honored him. He said they did not know his Father, but he did. He said he knew his Father, and he obeyed his words. Jesus told them they did not behave like the children of Abraham, since he was glad to hear the words of God.

His enemies asked Jesus how he could know anything about Abraham because he was so young. He told them that he always was, even before Abraham. The Jews who hated him didn't like it when Jesus suggested he always was, like God. They picked up stones to throw at him, but he hid himself among the people and quietly walked out of the temple.

G-40 What Happened to the Blind Man Jesus Healed
John 9

As Jesus left the area of the temple, where the angry Jews were getting ready to stone him, he saw a blind man begging by the roadside. This man was born blind and his parents lived in Jerusalem.

The twelve disciples were with Jesus when he passed by the poor blind man. They knew he had been born blind, and they asked Jesus if his blindness had happened as a punishment for his own sin or the sin of his parents. Jesus said it was neither, but he was born blind so that the works of God might be shown through him.

Jesus stopped. He rubbed a little clay on the blind man's eyes. He told him to go into the pool called Siloam and wash the clay away.

The blind man obeyed without hesitation. As soon as he washed the clay away, he began to see. Instead of returning to the roadside to beg, the happy man told everyone he knew how Jesus had cured him of his blindness.

Everyone was very surprised, especially since he had been born blind. Many could not believe that he was the same person, but he convinced them of who he was.

The Pool of Siloam in Jerusalem

Everyone in his neighborhood was excited, and they wanted to know how Jesus had helped him to see. He told them how Jesus had rubbed clay on his eyes, how he washed at the pool of Siloam, and how he could see again. They asked him where Jesus was, but the man did not know.

His neighbors brought the man who had been blind for the Pharisees to see, and they also questioned him. Because it was the Sabbath day, they thought Jesus had done wrong by anointing the man's eyes and sending him to wash in the pool. They thought Jesus must be a sinner. Others said a sinner couldn't do such a miracle. Some of the people thought Jesus was a great man, and others thought he was wrong and deceitful.

The Pharisees asked the man what he thought of Jesus, and he said, "I believe he is a prophet." Some of the people who hated Jesus thought that the man might be lying. They called his parents and questioned them.

His parents were afraid of these people. They thought that the Pharisees would kick them out of the synagogue if they said the wrong thing. His parents said that the man had been born blind, but they would have to ask him how he got his sight because they did not know.

Again they asked him what happened. He said he had already told them once and they chose not to listen. He asked them if they would become Jesus's disciples if he told them again. They became angry and said that they were disciples of Moses because they knew God spoke to Moses, but they did not know about Jesus and where he came from.

The man who had been healed said that Jesus must have come from God; otherwise he wouldn't be able to perform a miracle the way he had done. This made the enemies of Jesus even angrier, and they decided to kick the man out of the synagogue. He wasn't allowed to worship there any longer.

Jesus soon heard what had happened and he found the man. Jesus asked him if he believed on the Son of God. The man asked, "Who is he Lord that I may believe?"

Jesus said, "You have seen him with your own eyes, and now he is speaking to you."

The man smiled with joy and said, "Lord, I believe!"

G-41 JESUS BLESSES THE CHILDREN; THE RICH YOUNG MAN
MATTHEW 19:13-30; MARK 10:13-31

While Jesus was teaching the people out on the countryside not far from the Jordan River, some mothers brought their little children to him and asked him to bless the children. Jesus took them in his arms, put his hands on their heads, and prayed. The disciples thought Jesus had more important work to

Jesus Blesses the Little Children

do, and they told the mothers that they should leave Jesus alone.

Jesus was not happy with the disciples. He told them that the kingdom of God was for people with the attitude of a little child and that anyone who does not have this innocent, humble attitude will not be able to enter the kingdom. And he continued to bless the children.

Jesus knew that little children would gladly believe him and that they could even lead older people to believe in him. He knew the hearts of children were innocent and pure.

Jesus went with his disciples to a different place. As he was walking, a very rich young man in fine clothes knelt down before him and said, "Good Master, what shall I do that I may receive life in the other world?"

Jesus told him the only one who is good is God. Jesus said that he should keep the commandments. The boy said he did keep the commandments of Moses, but he knew he needed something else. Jesus told him to go home, sell all his riches, give the money to the poor people, and then he would have riches in heaven. Jesus told him if he did this, he could come back and be his disciple.

The young man changed from happy to deeply troubled. He bent his head down and walked away. Jesus watched him walk away, and Jesus was also sad. He turned to his disciples and said it was very hard for a rich man to enter the kingdom of God. He knew the young man loved his rich things more than he loved God. The young man knew he was missing something, but he was unwilling to do what Jesus told him to.

G-42 Seventy Other Disciples; The Good Samaritan
Luke 10:1-37

Jesus Sends Out the Seventy Disciples

Jesus knew that his days of preaching were coming to an end. He chose seventy other men who had followed him, and he gave them the powers to heal the sick and to cast out evil spirits. Then he sent them out in pairs into the country east of the Jordan River to preach in the cities and villages where he was planning to go later.

These men went out to heal the sick and to tell people about the kingdom of heaven. When their work was finished, they hurried back to Jesus, telling him they were glad that the evil spirits had obeyed them. Jesus told them not to be glad about that, but to be glad that their names were written in heaven.

The Samaritan Finds the Wounded Man

Jesus prayed to God. He told the disciples that they were blessed to see and hear what they had because many kings and prophets desired to see and

The Good Samaritan Carries the Man on His Horse

hear these things, but they would never be able to.

A Jewish lawyer wanted to tempt Jesus. He asked him what to do to inherit life in heaven. Jesus answered with another question. He asked him what was written in the Law of Moses. The man answered, "Moses wrote that we should love the Lord our God with all our heart, and with all our soul, and with all our strength, and with all our mind; and he wrote that we

The Arrival at the Hotel

should love our neighbors as ourselves."

Jesus said, "You have answered right. Do this and you shall have life in heaven."

The man was not satisfied. He asked Jesus, "Who is my neighbor?" Jesus told him the story of the Good Samaritan:

"One day a man started to travel from Jerusalem to Jericho. As he went along the lonely road he met some robbers. These men stopped him, took his money, tore off his clothes, and beat him until he was half dead. Then they ran off, leaving him by the roadside."

"A priest came along, and he saw the poor man lying there. But he did not stop to help the stranger. He did not even speak to him at all or ask if he might send someone else to help him."

"After the priest had left, a Levite passed by. He also did not even look twice at the poor man. He hurried on his way, leaving the poor man to die."

"No doubt the poor man would have died if a kind-hearted Samaritan had not come along the road soon afterward. When he saw the poor man he stopped his mule, climbed out of his saddle, and bent over the stranger to speak to him. He saw that the wounded man was a Jew, and he knew that the Jews were not friendly to the Samaritans. But he knew that this Jew was in deep trouble. He poured oil on his wounds and tried to bandage him. He gave the wounded man a drink to revive him, and he placed him onto his own mule's back."

"He brought the wounded man to a hotel, and he took care of him until the next day, when he started on his journey again. Before he left, he gave money to the innkeeper and asked him to take care of the man. He said that he would give him more money when he returned, if necessary."

Jesus asked the lawyer which of the three men had been a neighbor to the one who was attacked by the robbers. "The man who treated him kindly," answered the lawyer. Jesus said, "Go and do as the Samaritan did."

G-43 LAZARUS, THE MAN JESUS CALLED OUT OF HIS GRAVE JOHN 11:1-54

Lazarus was a Jew who lived with his two sisters, Martha and Mary. Their home was in the little village of Bethany, near Jerusalem, and Jesus often visited them while attending the Jewish feasts. They believed that he was the Son of God, and they always made him feel welcome.

One day while Jesus was in the country east of the Jordan River teaching the people, a messenger arrived and told him that Lazarus was very sick. The sisters had sent the messenger, and they believed that Jesus would come at once to help. Jesus did not go at once. He told the disciples, "This sickness of our friend Lazarus is for the glory of God."

So the messenger returned without Jesus. The disappointed sisters stayed by Lazarus's bedside and watched him grow weaker and weaker until finally he died. They wondered why Jesus had not come to help him.

They continued to wait because they knew Jesus had raised people from the dead. Time passed and still they saw no sign of Jesus arriving. Finally

Jesus at the House of Martha and Mary

the neighbors and friends who were there helped to wrap Lazarus's body in linens. They carried his body to the cave where he was to be buried. Martha and Mary followed, and they saw his body put in the cave and a giant stone placed in front of the cave opening. Still Jesus was nowhere to be found.

Four days passed by, and the sorrow of the sisters grew deeper. They believed that it was too late for Jesus to help even if he arrived. And they wished Jesus was there to at least comfort them. Finally they heard that

Jesus and his disciples were coming. Martha ran to Jesus and fell at his feet. She cried, "If only you had been here, my brother would not have died!"

Jesus knew how sad she was, and he told her that Lazarus would rise again. She said that she knew he would be resurrected at the end of the world. Jesus told her, "I am the resurrection and the life. He that believes in me, though he were dead yet shall he live. And those who live and believe in me shall never die."

He asked her if she believed this. She said that she believed he was the Christ and the Son of God. But she did not completely understand. She ran to get her sister Mary after Jesus asked her why Mary wasn't there.

Mary left her house and went to meet Jesus as soon as she heard that he was there. She found him by the roadside with her sister, outside the village. She also told him that Lazarus wouldn't have died if he had been there sooner. Other people from the village had followed her there and were watching as she cried.

Jesus was moved by the sorrow of all the people including the sisters, and he asked to be taken to Lazarus's body. Even Jesus cried as he approached the cave. Jesus asked a man to roll the stone away from the cave's opening.

The Raising of Lazarus

Martha told Jesus that Lazarus had been dead for four days and his body must already be decaying. Jesus answered, "Did I not tell you that if you would believe you should see the glory of God?"

They took away the stone, and while the people stood looking on, Jesus lifted his eyes to heaven and said, "Father, help me raise Lazarus from the dead so that the people watching will believe I am sent by you." He looked into the dark cave and called out with a loud voice, "Lazarus, come forth!"

The astonished people saw the still, white figure within the cave rise up and walk out toward them. Jesus told his friends to remove the linens that covered Lazarus. Lazarus was alive once again.

After the miracle, many of the people who had come from Jerusalem to comfort Martha and Mary believed that Jesus was the Christ. Soon the scribes and Pharisees and chief priests in Jerusalem heard what had happened, and they were greatly upset.

They thought that if they let Jesus continue, all men would believe in him, and the Romans would come and take away their land. From that time, the enemies of Jesus began to plan how they might capture him and kill him.

G-44 JESUS HEALS THE SICK AND TEACHES IN A PHARISEE'S HOUSE
LUKE 14:1-24

Jesus knew the plans of his enemies, and he did not remain in Bethany for very long. He took his disciples and returned to the country near the Jordan River. While there he continued to teach and heal the sick and possessed people who were brought to him.

One Sabbath day, a Pharisee who lived nearby invited Jesus to dinner at his house. Jesus went, and other Pharisees and lawyers were present, along with some people who had not been invited. The uninvited people had to stand, which was the custom.

One man standing had a disease called dropsy. He was there because he hoped that Jesus would heal him. Jesus felt sorry for the poor man when he saw him standing nearby. He turned to the Pharisees and lawyers and asked if it was permitted to heal someone on the Sabbath day, but they refused to answer him.

Jesus healed the man and sent him away. He told the Pharisees and lawyers that they would not permit an ox or ass that had fallen into a pit to remain there until after the Sabbath day. They understood what he meant, and they had sympathy for the poor man.

Those who were there expected to hear Jesus teach, and they were not disappointed. He noticed how the guests chose the best places for themselves when they arrived, and he tried to teach them a lesson in humility. He told them that when they are invited to a wedding, they should not choose the place of highest honor in case someone else should arrive who was more honorable. Otherwise they would be asked to move, and they would be embarrassed in front of all the guests. But if they chose the lowest place, they would be told to move to a better place, and they would be honored.

Jesus turned to the Pharisee who had invited him to his house and said, "When you prepare a feast, do not invite your friends and relatives and rich neighbors, because they will only reward you in the same way. If you wish to receive a reward at the time the righteous people are resurrected, then invite the poor, crippled, and blind to your feast. They cannot reward you themselves, but God will bless you for what you have done."

One of the guests heard the words Jesus spoke to the host, and he said, "Blessed is he who eats bread in the kingdom of God." Then Jesus told a parable or story with a message to all of them, about the kingdom of God:

The Great Dinner

"A man prepared a great dinner and invited many guests. When everything was ready, he sent his servant to call the invited guests to come and eat. But every one of them had an excuse for not going. The first said he had just bought a piece of land that he needed to go and see, and he asked to be excused. Another man said that he had bought two oxen and he was going to try them out for pulling a load, and he could not go. Another said he had just gotten married. Everywhere he went, the invited guests asked to be excused, and the servant returned to tell his master."

"The feast was ready, and the master was greatly disappointed to hear that no one would be coming. He became angry with them and decided they didn't even deserve to eat his good food. He sent the servant out to gather the poor people from the streets and also the blind and lame people. Still there was room for more guests, and he sent the servant out to the country to find more poor people. His house was filled with hungry people who enjoyed the good things he had prepared for his unfaithful friends."

G-45 THE PHARISEES TRY TO FRIGHTEN JESUS
LUKE 13:11 – 15:32

Jesus was teaching in the cities and villages where the seventy disciples had gone to preach and heal the sick. In one city he saw a woman with a crooked body in the synagogue on the Sabbath day. She had not been able to straighten her body for eighteen years and was stooped over. Jesus pitied her when he saw her. Calling her to him, he told her that she was set free from her problem that had afflicted her for so many years. Then he laid his hands on her bent back, and immediately she was able to stand straight up.

The woman was very happy, and she praised God because she had been made well. The ruler of the synagogue was unhappy because she had been healed on the Sabbath day. He told Jesus that people had six days out of the week when they could be healed, but they shouldn't do so on the Sabbath.

Jesus told the ruler of the synagogue that he was only pretending to be careful to please God. He told him he took care of his ox and ass on the Sabbath day. He said that the poor woman who was a daughter of Abraham should be taken care of, especially when she was so ill.

The enemies of Jesus were ashamed when they heard his wise reply. The others praised God because Jesus had healed the woman's crooked body.

One day, some of the Pharisees went to Jesus and pretended to be friendly. They told him that Herod, the king, was planning to have him killed just as he had John the Baptist killed. They urged Jesus to go far away, and in this way they hoped to get rid of him, at least for a while.

Jesus was not afraid of Herod. He knew that his greatest enemies were among the Jews, especially the religious rulers. They hated him because he taught the poor people and because he told them about their own sins.

He told the Pharisees to tell Herod that he would be healing the sick and casting out evil spirits for two more days, and the next day he would be made perfect; he would walk for three days, since no prophet had ever been killed outside of Jerusalem. Jesus meant that the Jews in Jerusalem would be

Jesus Preaching to the Multitude

responsible for his death, and not Herod.

Many publicans and sinners followed Jesus, hoping to hear his words. The Pharisees and scribes found fault, saying, "This man visits with sinners and even eats with them." Jesus knew that they were complaining about him, and he spoke to the people by parables.

First he told them the parable about the lost sheep. He knew that the Jews would understand because they kept so many sheep. He told them that

433

they would all look for one lost sheep out of a hundred, even though the other ninety-nine were safe, and they would rejoice when they found the lost sheep. He told them it is the same way in heaven: saving one lost sinner causes more joy than ninety-nine people who have no sin.

There were women in the crowd listening to Jesus's words. Jesus saw them there, and he told a story they might understand. He asked if any woman who had ten pieces of silver and lost one would not search her home carefully until she found the missing piece. He said that of course she would be overjoyed when she found the missing piece, and so it is in heaven when one lost sinner comes to God.

Both the men and women were listening very carefully now, and Jesus told the parable about the unthankful son who left his father's house and went to live among strangers:

"A man had two sons, and the younger son didn't want to live at home with his father and brother any longer. He asked his father to go ahead and give him the money that would be given to him someday as an inheritance. The father figured out how much he was going to give to each son, and he gave the younger son his share. The younger son took his part and went

The Prodigal Son Leaves His Father

434

away. He thought he was very rich, and he spent his money freely. He seemed to have many friends, and he wasted his money on foolish pleasures. But after a while, he had spent all his money and had nothing left at all. He grew hungry, but his former friends refused to help and left him."

"The desperate young man offered to care for a farmer's hogs, but he could scarcely keep from starving. No man pitied him or gave him any decent food to eat."

"Then the young man remembered his father and the hired servants who worked in his father's house. He knew that the servants were well cared for. He decided to return to his father's house and ask to be made a servant there. He returned home to beg his father's forgiveness and to ask permission to be a servant in his father's home."

The Prodigal Son Caring for Hogs

"The father loved the wandering boy, and his heart was very sad when he left home to live with strangers. Every day he longed for the boy to come back. When he saw him coming, clothed in rags, he ran out to meet him and cried tears of joy. The boy began to speak. He said, 'Father, I have sinned against heaven and against you.' But the father did not let him continue.

The Prodigal Son in the Arms of His Father

He told a servant to bring fine clothes for his son and to prepare a feast of celebration because his lost son had been found."

"The older son was working in the field. When he returned home and saw the excitement, he asked the servants what had happened. They told him that his brother had come back. The older son was displeased and would not go inside to see his younger brother. Then his father came out and told him the good news, but still he was displeased. He told his father that he had served him faithfully for years but there was no celebration for that, and his brother who had done nothing was receiving a big celebration."

"The father understood why the older son was jealous. He told him, 'Son, you have always been with me, and all that I have is yours. Whenever you wished, you could have prepared a feast. But your brother has been like a dead person to me, and now he is alive again. And it is right that we should be glad because he has returned to be with us again. He was lost, but now he is found.' "

G-46 FOUR STORY-SERMONS JESUS PREACHED
LUKE 16; LUKE 18:1-15

People from many different villages had been following Jesus. There were people of all types: both poor and rich, educated and uneducated. Jesus knew about their differences, and he wished to teach all of them. He knew from his experiences that people liked listening to stories, and he decided to preach four stories with lessons to be learned from them to the many people. The first was about an unfaithful steward:

"A certain rich man," said Jesus, "hired a servant to take care of his possessions and business affairs. This servant went to live in the rich man's beautiful house and was called his steward. He was supposed to handle his master's business wisely, but he did not. After a while, the master heard that the steward was wasting his money and other resources."

"Calling the unfaithful steward, the master told him what he had heard. The steward hung his head in shame, unable to deny his guilt. Then the master grew angry and said, 'No longer shall you be my steward!' He was about to dismiss the unfaithful servant and tell him to leave his home."

"The steward had nowhere else to live, and he wondered what he would do. He didn't want to work in the fields like a poor man, and he was too proud to beg for food. So he decided to make friends with the other servants of the rich man, hoping that they might allow him to live in their homes."

"Eventually the master heard what the unfaithful servant was doing, and he said, 'At least he can take care of himself, and he shows some wisdom that way.'"

By this story, Jesus was teaching the people that they would not always have homes in this world. Someday they would have to leave their homes and go to live in a different world. Just as the unfaithful servant had shown wisdom by preparing a home for himself, knowing that he would not always have a home in the rich man's house, everyone should begin to prepare for

Lazarus at the Rich Man's House

themselves a home in heaven by trying to please God.

The next story Jesus told was about a poor rich man and a rich beggar:
"There was a rich man who thought only of his own comfort and happiness.
He wore expensive clothes, like a king, and he ate the best kinds of food
every day. His servants looked after him all day and night, and he did
nothing except enjoy himself."

438

"And there was a beggar named Lazarus who had no home or friends. He was a good man although he was a beggar, and he came to sit at the gate of the rich man to ask for crumbs that might fall from his table. Finally the poor beggar became sick, and sores broke out all over his body. He could not even drag himself away from the rich man's gate. As he lay there suffering, dogs from the street came to lick his sores. But the rich man did not try to help him at all. He let him stay there day after day in his misery."

Angels Carry Lazarus to Heaven

"Eventually the poor beggar died, and angels came and carried him away to heaven. He was no longer a poor beggar, and he enjoyed the company of Abraham and the other good people who had left this world. The rich man

439

died too, and his friends buried him in a nice, new grave. But the rich man found himself in a place of torment after death. Now he was poor, so poor that he could not even get a drink of water to cool his burning tongue."

"In this place of torment, the poor rich man looked up and saw off in the distance the same Lazarus who used to beg at his gate. He remembered Lazarus, and he saw him resting comfortably with Abraham in a beautiful place. The miserable rich man cried out to Abraham and begged for mercy. He knew that he wouldn't get to go where they were, but he hoped Abraham would send Lazarus to give him just a drop of water to cool his burning tongue."

"Abraham called back that he could send no water. He said, 'Remember that you enjoyed fine things in your lifetime, while Lazarus had only poverty and suffering when he lived in the world. Now he is comforted and you are being tormented. I can send nothing to you because no one can travel from this place to your place of torment, nor can anyone go from your place to ours.'"

"The poor rich man remembered his brothers who were still alive and living on Earth. He did not want them to come to the place of torment, and he asked Abraham to send Lazarus back to the world to warn his brothers about the dreadful place. Abraham told him that his brothers had God's law to warn them, and it was not necessary for Lazarus to go. The poor rich man pleaded that his brothers might listen if someone rose from the dead to tell them about the place of torment. Abraham answered, 'If they will not hear the words in God's Book, neither will they listen if one should rise from the dead and speak to them.'"

Jesus knew that sometimes God does not answer prayers immediately because he wishes to have people pray very hard. He lets them ask more than once before he gives them the things they ask for. Jesus wished to teach men to keep on praying when their prayers are not answered, and so he told them the story about a poor widow and an unjust judge:

"There was a poor widow who had been wronged by a wicked enemy. She could not punish the enemy or get back what he had taken from her. She went to a judge who lived in her home city, and she told him about her problems. The judge was also a wicked man, and he did not care to help her. For a while he paid no attention to her, but she kept returning and asking for help. Finally he decided to punish the man only so that the woman would stop bothering him."

Then Jesus told everyone to learn a lesson from the unjust judge. God was not unjust, but he sometimes granted the wishes of those who called on him day and night, over and over again.

The Pharisee and the Publican

Some of the people listening to Jesus thought that they were righteous, and they despised those that they thought were not. Jesus taught them a lesson with the story about the pharisee and the publican in the temple:

"Two men went to the temple to pray. One of them was a Pharisee, and the other was a publican. The Pharisee stood and prayed aloud, saying 'God, I thank you that I am not like other men who are unjust, unrighteous, unfair in business dealings, and thank you that I am not like the publican over there. I fast twice, and I pay my tithes for what I earn every week.'"

"But the publican stood in a corner by himself and would not even lift his eyes toward heaven when he prayed. He bowed his head and hit his chest, saying 'God be merciful to me, a sinner!'"

Jesus said, "The publican, and not the proud Pharisee, went home to his house with God's blessing. Whoever lifts himself up in his own sight is not pleasing to God, but whoever humbles himself shall be lifted up."

G-47 WHAT HAPPENED ON THE WAY TO JERUSALEM
MATTHEW 20:17-34; MARK 10:32-52; LUKE 18:31-43

Jesus on the Way to Jersusalem

Once again it was time for the annual Passover Feast in Jerusalem, and Jesus knew that his life would be coming to an end. He took his twelve disciples aside from the crowd that followed him and told them once again that he would be condemned to die soon. The disciples did not understand, and they believed that Jesus soon would become the King of the Jews.

Two of his disciples, James and John, went to see Jesus with their mother. She knelt in front of him and asked Jesus to give her sons places of honor in his kingdom. Jesus knew that they didn't understand the kingdom of heaven would not be like an earthly kingdom, and he said that only God the Father

442

could give places of honor.

The other disciples felt jealous of these two and Jesus knew about their feelings. He told them that in his kingdom, those who would be great must be the servants of everyone else. He reminded them of how he had worked very hard for others, and he told them that they should be willing to serve others.

Many other people going to the feast walked along the same road with Jesus and the disciples. They had heard Jesus talk and seen him heal the sick. They hoped he would set up his kingdom in Jerusalem at the time of this feast.

Eventually the group reached a city called Jericho. The road to Jerusalem led through the streets of this city, and the people of Jericho were excited to see Jesus there. News that he was there spread throughout the city, and many people went out to see him.

A blind man named Bartimaeus sat by the roadside begging. He heard the sound of many people, and he wondered why there was such a large crowd. He asked someone and was told, "Jesus of Nazareth is going by."

Bartimaeus had heard about Jesus of Nazareth and his ability to heal people. He rose from his seat by the roadside and cried out, "Jesus, son of David, have mercy on me!"

Those who stood nearby were displeased to hear him yelling at Jesus in this manner. They told him to be quiet and that the crowd was too large for Jesus to hear him. But he only cried out more loudly.

Jesus knew about the poor beggar, and he knew how the men nearby had urged him to keep quiet. He stopped and told someone to tell the blind man to come to him. A messenger hurried to Bartimaeus, saying, "Be happy, because Jesus heard you and now he is calling for you."

Bartimaeus ran to the place where Jesus stood. Jesus asked him what he wanted. He said that he wanted to have his sight again. Jesus told him, "Go on your way. Your faith has made you well." At once his blind eyes opened, and Bartimaeus could see as well as those who had never been blind. He joined the crowd following Jesus.

G-48 THE MAN WHO CLIMBED INTO A TREE TO SEE JESUS
LUKE 19:1-29

A rich man named Zacchaeus, the chief of the publicans, was living in Jericho at the time. He had never seen Jesus, but he wanted to when he heard that Jesus would be passing through Jericho. He ran down the highway toward the large crowd.

Zaccheus Climbs a Tree to See Christ

Zacchaeus did not stop when the crowd stood still. He continued on a bit
further, and he climbed into a sycamore tree growing by the roadside. He
thought he would be able to see Jesus from the tree when he passed by. He
was a short man, and he wouldn't have been able to see Jesus otherwise.

Soon the large group moved down the road, including the people of
Jericho who had gathered tried to catch a glimpse of Jesus. The group went
on until they reached the sycamore tree, and Jesus and his disciples stopped
there. Jesus looked up into the tree and saw Zacchaeus clinging to its brances

and gazing down at him.

Jesus said, "Zacchaeus, come down at once. Today I must stop at your house." Zacchaeus was surprised to hear these words. He had hoped just to see Jesus, but now he would be able to talk with him in his own home.

Zacchaeus was very glad to lead Jesus and the disciples to his home. Others went along too, and some found fault, saying that Jesus shouldn't want to stop at the home of a publican because publicans were all sinful. The Pharisees refused to enter his home.

Although Zacchaeus was a publican, his heart was changed by Jesus's kind words. He told Jesus that he would give half his riches to the poor, and if he ever cheated anyone, he would give them back four times as much as he had taken.

Jesus was pleased with him, and he knew that his heart really had been changed. He said, "Today salvation has come to your house, for the Son of man is here to seek and to save those who are lost." Jesus had known about Zacchaeus's desire to see him, and he was willing to grant him forgiveness because he had received him into his home and was willing to try to right the wrongs he had done.

Others stood by listening, and Jesus told them another parable or story with a message. He knew that the people didn't yet understand that the kingdom of heaven was not like an earthly kingdom, and he wanted them to understand more about it.

Jesus said, "A nobleman went away to a far country to be made the ruler of a kingdom. Before he left, he gave each of his ten servants a sum of money, called a pound. He told them to use the money until he returned."

"After a while the nobleman returned, and he had been made ruler of the faraway kingdom. He called his ten servants and asked them how they had used the money he had given to them before he went away."

"The first servant came to him bringing ten pieces of money. He told him that he had been using the money to buy and sell goods at a profit, and he had gained ten pounds, which he showed to him. The nobleman was pleased with that servant and said to him, 'Because you have done this, I will make you the ruler of ten cities in my kingdom.'"

"The next servant had gained five pounds by using the money the nobleman had entrusted to him. The nobleman was pleased with him also, and he told him that he would make him the ruler of five of his cities."

"The third servant came, bringing only one pound. He told the nobleman he kept it wrapped in a napkin because he was afraid he might lose it, and he feared the master was harsh. The nobleman was displeased with that servant. He told him that he should have at least put the money in the bank so that it would earn interest. He told him to give the pound to the one who had ten pounds."

"The servants were surprised, and they asked why the one with ten pounds should have even more. The nobleman answered, 'To everyone who uses what he has, more shall be given. But those who refuse to use what they have shall have their own taken away.'"

After telling this parable, Jesus and his disciples left Jericho and went on their way over the mountains toward Jerusalem.

G-49 HOW MARY SHOWED HER LOVE FOR JESUS
MATTHEW 26:6-16; MARK 14:3-11; JOHN 12:1-11

"Simon the leper" was a friend of Jesus. He lived in the village of Bethany, not far from Lazarus and his two sisters. However, Simon was no longer a leper since Jesus had healed him of his leprosy.

News had reached the village of Bethany that Jesus and his disciples were traveling down the road from Jericho and would soon arrive. This was great news to his friends who loved him, and at once they began to plan how they would welcome him. Simon arranged to make dinner at his home for the tired guests, and Martha, the sister of Lazarus, went to help prepare and serve the evening meal. Simon invited Lazarus to eat with the other guests at his table.

Finally all the guests had arrived, and they were welcomed at the home of Simon. The food was placed on the table and the guests were brought into the dining hall. Some who were not invited stood around, waiting to see Jesus and also Lazarus, who had been raised from his grave after four days.

While the guests were eating, Mary, the other sister of Lazarus, arrived with a box in her hand. Going to the couch where Jesus was resting, she broke the box and poured the contents on Jesus's head and feet. The box contained expensive perfume, and she bent down and wiped the feet of Jesus with her long hair.

Soon the odor of the perfume filled the whole room. Everyone there could tell it was very expensive and of the very best kind. People began talking about this. One of the disciples, Judas Iscariot, said that she should have given the money to poor people who needed food instead of wasting the money on expensive perfume.

Jesus knew what everyone was saying and thinking. He saw them question Mary and speak unkindly to her. He spoke to them and said, "Leave this woman alone. She has done a good work, because she has come before my death to anoint my body with sweet perfume. You will always have the poor, but I will not be with you much longer. Mary has shown her love for

Judas Meets With the Chief Priests

me." And Jesus also said that wherever the gospel was preached, this deed by Mary should also be told.

It is possible that Mary understood Jesus was going to die even when the disciples refused to listen. She had done the best she could to show her love for him.

Judas Iscariot was even more displeased after Jesus said this. He was no longer a true disciple because he had allowed Satan's influence to enter his heart. Sometimes he took money that had been donated and kept it for himself, and he planned to be a rich ruler in the kingdom he expected Jesus to set up.

A wicked idea crept into Judas's mind. He planned to go to the enemies of Jesus in Jerusalem and promise to help them arrest Jesus if they would give him some money. After the dinner was over, Judas left Bethany and went to see the chief priests and scribes who lived in Jerusalem.

The enemies of Jesus had been talking for many days about how to capture him. After Lazarus had been raised from the dead, they were more anxious to capture him than ever, because more and more people had started to believe in him. They were glad when Judas Iscariot came to them, and they promised to give him thirty pieces of silver if he would take them to Jesus when his followers were not surrounding him.

G-50 How Jesus Rode Into Jerusalem As a King
Matthew 21:1-17; Mark 11:1-12; Luke 19:29-47;
John 12:12-19

It was a time of great excitement. People were flocking out of the city gate and hurrying along the road that led down the valley and up the slope of Mount Olivet, also known as the Mount of Olives, just outside of Jerusalem. They were rushing out to meet Jesus.

Many of these people did not live in Jerusalem. They were there to attend the Feast of the Passover, and they had heard about the miracles Jesus performed. Others lived in Jerusalem and they had heard how Jesus raised Lazarus from the dead, and they were eager to see him again. As they went, they took branches off of palm trees to wave and welcome him with.

That morning, Jesus had sent two of his disciples to a village near Bethany to get a colt, which he told them they would find tied up. He told them to bring the colt to him, and if the owners should question why they untied the colt, they should answer, "The Lord has need of this colt today." The disciples had found the colt tied by the roadside. They told the owners the message from Jesus, and they were allowed to take the animal.

The disciples had spread some of their clothes on the colt's back, and Jesus sat on the colt's back, on top of the clothes. Others threw their clothes along the road for Jesus to ride over. As the crowd from Jerusalem approached, to the Mount of Olives, the people who had followed from Bethany began to shout, "Blessed is the King who is coming in the name of the Lord! Peace in heaven, and glory in the highest!"

The people who came out of Jerusalem met Jesus and his disciples on the slope of the Mount of Olives. They heard those who followed Jesus shout praises to him, and they waved their palm branches and rejoiced loudly. Some threw their palm branches in the road for Jesus to ride over.

Christ Approaches Jerusalem

In the crowd were some Pharisees who were there only to find fault. When they heard the people shouting, they went to Jesus and said, "Master, make them stop shouting." But Jesus knew prophecy was being fulfilled, and he didn't want to make them stop. The prophet Zechariah had said that the Savior would ride into Jerusalem on a colt, with people shouting, and that was happening right then.

The crowd passed through the city gate, and Jesus rode up Mount

Christ Passing Through the City Gate

Moriah, where the temple stood. As he went, everyone shouted, "Hosanna to the Son of David." The people in the city streets were very excited and wanted to know what was happening. The crowd answered, "This is Jesus, the prophet of Nazareth, of Galilee."

Christ Drives the Buyers and Sellers Out of the Temple

When Jesus came to the temple, he saw men who were buying and selling animals to be used as sacrifices, and others who were called moneychangers. Once before he had driven these people out of the temple, and now he drove them out for the second time, telling them his house was not a den of thieves. The men were charging too much for their animals to be used as sacrifices, and Jesus thought this was stealing from the people.

451

Everyone in the city was still excited and eager to see Jesus. The blind and the lame went to him in the temple, and he healed them there. Little children came singing, "Hosanna to the Son of David!"

The chief priests and scribes in the temple saw Jesus heal the blind and the lame, and they heard the children sing praises to him. They were angry that more and more people were paying attention to Jesus and not to them. They asked him about what the children were saying, and he quoted Scripture, saying, "Out of the mouths of little children praise has been perfected."

In the evening, Jesus and his disciples returned to Bethany to be with Jesus's friends.

G-51 The Teachings of Jesus in the Temple
Matthew 21:18-46; Mark 11:12 – 12:12;
Luke 19:47 – 20:19

Early in the morning, Jesus and his disciples began to leave Bethany and headed for the temple in Jerusalem. Jesus was hungry, and he stopped to eat from a fig tree by the side of the road. He saw that there was no fruit and only leaves. As he walked away disappointed, he said, "Never again shall any man eat fruit from this tree."

When they came to the temple, many people had already gathered to hear Jesus teach. The chief priests and scribes were there also, waiting to ask him a question. They wanted to stop him from entering the temple. They asked him, "By what authority do you teach and work miracles? Who gave you this authority?"

Jesus answered them by asking them a question. He asked, "Was the baptism of John from heaven or of men? Tell me this, and I will answer your question." The enemies of Jesus did not know how to answer. They did not believe that John the Baptist was a prophet of God, but the many people listening did, and they were afraid to offend them and turn the people against them. The priests and scribes answered, "We cannot tell whether John's baptism was from heaven or of men." Then Jesus said, "I will not tell you by what authority I do what I do, either."

Jesus started to teach by parables or stories again. He told the people about a man who had two sons. He called his older son and told him to go out and work in his vineyard, but the boy refused. He soon apologized for refusing to obey his father, and he went out to the vineyard and worked.

The father told the younger boy to work in the vineyard also. He said he would go, but he didn't. Jesus asked the people which one of the two boys obeyed his father, and the people answered, "The first."

Jesus Heals and Teaches in the Temple

Jesus said that the two boys were like two groups of people – the people whom the Pharisees called sinners, and the Pharisees and other leaders themselves. The leaders claimed to be obedient to God but they were not, and the people they called sinners listened to John's words and had been baptized by him.

Jesus told another story about a man who planted a vineyard, planted a hedge around it, set up a winepress, and constructed a watchtower. He hired some men to take care of the vineyard, and he went away to a different country. When the time came for the fruit to be ripe, he sent servants to get some of the fruit and bring it back to him. But the keepers of the vineyard treated the servants unkindly. They beat the first servant badly and sent him away with no fruit. They threw stones at the second servant and wounded his head. And they killed the third servant. Later, other servants were sent, but the wicked people who were caring for the vineyard treated all of them badly.

The owner of the vineyard was very sad, and he finally decided to send his own son. He thought surely they would recognize his son and treat him with respect. When the keepers of the vineyard looked out from the watchtower and saw the son coming, they decided to kill him, since he would inherit the vineyard someday and they wanted to keep it for themselves. They caught him, killed him, and threw his body outside the vineyard.

Jesus asked the people what the owner of the vineyard would do when he found out what happened to his son. They all said that he would destroy those people and find much better men to care for his vineyard, men who would give him fruits when he wanted them.

Jesus looked at his enemies standing nearby and said, "The kingdom of God shall be taken from you, and it shall be given to a different nation, which will grow fruit." The priests and scribes knew this parable was directed against them, and they were angry. Still, they were afraid to attack Jesus because they knew almost that everyone there believed he was a great prophet.

In the evening, Jesus and his disciples returned to Bethany to be with his friends, and in the morning he returned to the temple to teach the people who gathered to hear him. On the way, the disciples saw that the fig tree that had no fruit had died and dried out completely. They were surprised that it had changed so soon and they mentioned it. Jesus taught them a lesson from the fig tree. He said that if they have faith that God hears them when they pray, they could do greater things than he did with his words to the fig tree. He told them if they ask anything in prayer and believe that God hears them, they would be given what they ask for.

G-52 Jesus's Last Days in the Temple
Matthew 22:1-24; Mark 12:13 – 13:1; Luke 20:20 – 21:4; John 12:20-36

While Jesus was teaching in the temple, he told the people that the kingdom of heaven is like a king who made a feast at his son's wedding. The king prepared a great feast and invited guests from a nearby city. When everything was ready, no guests came. He sent servants to remind them that they had been invited, but still no one came. They joked about it and went on with their own work. Some of them even treated the king's messengers badly and killed them.

The king heard what they had done to his servants, and he was very disappointed. He called out his army to destroy them and burn their city. Then he invited other guests to the feast, and all of them arrived on time.

There were poor people and rich people, the good and the bad, and the king gave each person clothing to wear. He wanted all of them to look good for the feast. When everyone had arrived and put on their nice, clean clothes, the king came in to welcome them.

One man there refused to put on the clean clothes given to him by the king. He stood there, clothed in dirty rags. The king saw him and asked why he came without putting on the clean clothes he had been given. The man hung his head and didn't know what to say. The king was displeased with him because he had disobeyed. He ordered his servants to take the man, tie him up, and carry him away to be punished.

The Pharisees and the other enemies of Jesus knew that these parables were showing the other people how they had refused to obey God and accept Jesus as the Messiah, and they were determined to stop his teaching. They decided to ask him questions to distract him from teaching. They sent some men who pretended to be good, and they asked Jesus if it was wrong to pay tax money to the Roman emperor, Caesar.

The Jews disliked paying taxes, and Jesus's enemies knew that if he told them to pay their taxes that no one would want to make him their king. And they knew the Roman rulers would be mad if they told them Jesus said not to pay taxes, and they would probably punish Jesus.

Jesus knew that these men were not sincere, and he would not allow himself to be tricked. He asked to be shown a piece of money that would be used to pay taxes. He showed them that Caesar's picture was on one side of the coin, and his name was on the other. He told them to give Caesar those things that belonged to him and to give to God the things that belong to God. Jesus's enemies were surprised that he could not be tricked so easily.

Others came to question Jesus, and one of them was a lawyer who asked, "What is the greatest commandment of the law?" Jesus replied, "You should love the Lord, your God, with all your heart, and with all your soul, and all your mind, and with all your strength: this is the first commandment. And the second greatest is this: You should love your neighbor as much as yourself. No other commandments are as important as these two." The lawyer said that he had answered well, and he said that to love God and love one's neighbors is surely more important to God than burnt offerings and sacrifices.

Jesus was pleased with the lawyer's reply. He saw that he understood God's Word better than many who pretended to be experts and teachers. He told the lawyer that he was near to the kingdom of God.

Christ and the Tribute Money

While Jesus was in the temple, some men began talking to the disciple Phillip, and they asked permission to see Jesus. These men were Greeks – not Jews – and they had come to worship the God of the Jews, therefore they were called proselytes. Because they were not Jews, they were not allowed into the part of the temple where Jesus was teaching. Phillip and the disciple Andrew told Jesus that strangers from Greece were waiting to see him.

When Jesus heard about the visitors from Greece, he said to Phillip and

Jesus Says the Poor Widow Gave the Most of All

Andrew, "The hour has come that the Son of man should be glorified." He told them that he would be killed for the sins of all people, but they did not understand. Because Jesus was a human and could feel pain like any other human, he did not want to be killed on the cross.

He felt troubled and prayed, "Father, save me from this hour." Then he remembered that his work would not be finished if he did not die for sinners, and he said, "Father, glorify your name." A voice spoke from heaven, "I have glorified it, and will glorify it again." Some people thought the voice was an angel's voice, and others thought it was thunder.

After teaching, Jesus sat down near a place in the temple called the treasury, where the money boxes for offerings were kept. Jesus saw the rich pass by and throw large amounts of money into the boxes. He saw a poor widow stop and throw two little coins into a box. Jesus told his disciples that the poor woman had given all she had and therefore had given more, while the rich people only gave part of their money. He wanted to teach them that God looks at the heart of the giver. God saw that the poor widow gave all her money because she loved him, while the rich people gave offerings because it was their duty.

Then Jesus and his disciples left the temple for the last time. They headed toward the Mount of Olives.

G-53 Jesus Teaching on the Mount of Olives
Matthew 23:37 – 25:46; Mark 13; Luke 21:5-38

As Jesus left the temple for the last time, the disciples spoke to him about the beauty of God's house. Like all other Jews, they took pride in their temple where God was worshiped. They were surprised to hear Jesus say, "The time is coming when the stones of these buildings shall be torn apart."

On the Mount of Olives, Jesus rested for a while before going on to Bethany. His disciples gathered around him there to ask when the beautiful temple would be destroyed. No one else was there, and Jesus talked for a long time about the things that would happen to Jerusalem and later to the whole world. He told them that there would be men who would claim to be the Christ of God and that many would believe in them.

He said that great wars would be fought between nations, and troubles of different kinds would come upon the people. He said that before the end of time the gospel would be preached to all people in every part of the world. The disciples were surprised to hear this, since they believed that salvation belonged only to the Jews.

Jesus told the disciples the parable of the ten young women, called virgins. Five of them were wise, and five were foolish. All had been invited

The Mount of Olives, Outside Jerusalem

458

The Ten Young Women

to the wedding of a friend. They took their lamps with them, as the wedding was to take place at night and only those carrying lights would be allowed to attend.

The rest of the people in the wedding party were slow to arrive. The young women grew tired of waiting and they fell asleep. At midnight it was announced that everyone else was arriving, and the young women woke up and began to adjust their lamps.

The five who were wise poured more oil into their lamps; they saw that their lights were growing dim, and they had brought an extra supply of oil with them. But the five who were foolish had brought no more oil, and they also saw that their lights were growing dim. "What shall we do?" they asked each other. Then they spoke to their wise friends and asked them to please give them some of their oil because their lamps were running out.

The wise young women did not have any oil at all to spare, and they told the foolish young women to go to the people who sell oil to buy more. While they were away buying oil, everyone else in the wedding party finally arrived, and the five wise young women went with them to the place where the marriage was to take place.

When all the guests had entered, the door was shut, and no one else could

459

enter. The foolish young women arrived after the door had been shut, and they knocked loudly. But they had arrived too late, and the groom would not allow them to enter.

With this story, Jesus wished to teach his disciples to watch and be ready since they would not know the time when he would call for them to leave this world and go to be with him. If they would not be ready when he calls, they would have no time left to get ready, and like the foolish young women, they would be left behind and shut out of heaven.

Jesus Speaking to His Disciples on the Mount of Olives

Jesus told the disciples what will happen at the end of the world. He said that the Son of man (Jesus) will come in his glory, bringing all the angels with him. And he will sit upon the throne of his glory. Before him, all the nations of the world will be gathered, and he will the separate the good from the evil. Those who have believed in him he will place on his right side, and those who have disobeyed will be placed on his left.

"Then shall the Son of man be King," said Jesus, "and he will say to them on his right, 'Come and dwell in the kingdom which has been prepared for you. For I was hungry, and you fed me; I was thirsty, and you gave me drink; I was a stranger, and you gave me shelter; I was shivering with cold, and you gave me clothes to keep warm; I was sick, and you visited me; I was in prison, and you came to see me even there.' And the ones on his right will reply, 'Lord, when did we see you in need and help you this way?' And the

King will answer, 'Whenever you helped one of my needy brothers, even the least of them, you helped me.'"

Jesus continued, "Then the King will turn to those on his left and will say to them, 'Depart from me, you who are cursed, and go away into everlasting fire which has been made ready for the devil and his evil demons. I was hungry, and you did not feed me; I was thirsty, and you gave me no water; I was a stranger, and you gave me no shelter; without clothes, and you gave no clothes to me; sick, and you did not visit me; in prison, and you did not come to me there.' And the ones on his left will reply, 'Lord, when did we see you hungry, or thirsty, or without clothes, or a stranger, or sick, or in prison, and not help you?' And he will say to them, 'Whenever you refused to help one of my brothers, even the poorest of them, you refused to help me.'"

"Those on the right," said Jesus, "will have everlasting life in heaven, while those on the left will have everlasting suffering and torment."

G-54 THE LAST SUPPER
MATTHEW 26:17-30; MARK 14:12-26; LUKE 22:3-39; JOHN 13

Two disciples, Peter and John, were hurrying along the road from Bethany to Jerusalem. They were going on an errand for Jesus. It was time to kill a lamb for the Passover Feast, and Jesus had chosen those two disciples to go to Jerusalem and prepare the feast that he and his twelve disciples would eat that evening.

After they passed through the city gate, they looked around and saw a man carrying a pitcher of water. At that time, usually only women carried pitchers of water in the streets. Jesus had told them that they would see a man carrying a water pitcher, and they were to follow the man to his house.

The City of Jerusalem in Christ's Time

Jesus and the Disciples in the Upper Room - The Last Supper

At the house they met the man, and they gave him the message that Jesus had sent: "Our master asks permission for him to use your guest room in which to eat the Passover supper with his disciples." The owner of the house led them to a nice room upstairs. It was furnished with a table and couches where guests could relax while they ate. The owner knew of Jesus, and he was glad to help him and his disciples.

When evening came, Jesus and the other ten disciples joined Peter and

John, and they all sat around the table in the quiet room upstairs. They were sad because Jesus kept speaking to them about going away soon. It was hard for them to believe this since they had seen him do so many wonderful things. They believed that no one would be able to kill him. Soon they were talking about other topics, including who would be the greatest in the kingdom Jesus would set up.

Jesus knew what they were thinking, and he wished to teach them more about the kind of kingdom he was bringing to mankind. He rose up suddenly from the table, took off his cloak, and tied a towel around his waist. He took a basin of water and began to wash the disciples' feet.

Jesus Washes the Disciples' Feet

The disciples didn't know what to make of this. They had already washed their feet before going upstairs, and they could not understand why he would want to do this humble act of service. Finally Jesus went to Peter with his basin, and Peter said that he would never allow Jesus to wash his feet. "Then," said Jesus calmly, "you shall never have a part in my kingdom." Peter changed his mind, and he said, "Lord, you may wash my feet, and even my hands and head." He said to all of the disciples, "You are clean already, but not all." Jesus knew which one of them was not a true disciple.

When the strange washing was over, Jesus laid aside the towel and picked up his cloak again. He returned to his place at the table beside John. He began to explain to his disciples what he had just done to them: "You call me Lord and Master, and so I am. If I, your Lord and Master, have washed your feet, then you should wash each other's feet. I have given you an example of what you should do to each other, as I have done to you. The servant is not greater than his master, and if you would be good servants you will obey my words. If you know my words, you will be happy when you obey them."

Jesus also said that one of them would turn him over to his enemies, who would take his life. This seemed hard for them to believe, but the disciples knew that Jesus always spoke the truth. Instead of looking at each other, each man thought of himself and asked, "Lord, is it I?"

John, the disciple who liked to be near Jesus, was reclining next to his master at the supper. Peter motioned to John and whispered, "Ask him which one of us will do this dreadful deed." So John asked Jesus, and Jesus whispered to him, "The one I give a piece of bread to, after I have just dipped it in the dish." John watched carefully. He saw Jesus dip a piece of bread in oil and give it to Judas Iscariot.

After Judas had taken the bread that Jesus handed him, Jesus said, "Do quickly what you are going to do." This made Judas more anxious to get rid of his master, and he hurried away into the night. None of the disciples understood what Jesus meant, but they thought Judas must have been running an errand for him, since Judas carried the moneybag.

After supper, Jesus took bread, blessed it, and broke it into pieces. He gave a part to each of the disciples, saying, "Take this bread and eat it, for it is my body which is broken for you." Then he took the cup, and when he had given thanks, he passed it to them, saying, "Drink this, for it is my blood which is shed for you."

They lingered a while longer in the upper room, and Jesus told them that he would soon have to leave them alone. He urged them to remember his commandment to love each other as he had loved them, and he told them that he would prepare a place for them in his Father's house.

Peter insisted that he would never leave Jesus but instead he would go with him. Jesus told him that he could not go now but that he might be able to later on. He also told Peter that he would prove himself to be a coward before daylight returned. He would forsake Jesus and deny three times that he had ever known him. Jesus and his disciples sang a song together, and they quietly left the upper room, going out of Jerusalem and into a nearby garden.

G-55 How An Untrue Disciple Sold Jesus
Matthew 26:36-75; Mark 14:32-72; Luke 22:39-71;
John 18:1-27

The greedy, evil-minded disciple, Judas Iscariot, hurried along the dark streets toward a large room where the enemies of Jesus were gathered together, waiting. Soon Judas arrived and was admitted to the room. Following a short conversation and some arguing, thirty pieces of silver were counted out and handed to Judas. Then the assembly broke up, each man hurrying to get a torch or to summon soldiers.

While this was taking place, Jesus and the other eleven disciples had left the room where they had eaten their last Passover dinner together, and they had gone outside the city to a garden across from the brook of Kidron. He told eight of the disciples to remain at the entrance to the garden, which was called the Garden of Gethsemane. Peter, James, and John went with him into the shadows of the trees to pray.

While Jesus prayed, the disciples fell asleep. They could not understand why he was so troubled, and they did not know what to do. Jesus tried to wake Peter, James, and John three times, but they did not offer him the comfort and support he wanted.

The Garden of Gethsemane, Surrounded by a Wall

465

Jesus Prays in the Garden

God sent an angel from heaven to strengthen and comfort Jesus while he prayed alone. He knew the sorrow that was soon to come. He knew that he would suffer as he was made to die on the cross in a painful way.

An Angel Appears to Jesus

Jesus asked God to take away the suffering from him - if that was possible. He said that he wanted this only if it was God's will.

Jesus and the Three Disciples Leave the Garden

When Jesus awakened the sleepy disciples for the third time, he said that it was time for all of them to leave. They got up and started to follow Jesus out of the garden. Off in the distance, they saw a group of men carrying torches, looking as if they were searching for someone. Jesus walked up to them and asked them whom they were searching for. They answered, "Jesus of Nazareth."

"I am he," answered Jesus. The men fell backward. When they got up, Jesus asked them again for whom they were searching.

And again they answered, "Jesus of Nazareth." Judas was with the men. Judas stepped forward and cried, "Hail, Master!" and kissed Jesus on the cheek. Jesus knew the evil thoughts in Judas's mind, and he asked him whether he had betrayed him with a kiss.

Judas had told the men that he would kiss Jesus when he found him. The men grabbed Jesus and prepared to lead him away. Peter took out his sword and cut off the ear of one of the soldiers. Jesus didn't like this and told Peter to put away his sword. Then Jesus healed the soldier's severed ear.

The soldiers bound their prisoner, and they started walking toward the room where the enemies of Jesus were waiting. Peter followed far behind, fearing that the soldiers might capture him also.

First the soldiers brought Jesus to the house of a man named Annas, who was the father-in-law of the high priest Caiaphas, and the trial began there.

Judas Betrays Jesus With a Kiss

John, one of the disciples, was allowed to enter because he knew the high priest, and he went inside where Jesus was. Peter was a stranger, and he was not allowed to enter the home.

John spoke with the doorkeeper, and Peter was allowed to come inside out of the cold. When Peter was inside a girl asked him if he was a disciple of Jesus. Peter was afraid and said, "No, I did not know the man."

Peter went to warm himself near the fire, and other men were there also. One of the men asked him if he was a disciple, and again he said he was not. One of the soldiers who had been in the garden told the others how Peter had used his sword, and again Peter denied the truth.

While this was happening, the high priest and others had been asking Jesus questions about his teachings and had been treating him shamefully. The enemies of Jesus led their prisoner out of the high priest's house, and as he passed he looked sadly on Peter.

Peter recalled how Jesus had told him that he would deny him three times before the morning. Tears filled Peter's eyes, and he turned away from the fire and ran out the door, crying. He saw himself as a coward, afraid to admit that he once had proudly followed Jesus.

469

Peter Denies Christ

G-56 THE DARKEST DAY
MATTHEW 27:1-54; MARK 15:1-39; LUKE 23:1-47;
JOHN 18:28 – 19:31

After the long, sad night when Jesus was captured in the garden, morning came, and the news that Jesus was now a prisoner began to spread. His friends were terrified and his enemies were overjoyed. Jesus first was brought before the council of priests and elders. They punished people who had disobeyed the Law of Moses.

Jesus's enemies had false witnesses speak against him. These liars said that Jesus had talked about destroying the temple. Jesus would not speak in his own defense. Before the council could put anyone to death, they had to have the consent of the Roman governor.

Jesus Before the Council of Priests and Elders

From there, the soldiers led Jesus before the Roman governor, Pilate, who had taken the place of Herod. Pilate knew nothing about Jesus. He brought him into his judgment hall and talked with him for a while.

He was surprised to hear the wisdom of the one the Jewish leaders wanted to die. He went out and told them, "I find no fault in this man." But the Jews cried more loudly that Jesus should be put to death, saying that he had stirred up the people throughout the country, even those in Galilee.

Jesus Before Pilate, the Roman Governor

A Roman Hall of Justice

When he heard that Jesus was from Galilee, he said, "This man belongs to the country that Herod rules." This Herod was a son of the Herod who wanted to kill Jesus when he was a baby. Herod was also in Jerusalem, and Pilate immediately sent Jesus to him.

Herod had John the Baptist killed. He had heard much about Jesus, but he had never seen him. When the soldiers brought him, Herod hoped that Jesus might do some miracle for him to see. He asked Jesus questions, but he refused to answer any of them. The chief priests and scribes said many evil and untrue things about Jesus, but he refused to speak in his own defense.

472

Christ Is Mocked

Herod grew impatient with the silent prisoner, and he began to make fun of Jesus. He mocked Jesus with the help of his soldiers, dressing him in a purple robe and pretending to honor him as a king. Then he sent him back to Pilate.

Pilate's wife had heard about the trial of Jesus, and she was greatly troubled because she had dreamed about him that night. She sent a message

Christ Before the People

to her husband, urging him to set Jesus free. Pilate also wanted to set Jesus free because he thought he was guilty of nothing. He told the accusers that neither he nor Herod thought that Jesus deserved to be punished by death. But the mob told him that they would have Caesar replace him if Jesus was set free, and Pilate feared losing his job.

As the trial went on, Judas Iscariot saw that Jesus was condemned to

Jesus Is Held Prisoner

die, and he began to feel terribly guilty. He had hoped that Jesus would free himself by some miracle, but he saw that Jesus was allowing them to keep him as a prisoner. Judas no longer wanted the money, and he told the priests and scribes that he had sinned by selling them an innocent man.

The chief priests and scribes told him that he was responsible for his own sin. And they refused to take back the money that Judas no longer wanted. Judas threw down the money on the floor of the temple, ran to a place with no one around and hanged himself.

Before giving Jesus up to die, Pilate talked to the mob about another prisoner he had – a wicked man named Barabas, a robber who had caused much trouble for the Jews. At the time of the Feast it was customary to release a prisoner, and Pilate asked which prisoner he should release – Barabas, the criminal who was feared, or Jesus, the innocent man they hated.

The Crown of Thorns and Reed

The people answered, "Set Barabas free!"

Pilate asked what he should do with Jesus and the people answered, "Crucify him! Crucify him!"

The trial came to an end. Pilate, wishing to please the people, called some Roman soldiers and told them to lead Jesus away to be crucified. First he took water in a basin and washed his hands before the Jews, saying, "I am not guilty of the death of this innocent man."

The Jews cried out, "We will accept the blame!"

Jesus had a crown of thorns on his head. They put a reed in his hand, and they mockingly called him the King of the Jews. They blindfolded and hit him, saying, "Tell us prophet, which of us struck you?" And they spat on him. Still Jesus said nothing. He was suffering for those who deserved to suffer for their own sins.

Finally the soldiers took off the purple robe and dressed Jesus in his own clothes again. Then they led him outside the city to nail him to a cross. They took two other prisoners, men who had been thieves, and made them all carry their own crosses. They were led away with Jesus to die.

A crowd of onlookers followed the soldiers through the gate to the hillside where the crucifixion was to take place. Many in the crowd were enemies of Jesus, and others were friends who wanted to help but couldn't.

As they walked, Jesus couldn't carry his cross any longer. The soldiers allowed someone from the crowd to carry the cross for Jesus, as he was too exhausted to continue.

Christ Cannot Continue Carrying the Cross

477

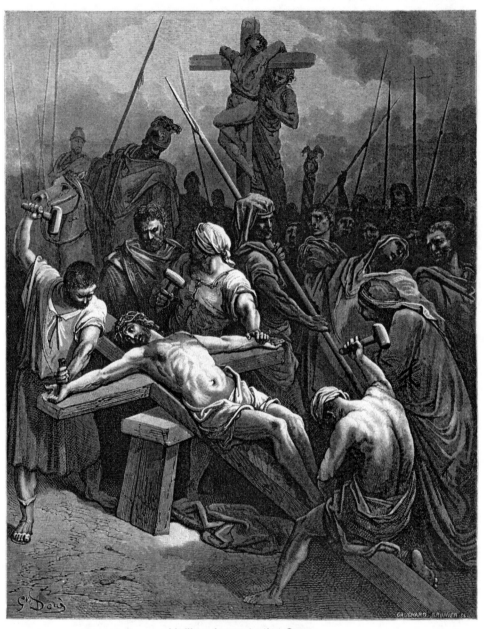

Nailing Jesus to the Cross

The crowd stopped on the hillside of Calvary, and the soldiers began to strip the prisoners of their clothing and nail their hands and feet to the crosses.

Erecting the Crosses

Then they raised the crosses high into the air and planted them in the ground, leaving the prisoners to hang there until they died. Jesus prayed, "Father, forgive them, because they don't know what they are doing." The soldiers cast lots – a form of gambling – to decide who would keep Jesus's coat. They divided his other belongings.

The Crucifixion

Jesus's cross was in the middle of the two thieves, and above his head was nailed a sign that said in three languages, "This is Jesus, the King of the Jews." When the Jews read the writing they were displeased and asked Pilate to change it to: "He called himself the King of the Jews." But Pilate refused to change it, and everyone passing by could read what it said.

Darkness at the Crucifixion

While Jesus hung on the cross, one of the thieves began to mock him, but the other thief begged to be forgiven and to be remembered in the kingdom of heaven. He believed that Jesus really was the King from heaven, which the Jews refused to believe. Jesus saw his faith and said, "Today you shall be with me in paradise." The thief knew his sins were forgiven, and he was glad in his heart, even though he was suffering and in pain.

From his cross, Jesus saw a group of sorrowful friends standing at the edge of the crowd, and his mother was there. John, the disciple who loved him so much, was also there. Jesus asked John to always take care of his mother.

The enemies of Jesus stood around the cross, making fun of him and telling him to come down if he was the Son of God. Even the chief priests and scribes were there, and they said, "He said he could save others, but he cannot save himself! If he is the king of Israel, let him come down, and we will believe in him, too."

At about noon the sky suddenly grew dark. For three hours the darkness lasted, and then Jesus cried out with a loud voice, "It is finished!" and soon he died.

The Roman soldiers often showed mercy to those being crucified by breaking their legs, which caused them to die more quickly. They did this to the two thieves, who were still alive. Jesus appeared dead, and they stabbed his side with a spear to make sure. Both blood and water came out of his side indicating he was already dead, and there was no need to break Jesus's legs.

The Roman captain who stood near the cross and the soldiers who were with him saw the rocks torn apart by a terrible earthquake, and they were frightened. The captain said to his soldiers, "Truly this man was the Son of God!"

G-57 THE WATCHERS AT THE TOMB OF JESUS
MATTHEW 27:55 – 28:1; MARK 15:42 – 16:5;
LUKE 23:50 – 24; JOHN 19:31 – 20:1

The Jews who were so happy when Jesus was taken prisoner and crucified still felt troubled about him. The Sabbath was the next day, and they did not want to have him hanging on the cross with the words "This is the King of the Jews" written above his head.

A rich man named Joseph of Arimathea, who was also a ruler among the Jews, asked Pilate for permission to take the body of Jesus and bury it. Although he was a ruler, he loved Jesus and did not take part in the plot to kill him. Along with Nicodemus, the Pharisee, he had long believed in Jesus, but they both were afraid to tell the other Jews of their belief.

With Pilate's permission they went to Calvary. They wrapped Jesus's body in rich linen clothes and applied sweet spices and perfumes that Nicodemus had brought with him.

They laid the body in a new tomb that had been cut out of a large rock. This grave opened into a garden, and it was to be Joseph's burial place when he died. Some of the women who often listened to Jesus when he taught

482

Taking Jesus's Body Down From the Cross

watched as Joseph and Nicodemus placed the body in the dark tomb and rolled a heavy stone in front of the entryway.

Preparing Jesus's Body for Burial

Night had fallen and the Sabbath had begun. The friends of Jesus had returned home to keep the Sabbath the way that Jews were supposed to. But the enemies of Jesus began to fear that his friends might disturb the grave. They remembered Jesus had said that he would rise on the third day, and they thought his disciples might steal his body to make it appear he had risen, which would cause more problems for them.

They asked Pilate for permission to place his Roman seal on the tomb, and they also asked Pilate to have Roman soldiers guard the tomb. The seal was placed on the stone, and soldiers were stationed to guard the grave day and night.

The women who had watched Joseph and Nicodemus bury his body wanted to show their love for Jesus, and after sunset the next day they hurried to prepare some sweet perfumes. They planned to go early the next morning to anoint the body of their dear friend, even though he had been buried already. The eleven disciples were very sad. They hid themselves from passersby, and they had forgotten that Jesus said he would rise again on the third day. It seemed that nothing was left for them, and all they did was mourn and weep.

The Burial of Christ

Early in the morning of the third day following Jesus's crucifixion, a group of women went toward the tomb. They planned to have someone roll the stone out of the way so that they might anoint the body with perfume. When they arrived, they saw that the stone had been moved and that the tomb was empty. The body of Jesus was not there.

G-58 WHEN JESUS AROSE FROM THE DEAD
MATTHEW 28:2-16; MARK 16:5-14; LUKE 24:4-12;
JOHN 20:2-18

The Roman soldiers grew tired while watching the tomb where the body of Jesus was. As the sun was beginning to rise in the morning, they felt the earth tremble beneath their feet. Then they saw an angel appear and move the great stone that was the door to the tomb. The angel had a face like lightning, and his clothes glowed very brightly. The soldiers fell down on the ground in fear. Jesus had come back to life, and he was gone.

An Angel at the Door of the Tomb

486

The Angel Tells the Women of Christ's Resurrection

When the women arrived at the tomb, Jesus's body was already gone, and the angel was still inside the tomb. At first they did not see the angel, and Mary Magdalene left the others to find Peter and John and tell them that the body of Jesus was missing.

The other women noticed the beautiful angel in the tomb. They were afraid and bowed down on the ground. The angel told them that Jesus had been raised from the dead and was not there. The angel said that they were to tell the disciples that Jesus was alive and would meet them in Galilee.

The women ran from there, filled with joy but trembling with excitement and fear. The news from the angel seemed too good to be true; still they believed and hurried to tell the others. But the disciples refused to believe the news.

Peter and John ran to see the empty tomb for themselves, and they found no one there. The soldiers had run to the city to tell the enemies of Jesus what had happened. They went inside the tomb, and all they found was the linens that Jesus had been wrapped in.

Mary Magdalene had not stayed in the garden long enough to hear the angel's message, and she returned, hoping to find the missing body. She

John and Peter at the Tomb of Jesus

488

Inside the Tomb

stood by the empty grave and cried. Then she saw two angels sitting, one at the head and another at the foot of where the body of Jesus had lain. They asked her why she was crying, and she said it was because she didn't know where the body of Jesus had been taken.

As she turned around, she saw Jesus himself standing there. She was crying so much that she couldn't see clearly, and she thought he was the man who cared for the garden. She asked him what he had done with the body of Jesus. Then Jesus said, "Mary!" and she knew his voice. She was overcome with joy. She fell at his feet and cried, "Master!" He told her to go at once and tell her grieving friends that she had seen him and that he would soon ascend to heaven.

While these things were happening, the soldiers went into the city and told the chief priests what had taken place in the garden tomb. The chief priests were alarmed. All the enemies of Jesus gathered together and wondered what to do. They offered to pay the soldiers a large sum of money if they would tell no one what really happened and lie about it instead, saying that the disciples had stolen the body while they were sleeping.

The Roman soldiers gladly took their money and went away. When they were questioned about it, they said that the disciples had stolen Jesus's body from the grave while they were sleeping.

G-59 THE STRANGER ON THE ROAD TO EMMAUS; DOUBTING THOMAS
LUKE 24:13-48; JOHN 20:19-31

The Passover Feast had ended, and some of the visitors to Jerusalem were returning to their homes. Along the road leading from Jerusalem to the village of Emmaus, two men were walking slowly with bowed heads. They were friends of Jesus, and they were upset that he had been crucified and killed. They met a stranger on the road, and the stranger asked why they were so unhappy. The men were surprised that the stranger didn't know already, and they told him everything that had happened with the trial of Jesus, his crucifixion, and burial. And they told him that Jesus was supposed to arise on the third day and that they had heard he arose, but when they went there themselves, they only found an empty tomb and no angels.

The stranger listened patiently, and when they had finished, he told them about the writings from the Old Testament which predicted that all of these things would happen. The men wondered who this stranger could be. When they reached their village of Emmaus, the two men invited the stranger to stay with them until the next morning, as it was nearly dark. When they sat down to eat, the stranger took bread, blessed it, and gave it to them. They knew at once that it was Jesus, and he disappeared from their sight.

The two men understood why the women who had seen the angels seemed so filled with joy. Their own hearts were filled with gladness after

The Journey to Emmaus

seeing the risen Jesus. They got up and ran back to Jerusalem to tell the disciples what they had seen.

It was very dark when they reached the house in Jerusalem where the disciples and some of their friends had gathered. They noticed all of them seemed happy instead of sad. They said that Peter had seen Jesus, and they were even happier to learn that these two men had also seen Jesus.

While they were talking, suddenly Jesus himself appeared to all of them.

Jesus Appears to the Disciples

They were frightened because all the doors were closed, and they thought he must have been a spirit. He knew what they were thinking, and he told them to touch his hands and feet, as a spirit does not have flesh and bones. He asked for something to eat, and they gave him a piece of fish and some honey, which he ate. They were simply overjoyed to see him there after seeing him tortured and killed.

Thomas, one of the disciples, was not there and did not see Jesus himself, and he did not believe that the others had seen him when they told him. He

Thomas Sees Jesus

said, "Unless I see and put my fingers in the holes in his hands where the nails pierced him, and put my hand into the place where the spear cut his side, I won't believe it."

A week passed by, and again the disciples were together in a room with a closed door. This time, Thomas was with them. Jesus appeared to them as he had before, and this time he said, "Peace be to you!" He singled out Thomas and said, "Look at my hands, and put your fingers in the holes made by the nails; and put your hand into the hole in my side made by the spear. And do not doubt, but believe."

Thomas worshiped Jesus, saying, "My Lord and my God!"

Jesus said to Thomas, "You believe because you have seen. But blessed are those who will believe even though they do not see me."

G-60 JESUS'S LAST MEETING WITH HIS DISCIPLES
MARK 16:15-19; LUKE 24:50-53; JOHN 21;
ACTS 1:1-14

Far up in Galilee, a group of men and women had gathered together on a mountainside, waiting for Jesus to appear. Jesus appeared to them there and talked with them, as he had done on other days. They were elated to see him once more and worshiped him.

One day after this meeting, some of the disciples returned to the Sea of Galilee. The familiar sight of the water and fishing boats made Peter want to go fishing again. The other disciples all agreed to go fishing with him.

They fished all night but did not catch a single fish. When it was morning, they approached the shore, and they saw a stranger standing by a campfire. He called out and asked them whether they had any fish.

The Men See a Stranger by the Shore

They said that they had caught nothing. He told them to cast their net one more time, on the right side of the boat. They obeyed, and this time the net was filled with fish.

John, who often traveled with Peter and James, now whispered to his companions, "It is the Lord Jesus." Immediately Peter wrapped his coat around him, jumped overboard, and began swimming to the shore. The others remained in the ship and steered it to the dock. Jesus commanded them to bring some of the fish they had caught, and Peter lifted the net out of the water. They had caught 150 large fish, but the net had not broken at all. Jesus asked the men to come and eat, as he had already prepared fish and bread on the burning coals of his fire.

After they had eaten, Jesus talked with Peter, the disciple who had denied him at the time of his trial. He asked Peter three times if he loved him, and each time Peter replied, "Yes, Lord, you know that I love you." Peter believed that Jesus knew everything, and he felt sad because Jesus asked him

The Fishermen Catch Many Fish

the same question three times. Then he remembered that he had denied Jesus three times, and he had just said three times that he loved him. Jesus told him to go and feed his lambs and sheep.

Peter had heard Jesus speak a parable one day about the Good Shepherd, who gave his life for his sheep, and he knew that Jesus had called himself the Good Shepherd. Peter understood that Jesus had died for the sins of

Jesus Begins to Ascend to Heaven

496

all people, and he believed that men and women were the sheep that Jesus meant he should feed. Not their bodies, but their souls, were hungry to be fed, and Jesus wanted Peter to leave his work as a fisherman and become a preacher of the gospel.

Jesus told Peter that when he was young, he went wherever he went; but as an old man, he would be carried, but not to a place he wanted to go. Jesus was telling Peter that he would be put to death for his beliefs when he was an older man. Then he said to Peter, "Follow me."

Peter turned around and saw John standing there. Then Peter asked him what his friend John should do. Jesus told him, "Never mind about John, you just make sure that you follow me."

Forty days passed by, and during those days Jesus often spoke with his disciples about the kingdom of God. Still they didn't realize that it would not be an earthly kingdom like David's. Finally it was time for their farewell meeting.

Jesus appeared to his disciples again, and when they saw him, they worshiped him. But some doubted. Jesus spoke to them, saying, "All power is given unto me in heaven and in earth. Go and teach all nations, baptizing them in the name of the Father, and of the Son, and of the Holy Ghost."

While they talked together, Jesus said, "John the Baptist baptized you with water, but you will be baptized with the Holy Spirit in a few days." Some of the disciples asked, "Will you restore the kingdom of Israel then?" Jesus answered, "It is not for you to know the plans of God the Father; but you will receive power from heaven when the Holy Spirit comes to you, and this power will cause you to witness boldly for me in Jerusalem, in the whole country of Judah, in Samaria, and in the farthest parts of the world. But do not leave Jerusalem until the Holy Spirit is given to you."

While Jesus talked to them as they were standing together on the Mount of Olives, suddenly the disciples saw him being pulled up into the sky. They watched until he disappeared from sight in bright clouds, after which time they saw him no more. Still they stood gazing upward, hoping to catch one last glimpse. Then two angels came and stood beside them, wearing beautiful white clothes. They said, "Men of Galilee, why do you stand gazing up into heaven? Jesus will someday return to you in the same manner in which he left you."

The disciples left that place and went to a home in Jerusalem and into an upstairs room. They met together with other friends of Jesus to pray and wait for the promised Comforter or Holy Spirit to be given to them. They weren't sad at all anymore because they knew that Jesus really was the Christ.

Jesus Disappears Into Bright Clouds

PART H: STORIES ABOUT THE APOSTLES
ACTS; THE EPISTLES; THE BOOK OF REVELATION

H-1 A SOUND LIKE RUSHING WIND AND WHAT IT BROUGHT
ACTS 1:25 – 2:47

In a large upstairs room in Jerusalem, 120 men and women gathered every day to pray. They were disciples and friends of Jesus while he lived on Earth. Jesus had told them to wait in Jerusalem for the promise of the Holy Spirit. They were obeying his command.

The 120 people were happy even though they could no longer see or hear Jesus. They remembered his words: that power from heaven would soon be given to them. They were waiting to receive this power, which would come with the gift of the Holy Spirit.

Ten days passed after Jesus ascended to heaven, and it was time for another Jewish feast day. This was called the Pentecost, and religious Jews from other lands had come to worship at the temple. The city was once again crowded with strangers from many different parts of the world.

One morning the friends and disciples of Jesus were gathered together in the upper room, praying as they did every day. Suddenly there was the sound of rushing wind. They understood the meaning of the sound from heaven, and at that very moment the Holy Spirit came to them.

They saw what appeared to be tongue-shaped flames of fire resting on each other's heads. They knew that the promise of the Holy Spirit had been fulfilled, and they began to praise God. No longer were they afraid of Jesus's enemies. The Holy Spirit gave them the boldness and courage to tell others that Jesus was really the Christ and Messiah.

Their rejoicing was so loud that it was heard in the street down below, and a crowd gathered to learn what had happened in the upper room. In the crowd were strangers who had come to Jerusalem from faraway countries where people spoke different languages. These people were surprised to hear the men and women in the upper room praising God in the languages of their homelands. They looked at each other with amazement and asked, "What does this mean? How can these people from Galilee know all of our languages?"

Others in the crowd were Jews who had lived in Jerusalem for a long time. They had been there when Jesus was crucified and when he arose from the grave. They knew these Spirit-filled men and women were friends

The Descent of the Holy Spirit

of Jesus. But they refused to believe in him. So, they said to the strangers, "These men who are speaking your languages are drunk. Pay no attention to them."

Then Peter stood up boldly where everyone could see him and said in a loud voice, "Men of Judah and strangers to Jerusalem, we are not drunk as you think. God has poured out his Holy Spirit on us, as he promised to do in the prophecy of Joel in the Scriptures: 'And it shall come to pass in the last

The Apostles Preaching the Gospel

days, said God, I will pour out my Spirit upon all people, and your sons and your daughters shall prophesy.'"

When Peter began to speak, the people became quiet and listened to his words. He preached a great sermon, telling them how God had sent his Son into the world to be their redeemer. He told them how people had refused to believe in Jesus and had turned him over to the Roman soldiers to be killed, how God had brought him back to life after three days, and how he had ascended to heaven. The people listened quietly, and Peter continued to preach, explaining to them why the Holy Spirit had come to the friends and disciples of Jesus that day. He proved to them that God had made Jesus, and many people there had helped crucify him.

Peter's words brought fear to some of the people listening. They felt guilty, and they cried out, "What can we do?" Peter told them, "Turn away from the wrong that you have been doing, ask forgiveness, and be baptized in the name of Jesus Christ. Then God will forgive your sins and will give you the Holy Spirit, as he has given us. The promise of the Holy Spirit is not only for us but for everyone who believes."

Many people believed in Jesus as the Son of God because of Peter's sermon. 3,000 believers were added that day to the original 120 who had gathered to worship God. They were baptized in the name of the Lord Jesus, and they celebrated because they knew their sins had been forgiven.

With the power of the Holy Spirit, the apostles now worked many signs and wonders in Jerusalem, and respect for God came to the people who saw and heard them. Every day more believers were added to their number until the number of believers was very large.

Many of the people who believed in Jesus as their Savior decided to sell all of their possessions. They divided their money with those who were poor. They met every day to praise God and worship him in the temple, and others who saw and heard them also believed. This was the beginning of the early Christian church, which is called the "church of God" in the Scriptures.

H-2 THE CRIPPLED BEGGAR'S GIFT
ACTS 3:1 – 4:31

Just outside the gate that led into the temple sat a poor crippled man who had never walked a step. Ever since he was a baby, he had never been able to walk on his own. Now that he was a grown man, forty years of age, every morning his friends carried him to the place where he would lie just outside the gate of the temple.

Because he could not walk or do any kind of work, he begged for a living. His friends carried him to the temple gate, where many people entered each day to pray. Many people saw him there, felt pity for him, and gave money to him.

One afternoon Peter and John went to the temple to pray. As they were about to enter the gate, the crippled beggar saw them. He called to them and asked for a gift of money, as he had done to everyone else who passed by. The two apostles stopped and turned to look at him. Seeing his pitiful

Peter and John at the Temple Gate

condition, Peter said to the man, "Look at us."

The man looked up, expecting to receive at least a small coin. Peter said to him, "I do not have silver or gold, but I give you what I have." Then with a tone of command he said: "In the name of Jesus Christ of Nazareth, rise up and walk!"

Peter took the surprised man by his right hand and lifted him up, and at once strength entered his feet and ankles. The man sprang up and walked and leaped around, praising God. He went with Peter and John into the temple and he rejoiced aloud. The people who saw him walking and leaping for joy were amazed because they knew that he was the same beggar who had always asked them for money at the gate, year after year.

Wishing to express his great joy, the happy man hugged Peter and John. While the three stood there, the astonished people gathered around to look at them. Seeing the people gathered, Peter spoke to them and said, "Men of Israel, why do you question what happened to the lame man? And why do you think that we have healed him? You denied Jesus to the point of killing him, and now you are denying his power once again. It is by the name of Jesus that this crippled man was made to walk again and given the strength of a well man."

The people were sad when they realized that they had not believed in Jesus while he was with them. Seeing their sorrow, Peter said to them, "I know you did not realize what you were doing when you cried out as a mob to crucify him; nor did your rulers know. But God has shown by the prophets' writings how these exact things would happen to his Son. And now you have the chance to repent of your sins, and they will be forgiven. God will forgive them and you will be free from guilt." Peter spoke more to the people, and many of them decided to believe in Jesus and were saved.

Before long, the rulers who had caused Jesus to be put to death heard about the lame man being healed. And they heard Peter preaching to the people there. For a while they listened, and they went away angry because Peter was teaching that Jesus had risen from the dead. They had paid much money to the Roman soldiers to keep this a secret, and they were displeased to hear Peter and John boldly declaring that God had brought the one they had crucified back to life. They decided that Peter and John must be stopped, and soon they returned to take them both to prison.

The next day, these angered rulers brought their prisoners before the same wicked men who had tried Jesus, and the wicked men questioned Peter and John. First they asked, "By what power, or in what name, have you done this miracle?"

Peter was no longer afraid of these men. He was filled with the courage the Holy Spirit had given to him, and he stood up boldly to speak. Peter said, "In the name of Jesus Christ of Nazareth, whom you crucified, whom God raised from the dead, by his name does this man stand before you healed." The rulers looked on, amazed. They saw the man who had been healed standing with Peter and John, his face beaming with joy.

Not knowing exactly what to do, they dismissed the prisoners for a few moments to discuss the matter. They could not deny that a great miracle had taken place, and they marveled at the boldness of the apostles, who were uneducated men. They knew that these apostles had been with Jesus, and they knew that they were doing the same works Jesus had done. Although they had killed Jesus, now they saw that they had not stopped his great work. Still they hoped to stop it, so they called the prisoners back and commanded them to teach no more in the name of Jesus.

Peter and John would not promise to obey them. They answered, "Whether it will be right for us to obey you instead of God, judge for yourselves. We cannot keep from telling about the wonderful things that we have seen and heard."

The rulers threatened to punish them severely if they should catch them teaching more in Jesus's name, and then they let Peter and John go free. Peter and John returned to the large group of believers and told them all what had happened.

Instead of complaining about this persecution, they all knelt down to pray. They talked to God and told him how the wicked rulers who had killed Jesus were threatening to punish them if they continued to preach about his resurrection from the dead. They did not ask God to protect them from the wrath of these wicked men, but they asked for more boldness so that they might continue to preach about Jesus. They asked God to help them work more miracles in the name of Jesus.

God was pleased with their prayers. He caused the place where they gathered to be shaken by his great power. Again the Holy Spirit came upon them, giving them more courage and boldness to preach the gospel.

H-3 Two Hypocrites in the Early Church
Acts 4:32 – 5:11

The people who worshiped with the apostles now numbered about 5,000. They met to worship God on the porch of the temple, called Solomon's porch, where Peter had preached after the lame man was healed.

These people were not selfish at all. Some had a little bit of money, and others had none. Still others had plenty and some to spare. Those who had plenty shared with those who had none, and every person's needs were supplied. Love in the hearts for their fellow men caused the rich to be kind to the poor and to take care of them as if they were needy brothers.

Many of the rich sold their houses and their farms. Then they took the money to the apostles for them to divide among the poor people who worshiped with them, so that no one would be hungry or without shelter.

In the group of worshipers were a man and his wife named Ananias and Sapphira. They saw the others selling their property and bringing their money to the apostles, and they decided to do the same. But they did not want to give all the money to the apostles.

The tempter, Satan, who came to Adam and Eve in the Garden of Eden, whispered to this man and his wife. They listened and Satan said, "Sell the property, but keep back some of the money and say that you are giving it all. Peter and the other apostles will believe that you have given everything, just as the others are giving everything, and they don't need to know that you saved some money for yourselves."

Ananias and his wife thought that this was a good plan. They both agreed to tell the apostles that they had brought all their money. Ananias hurried to them, carrying his bag of gold. God saw the desire in their hearts to deceive the apostles and appear very self-sacrificing, and he was not pleased.

Ananias brought his bag of gold to the apostles and laid it down before them, saying that he had sold his property and had brought the money to them. He felt guilty, but he expected to be believed. Instead of praising him, Peter looked at him and said, "Ananias, why has the tempter filled your heart with the idea to lie to the Holy Spirit and keep back part of the money? You are not lying to men, but to God."

When Ananias heard these words, he fell backward and died. And the people who were there watching realized what a terrible thing it is to try to deceive God. Some young men who were there took the dead man's body away to bury it.

Three hours later, Sapphira came into the room where the apostles were working. She had no idea what had happened to her husband. Peter saw her and knew who she was. He called her to him, and she approached him. Peter did not look pleased. He asked, "Did you and your husband sell your property for this sum of money?"

She saw the amount and answered, "Yes." Then Peter said, "How is it that you agreed to both tempt the Spirit of the Lord? The men who buried your husband are at the door, and they will bury you, too." Sapphira heard these words and immediately fell down and died, in the same spot as her husband.

Everyone was afraid to pretend to be a believer in Jesus – unless he or she was truly sincere in his or her beliefs.

The Death of Ananias

News of the teachings of the apostles had spread throughout Jerusalem. People had heard how God was showing his power through these men and the miracles they performed. More believers were being added to the church every day, until thousands more had been added. The disciples healed those who were brought to them and cast out evil spirits, and their ability to perform miracles never failed. People came from far away to be healed.

The wicked rulers of the Jews were becoming more angry and jealous every day. They saw how the works of Jesus were spreading further and further. The apostles and their teachings about Christ were being honored more than the Jewish rulers. The rulers decided to put them in prison. All of the apostles were caught and throw into prison, and the rulers waited to see what their followers would do, if anything.

While the rulers were home sleeping, an angel appeared to the apostles and set them free. The angel told them to go to the temple in the morning and speak boldly to the people.

The next morning, the high priest and his counselors gathered together and prepared to conduct a trial. When the prisoners were sent for, they were told that they had vanished from their cells while the doors were closed and locked.

An Angel Sets the Apostles Free From Prison

The high priest and the other rulers didn't know what to think. While they were discussing it, someone came in and told them that the apostles were once again teaching in the temple, as bravely as ever.

The rulers were afraid to capture them with force because they feared that the large group of people there might protect them. They did send men to bring them quietly to the council room.

When the apostles were brought to the council room, the rulers looked angrily at them and told them that they had been warned not to teach in Jerusalem about Jesus. The apostles told the rulers that they had been not only teaching but also saying that the rulers were guilty of killing Jesus.

Peter and the other apostles stood up boldly and said that they should obey God instead of men. God had given them Jesus and the Holy Spirit, and they would worship and honor God.

The rulers were enraged by these words and talked excitedly with each other. They wanted to turn the apostles over to the Romans or kill them some other way.

One ruler asked that the apostles be removed from the room. After they had left, he told the other rulers they should just leave them alone. If their work wasn't of God they would fail on their own, he said, and if it was of God, it would be wrong to stop them.

This man was very wise and intelligent, and the others respected him. They decided to do as he suggested, but they gave the apostles severe beatings before setting them free this time. They told them never to speak about or teach about Jesus ever again.

With bleeding backs, the apostles left the wicked rulers. But they were happy to suffer for Jesus since he had suffered so much more for them when he was killed. They continued teaching in the temple even after they had been beaten, and they taught in the homes of the people.

H-5 THE PREACHER WHO WAS STONED TO DEATH
ACTS 6:1 – 8:2

The number of believers in Jesus was now many thousand, including Jews from different parts of the world. Some were called Grecians because the people in their homelands spoke Greek, and others were called Hebrews because their peoples spoke the Hebrew language and lived in Palestine. There had been an unfriendly feeling between the two groups for a long time. They did not help to care for each other's poor, and this became an issue between them.

The apostles wanted to address this problem. They called all the thousands of believers together and said, "It is not right that we should spend all of our time looking after the poor. Pick seven wise men from among you who are filled with the Holy Spirit, and let them do the work of helping the poor so that we may pray, preach, and heal."

This plan pleased all the people, both the Hebrews and the Grecians, and they selected seven people to divide the money collected for the poor. These men were brought before the apostles for their blessing.

Stephen and Phillip were the names of two of the five men. We do not know much about the other five.

Stephen's faith in God showed itself through the miracles he performed among the people. He spoke with courage given to him by the Holy Spirit even when the enemies of the apostles were around.

There was a synagogue in Jerusalem where Jews from foreign lands met together to study the Scriptures. Stephen went there to preach the gospel. Some of the leaders of the synagogue argued against him and tried to prove that Jesus was not the Christ. But they could not win the argument because God gave Stephen so much wisdom and knowledge about Jesus. When those evil men heard Stephen speak so wisely, they were angered and wanted to do something to destroy him.

Stephen Appears Before the Council

510

They paid money to some of their evil friends to publish a report that Stephen was teaching against the Law of Moses and saying terrible things about the temple. As soon as the rulers and scribes read this report, they caught Stephen and brought him to the council room where the apostles had been put on trial.

Still, Steven was not afraid to speak bravely to his enemies about truth and what is right. He told them the story of the Israelites, beginning with the time of Abraham. He showed them how their ancestors had repeatedly disobeyed God, even when God had blessed them so much.

As Stephen talked, his face began to shine like an angel's. Those who stood in the council room saw the heavenly light but they didn't say anything. When Stephen told them about the sins of their ancestors, the rulers grew angry, and Stephen knew that they were planning to kill him. Still he was not afraid.

Looking up, he saw heaven and Jesus standing next to God's great white throne. God permitted him to see this vision to give him more courage to face his enemies. He said to everyone there, "I see the heavens opened, and Jesus standing on the right hand of God."

Stephen Is Stoned to Death

511

This made them even angrier. The rulers dragged Stephen outside and began to hurl large stones at him. Stephen's courage did not fail. He looked toward heaven and asked God to take his spirit. As he was dying, he also prayed, as Jesus had done, for the people killing him not to be blamed. When he died, he was the first one to be killed by God's enemies in their efforts to destroy the church of God. Someone killed for his or her beliefs is called a martyr, and we call Stephen the first martyr for Christ.

Some men who had known Steven heard about his death, and they took his body and buried it. They missed him greatly and mourned for him.

H-6 THE MAN WHO TRIED TO BUY THE HOLY SPIRIT
ACTS 8:1-25

In the city of Samaria, about thirty miles north of Jerusalem, lived a wicked man whose name was Simon. He performed magic, and the people assumed that he was receiving his power from God. However, his power was coming from Satan.

One day a preacher went from Jerusalem to Samaria. He was Philip, one of the seven men chosen to distribute the money to the poor. After Stephen was killed, the enemies of Jesus became braver, and they threw many of the believers into prison. The believers no longer gathered in Jerusalem but had split up and gone to different cities, to live and worship. They were not sad about this, and in fact it helped to spread the gospel to many different lands. This was why Philip decided to go to Samaria.

The people of Samaria listened closely to Philip's preaching. They saw Philip perform miracles in the name of Jesus, and they were impressed at the power of God. Many of them began to pay no more attention to Simon after they saw Philip healing the sick and the crippled.

Simon also went to hear Philip preach and see him perform miracles. He watched the preacher from Jerusalem heal the sick and cast out evil spirits. Realizing that Philip's power was greater than his own. He joined the other believers and was baptized. But he had never repented from his sins and wicked ways.

When the apostles in Jerusalem heard that Philip's preaching had caused many people to accept Jesus as their Savior, they sent Peter and John to Samaria. They went to tell the Samaritans more about the power of God, and the believers among them were given the Holy Spirit by God.

Simon looked on in wonder when he saw how Peter and John prayed and laid their hands on the people who received the Holy Spirit. The thought in his heart, "If only I had such power, the people would think that I was great, too. Maybe I can persuade the visitors from Jerusalem to sell this power to me." He offered money to the apostles if they would give him the power to fill people with the Holy Spirit by laying his hands on them.

Peter told him he was wicked and that he would surely lose all his money if he thought money could buy God's power. He told him that he needed to repent for all his sins and wicked acts or he would be lost forever. Simon was frightened, but he did not know what to do. He asked Peter to pray for him.

After their visit to Samaria, Peter and John returned to Jerusalem, passing through other villages along the way and preaching the gospel to everyone who would listen. More and more believers were being added to God's church.

H-7 PHILIP PREACHES TO A STRANGER ON A LONELY ROAD
ACTS 8:26-40

After Peter and John went back to Jerusalem, an angel spoke to Philip one day and told him that he must leave Samaria and travel south on an errand. Philip did not know what the errand would be, but he got up at once. He traveled south on the dusty roads until he reached Jerusalem. He kept going further south toward the desert of Gaza, where few people went.

Philip was not the only traveler on the road that day. A stranger in a chariot was riding ahead of him. He had come many miles to worship God at the temple. He was returning to his own land of Ethiopia, where he served as an officer of the queen.

God knew that this Ethiopian man truly wanted to worship and serve him, and God knew that the rulers in Jerusalem would not help him because he was from Ethiopia. God had sent Philip to help him understand the true religion. When Philip went up to his chariot, the Holy Spirit caused Philip and the Ethiopian to be able to understand each other.

While in Jerusalem, the Ethiopian had bought a copy of the Scriptures to take with him to his country. As he rode along, he read from God's book. When Philip came near, he heard the man reading from the book of Isaiah.

Philip asked the man if he understood what he was reading, and the man said that he needed someone to teach him. He invited Philip to ride with him in the chariot and tell him the meaning of the words.

They read the prophecies of Isaiah about Jesus, and Philip told him that the lamb Isaiah had written about was really Jesus. The story of Jesus was new to the Ethiopian, and he was eager to learn.

Philip Talks to the Ethiopian

Philip eventually baptized the man when they rode near some water. After he was baptized, God caused Philip to disappear from that place, but the Ethiopian went home rejoicing, knowing that his sins would be forgiven because he had found the true religion. And he told others who also became believers.

Philip went to a place called Azotus, and he preached the gospel in every city along the way until he finally arrived at Caesarea, a city on the shore of the Mediterranean Sea.

H-8 THE EVIL PLAN THAT WAS SPOILED BY A VISION
ACTS 9:1-21

Saul was from a different country, and he had gone to Jerusalem when he was a young boy to study the Jewish religion. He had learned everything so well that he became a Pharisee. He believed in the Law of Moses, and he thought that the new religion of Jesus was a threat to his traditions. He was angry with the believers in Jesus and even wanted to kill all of them.

The chief priests and scribes were glad to have someone as serious as Saul defending their cause. They gave Saul permission to treat the disciples badly, hoping that this would discourage others from wanting to follow their new religion. Saul had put so many people in prison that few were left to listen to the apostles teach near the temple.

514

News traveled to Jerusalem that the religion of Jesus was spreading to other cities. Saul became angrier than ever when he realized that the religion was still growing quickly. Saul asked for permission to go to Damascus and search for disciples of Jesus. He planned to kill them or bring them back to Jerusalem as prisoners. The high priest wrote letters to the rulers in Damascus, commanding them to assist Saul. Eventually Saul had nearly reached Damascus, carrying the letters to show to the rulers.

Messengers from Jerusalem had already arrived to warn the disciples in Damascus about Saul's intentions to kill or capture them. The believers were afraid after they heard about Saul's plans.

The Conversion of Saul

515

As Saul and his companions were nearing the wall surrounding the city of Damascus, a very bright light began to shine, and they all fell to the ground. With the light came a voice, but only Saul was able to understand it. The voice said, "Saul! Saul! Why are you persecuting me?" Saul was greatly surprised because he thought he was defending the one true religion. Saul cried out, "Who are you, Lord?" The voice answered, "I am Jesus of Nazareth, whom you are fighting against. It is difficult for you to oppose me."

Saul felt very ashamed when he thought about how badly he had treated those who believed in Jesus. He cried out, "What shall I do, Lord?" Jesus answered, "Rise up and go to Damascus, and there you will be told what you must do." Saul stood up, but he could not see which way to go. The strong light had blinded his eyes.

The men who were with Saul had also seen the light, but they were not blinded by its brightness. They led Saul into the city. They took him to the house of a man whose name was Judas, and they left him there.

Saul Approaches Damascus

Three days passed by and Saul was still blind. He would neither eat nor drink, and he still felt very bad for the way he had treated the believers in Jesus. One night God gave Saul a vision. He saw a believer named Ananias coming to put his hands on his blinded eyes in order to heal the blindness.

There was a believer named Ananias in the city of Damascus, and he also had a vision from God. In the vision, he heard God's voice calling to him, and God told him to go to the home of Judas on Straight Street and ask for Saul of Tarsus. God also told him about Saul's vision.

Ananias was frightened because he had heard about Saul's persecution of believers. But God told him that Saul was now his servant and not to be afraid of him anymore. Ananias found Saul and placed his hands on his eyes to heal his blindness. What seemed to be scales fell off of Saul's eyes.

Saul could see again, and he went out to be baptized. He was eager to please God and he no longer hated anyone. His friends brought food to him and strength returned to his body. He went to the synagogues to worship with the believers in Jesus. He talked about his vision on the road to Damascus, and he began to teach that Jesus is the Christ and Son of God.

H-9 HOW A BASKET HELPED TO SAVE A MAN'S LIFE
ACTS 9:21-31; ACTS 22:17-21; GALATIANS 1:17-24

The Jews of Damascus were very surprised to hear that Saul was worshiping with the believers in Jesus, and they were even more surprised to hear him preaching. They expected him to kill and imprison the believers instead of joining them.

Saul continued to teach every day, and eventually he told his new friends that he had to leave to go to a country called Arabia. In Arabia, he prayed much and studied the Scriptures until he understood how the prophets had predicted the coming of the Messiah. He understood clearly that Jesus of Nazareth was the one the prophets had written about.

After leaving Arabia, Saul returned to Damascus where he preached even more boldly than before. The Jewish teachers who did not believe in Jesus were unable to prove him wrong. When they realized that Saul was converting many people from the Jewish religion to the religion of Jesus, they became angry and wanted to kill him. They placed men at the gates of the city who were told to kill Saul if he should try to leave through one of the city gates. Then they decided to go ahead and capture him before he could even try to get away.

Saul and his friends knew about their plans. His friends hid him away until it was night, and then they lowered him down over the wall in a large basket. Once he was outside the city, he was able to find a safe place.

Saul wasn't sure where to go next. He had been gone from Jerusalem for three years, and he knew the priests and scribes there would consider him an enemy. He wanted to meet with the people he used to persecute in Jerusalem and tell them how God had changed him. So, he went to Jerusalem, trying

Saul Escapes in a Basket

not to be noticed by his enemies, and he found the apostles.

The apostles had not heard about how God had changed Saul, and their reaction to seeing him was not good. They thought that he might have only been pretending to be a disciple in order to capture and kill more believers. Saul was sad that they did not trust him.

Saul found a friend in a kind-hearted man named Barnabas, who was also a believer. Barnabas listened to Saul's story about his vision on the road to Damascus and how this had changed him. Barnabas convinced the apostles that Saul truly had been changed and was a believer.

The church in Jerusalem now rejoiced because God had changed their enemy into a true friend. Saul visited with Peter for fifteen days. During this time, he went to the synagogues where he used to seize the disciples and beat them. He taught there boldly in the name of Jesus. His old friends were amazed to see this, and soon they planned to kill him.

Saul knew about their feelings, but he was willing to give up his life for Jesus, if necessary. God had plans for Saul to do much more work before he died. God told Saul to prepare to leave the city because his old friends would not believe his story about his vision on the road to Damascus. God told Saul that he must preach the gospel not only to the Jews but also to the Gentiles, since Jesus was the Savior of all people.

The apostles helped Saul escape to the city of Caesarea on the coast, where Philip was living. From Caesarea Saul sailed to Tarsus, the place where he had been born.

After Saul had left Jerusalem, many of his enemies forgot about their plans to kill him, and they mostly left the other believers alone. The church continued to grow in numbers in every city and village where the gospel had been taught.

H-10 A Sick Man Healed and a Dead Woman Revived
Acts 9:32-43

When the disciples spoke about their fellow believers, they called them "saints." They had their hearts purified by their faith in Jesus, and therefore they also lived holy lives, as true saints do.

The apostles in Jerusalem were pleased to hear that there were so many disciples or saints in other cities throughout the land. Sometimes they visited different cities and encouraged the people to serve the Lord.

One day while Peter was visiting the saints in Lydda, a city near the Great Sea, he saw a man named Aeneas who had been sick with palsy and unable to leave his cot for eight years. Peter looked with pity at the poor man, and then he said to him, "Aeneas, Jesus Christ makes you well! Get up, and make your bed."

Aeneas was glad to hear these words. He believed them, and he had enough strength to get up. He was totally cured of his palsy. This was Peter's first miracle in Lydda, and many people who knew Aeneas believed in Jesus after what they had witnessed.

Peter Visits in Lydda

In a city called Joppa, not far from Lydda, there were more believers. One of them was a woman named Dorcas. She was loved dearly because of her kind words and helpful deeds for the poor. While Peter was visiting, Dorcas became very sick. Soon she died. Her death brought great sorrow to the hearts of her friends because they thought that no one could ever replace her. They sent messengers to find Peter, hoping that he would help.

Peter Restores Life to Dorcas

Peter returned with the messengers. They brought him to the house where Dorcas had died and led him to the room upstairs, where her body was lying. Many of her friends were there crying. Everyone tried to convince Peter that she must not be allowed to stay dead.

Peter knew what Jesus would have done at a time like this. He told everyone to leave the room, and then he prayed. Turning toward the body, he said, "Tabitha, arise!" and the woman opened her eyes. Seeing Peter, she sat up, and he took her hand, helping her to get up. Then he called for the saints and the poor widows to return to the room. They were so happy to see their dear friend alive again.

The news of this fantastic miracle spread rapidly throughout Joppa, and many people became interested. When they heard the gospel preached, they believed in Jesus and were saved from their sins. Peter visited Joppa for a long time, staying at least part of the time in the home of a man who was called Simon the tanner.

H-11 Peter's Vision of a Great Sheet
Acts 10:1 – 11:18

Cornelius was a Gentile man who lived in the city of Caesarea, about thirty miles north of Joppa. He was an officer in the Roman army and had command of over one hundred soldiers. His rank was called centurion or captain.

Although Cornelius was a Gentile, he feared or respected the true God and worshiped him. He taught his family to serve God instead of worshiping idols. Because of his example, some of his soldiers stopped worshiping idols and started worshiping God. Cornelius tried to help the poor people, and he prayed every day.

Simon Peter's Vision of the Great Sheet

One afternoon while Cornelius was praying, an angel appeared to him. The angel told him, "Cornelius, your prayers are heard in heaven, and your good works have been seen by God. Now send men to Joppa to the house of Simon the tanner, and bring back Simon Peter. He will tell you what you need to do." When the angel went away, Cornelius quickly sent two of his servants on this mission.

The next day as Cornelius's servants were nearing Joppa, Simon Peter had a vision from God. He had become very hungry, and while dinner was being prepared he went up on top of the house to pray. He fell asleep there, and he saw hanging down from the sky a great sheet held at the four corners. This sheet was filled with all kinds of animals. As it came down to the ground, a voice from heaven said, "Rise up, Peter! Kill and eat."

Peter looked into the sheet and saw that every type of animal was in it. Peter knew that the Law of Moses forbade the Jews to eat certain animals that were considered unclean, and he said he could not eat those animals. The voice told him that no animal God made should be called unclean.

The sheet filled with animals was lifted back to heaven and lowered a second and third time because Peter refused to touch the animals that the

Jews were not allowed to eat. Then the sheet disappeared out of sight, and Peter awoke. While he was wondering what this strange dream meant, the visitors sent by Cornelius stopped at the gate of Simon the tanner's house and asked for Peter. Right then, the spirit of God spoke to Peter and told him to go down and join the men who were seeking him because God had sent them. Peter promptly obeyed.

He went down and asked the men what they required of him. They told him how Cornelius had been commanded by the angel to send for Peter. Peter invited them to stay until the next day, when they would all leave.

Peter took six men with him and went with the servants of Cornelius to Caesarea. They followed the winding roadway by the seashore and did not arrive at Cornelius's home until the fourth day after the angel had spoken to Cornelius. They arrived to find a house full of people waiting to meet Peter and hear his words.

Peter at Cornelius's Home

This was the first time that Peter had been invited into the home of a Gentile. The Jews and the Gentiles usually did not socialize together, but Peter trusted in God. Cornelius fell down at Peter's feet to worship him. Peter stopped him and told him that he was only a man. Cornelius led him to a room where his relatives and friends were waiting. They were Gentiles, but they worshiped the God of the Jews. They were eager for Peter to teach them how to better serve the Lord.

Peter told them that even though the Jews did not go into homes of people of other nations, God had shown him that no people are unclean or unworthy. Peter asked Cornelius the reason he sent for him.

Cornelius told him about the angel he saw while he was praying. The angel told him that he should send for Simon Peter, and he would tell him what to do if he wished to please God.

Peter told him that he knew God accepts people of every nation who wish to serve him. He began to tell Cornelius and his friends about Jesus. He told them how Jesus had suffered and died to save people from their sins and that whoever would believe in him would be saved. While he was talking, God gave the Holy Spirit to everyone listening.

The six men who came with Peter were amazed that God gave the Holy Spirit to the Gentiles also. They had always been strict Jews and believed that salvation from sin was only for Jews, but they saw that God's plan truly was for everyone.

Peter decided to teach all of them about baptism, and he baptized everyone who believed. Peter and his companions spent several days in Caesarea teaching the people there about Jesus, and then eventually they returned to Jerusalem.

News of the events in Caesarea reached Jerusalem before Peter arrived. Some of the Jews were disappointed to hear that Peter had entered the home of a Gentile. Peter told them about his strange dream and what God had told him. He told them that God gave the Gentile people the Holy Spirit, just as he had given the Holy Spirit to the Jews who believed in Jesus.

When the believers in Jerusalem heard all of this, they rejoiced, knowing that God's plan of salvation was for everyone.

H-12 PETER'S ESCAPE FROM PRISON
ACTS 12

It was midnight, and the streets were quiet and deserted. But not everyone was asleep. A group of men and women were having a prayer meeting in the home of a widowed woman named Mary. They believed in Jesus, and they had to meet in secret because the new Roman ruler of the Jews, King Herod Agrippa, was persecuting them. He was a grandson of the King Herod who killed all the babies in Bethlehem when Jesus was very young. He was also a nephew of the Herod who killed John the Baptist.

Wishing to please the Jews, this King Herod became friendly toward the

Peter Is Delivered From Prison

religious rulers of the people. Soon he heard about the hatred that the chief priests and scribes had toward those who had accepted Jesus as the Savior of men. He commanded his soldiers to kill James, one of the apostles.

Because this pleased the Jews, he decided to kill Peter, too. He caught Peter and put him in prison, intending to have him killed publicly after the feast days were over.

The church was very upset that James had been killed and Peter was imprisoned. They prayed and prayed for Peter's release. That was the reason everyone was meeting to pray at Mary's house on the day before Peter was to be killed.

When Peter was sleeping, an angel of God came into the dark cell where he lay, touched him, and told him to get up. The guards could not see or hear the angel. Peter obeyed, and the heavy chains fell off his hands. The angel told him to put on his shoes and get dressed. The angel then told him to cover himself with his cloak. He walked out of his cell, past the guards, and through the great iron gate of the prison.

The iron gate swung open and allowed Peter to exit, although it had been locked. The angel told Peter which way to go and then the angel disappeared. Peter decided to find some of his friends before leaving the city and tell them what had happened.

He went to the home of Mary to visit her son John Mark, who was a friend of his. When he arrived, a woman asked him who he was, and he told her that he was Peter. Everyone was gathered there, praying. They were all very excited to hear that Peter had arrived, but they did not believe the woman, whose name was Rhoda. Rhoda was so excited that she forgot to open the gate to the house and let Peter inside.

The people praying thought that she must be crazy. Soon someone went outside to check, and they found Peter knocking at the gate. They let him inside, and he told them all to be quiet. He told them the story of how God had answered his prayer and how he was set free from prison.

Peter knew he had to keep running or he would be caught, so he told them goodbye. He asked them to send James, a brother of Jesus, and the other disciples the news of his escape from prison and execution.

King Herod was very angry to hear that Peter had escaped. He questioned the guards, and he saw that all the doors were tightly locked. Even though they had stayed at their posts and done their jobs, the king ordered that the guards be put to death.

Soon after, King Herod died suddenly. His death was punishment from God for the way he treated James, Peter, and the others who believed in Jesus. From that time, after King Herod Agrippa died, the disciples and believers in Jerusalem were no longer persecuted as much.

After Stephen was killed in Jerusalem, believers there had fled to other cities, and the message of Jesus spread with them. To the north of Jerusalem, in the country of Syria, was a large city called Antioch. Some of the believers went to Antioch and preached to the Gentiles as well as the Jews there. Many of the people who listened to the preaching became convinced that Jesus was the Christ or Savior. Others called them "Christians," mocking them.

In those days it took much longer for news to travel than it does today, and it took a long time before the church in Jerusalem heard about the Gentile believers in Syria. When they finally heard the news, they decided to send some people to help the new believers in Antioch. They chose Barnabas, who had befriended Saul when no one else trusted him.

Barnabas Preaches in Antioch

After many days he arrived there and met with the believers. He was glad to see so many people with so much faith. Barnabas preached, and even more people became believers in Jesus as their Savior.

Barnabas realized that he needed more help when he saw how rapidly the church was growing. Then he remembered Saul back in Jerusalem. Barnabas knew that Saul had gone to Tarsus to preach to the Gentiles. Tarsus was not far from Antioch, and Barnabas decided to try to find him there.

Saul was glad to see Barnabas again, and he agreed to go to Antioch to preach. For a whole year Saul and Barnabas lived together, preaching the gospel to the Gentiles and encouraging the believers.

Some visitors from Jerusalem arrived at the church. They were men who had been given a gift from God; they had the ability to see the future. They told the people in the church that a famine was coming and that there would be no food for a long time.

The people in Antioch saved their food, and before long there was a famine. They heard that the people in Judea were starving and dying. They put together an offering of food. Each family gave what they could. Saul and Barnabas were chosen to carry the food to the people in Judea, and they decided to send it all to the leaders of the church in Jerusalem.

Saul and Barnabas asked John Mark to return with them to Antioch, and he gladly accepted. John Mark was related to Barnabas, and it was his house where the midnight prayer meeting had been held. He was very helpful to those who preached the gospel in unfriendly lands. When he was older, he wrote the Gospel of Saint Mark, the second book of the New Testament.

H-14 THE FIRST MISSIONARIES IN THE EARLY CHURCH
ACTS 13:1 – 14:7

The church in Antioch grew until many Christians were there. God spoke to Saul and those around him, and God told him that Saul was to be called "Paul." From that time on, everyone called him by his new name, Paul.

God told Paul that he was to begin the great work of preaching the gospel to the Gentiles in faraway countries where most people didn't know about Jesus and the one true God. Paul, Barnabas, and John Mark, the young disciple from Jerusalem, started on their first journey as missionaries.

The Island of Cyprus in the Mediterranean Sea was the first place they stopped. They preached in two cities, Salamis and Paphos. The governor of Paphos, Sergius Paulus, sent for them while they were there preaching. He wanted to hear the message of God and listened carefully as they preached to him. He was beginning to believe when a wicked man told him not to trust the missionaries.

The Holy Spirit gave Paul the wisdom to know this wicked man's purpose. Paul told him he was evil and that God would make him blind.

Paul Preaches at the Synagogue

As soon as Paul said this, the man went blind, and someone else had to take his hand and lead him away. When the Roman governor saw this, he immediately became a believer that Jesus was the Son of God.

The missionaries left, sailing their ship toward the city of Perga in the country of Asia Minor. John Mark left from there and returned to his home in Jerusalem. Paul and Barnabas continued on toward a different city with the same name of Antioch.

Paul and Barnabas found a Jewish synagogue, and they went to talk to the Jews who worshiped there on the Sabbath day. The rulers of the synagogue welcomed them and invited them to speak. Paul told the story of Jesus and God's plan for salvation. Many of the Jews were not happy and left. Others, including some Gentiles, encouraged them to continue preaching. Those people followed Paul and Barnabas, wishing to learn more.

Many people gathered on the next Sabbath day to hear the missionaries speak about Jesus. The Jewish leaders were angry that so many Gentiles were listening to Paul and Barnabas, and they began to speak unkindly to them. Paul told them that salvation was first for the Jews but now for everyone, in all parts of the world.

The Gentiles were glad to hear this, and it caused many of them to become believers. The people formed a church in this city, also called Antioch.

After a while the Jewish leaders conspired with the rulers of the city to have Paul and Barnabas thrown out of the city. They left, but they left joyfully, knowing that their work there was done and that they had accomplished much.

Their next stop was the city of Iconium. Many Christians were there already, both Jews and Gentiles. The missionaries stayed there for a long time, preaching to them.

But there were enemies in this city also. Some Jews who did not believe told their Gentile neighbors some untrue things about the missionaries. The Gentiles grew to dislike Paul and Barnabas because of these false stories, and eventually they wanted to stone the missionaries.

Barnabas and Paul heard about the plan to kill them and they fled from the city. They went to another town, Lystra, to preach the gospel.

H-15 How Idol-Worshipers in Lystra Treated Paul and Barnabas
Acts 14:8-28

The people of Lystra worshiped idols. Most of them had never heard of God or Jesus. The words of Paul and Barnabas sounded strange to these people at first. After they saw Paul heal a crippled person, they began to pay more attention. The people were so excited by this miracle that they began to treat Paul and Barnabas like gods. They were speaking in their own language, which Paul and Barnabas could not understand.

When Paul and Barnabas saw the people bringing sacrifices and offerings for them, they knew that the people were treating them like they were gods instead of servants of the true God. It turned out that the people believed that they were Jupiter and Mercury, two Greek gods. Paul and Barnabas told them to stop at once because they were not gods but there to serve God. They also tried to get them to stop worshiping idols.

At first the people would not even listen to them, but finally they stopped treating them like they were gods. Most of them were not open to the idea of Jesus and salvation, and only a few became believers.

When the missionaries had been in Lystra for a while, the sinful Jews in Iconium heard that they were there, preaching to the idol worshipers. They sent men to Lystra to tell untrue stories about the missionaries. Some of the

The People Throw Stones at Paul

people threw stones at Paul until he fell down and appeared dead, and then they threw his bleeding body outside the city.

The believers stood by Paul's body, crying. Then they saw him move and realized that he was not really dead. Soon Paul stood up and walked with them back to the city. He and Barnabas left the next day, and they went to a place called Derbe. They continued to preach the gospel there.

After spending some time in Derbe and seeing many people become Christians there, the missionaries started their journey home. They stopped at the places where they previously had been. Finally they returned to Antioch, in Syria, the place where they had started their journey. They told the people of the church there how God had helped them to preach in faraway lands. Everyone was happy to hear that many more people had become Christians and were worshiping the true God.

H-16 THE ANSWER TO A PUZZLING QUESTION
ACTS 15:1-34

After Paul and Barnabas had returned from their missionary trip, some visitors from Jerusalem arrived at the church at Antioch. They were Jews, and they couldn't understand how Gentiles could be saved the same way as Jews without having to obey the law given by God to Moses. These visitors acted unkindly toward the Gentile believers and told them that they could not be saved without first keeping the Law of Moses.

Paul and Barnabas had seen many Gentile believers receive the Holy Spirit from God, even though they knew almost nothing about Moses's Law. The missionaries told the visitors that they knew that Gentiles had been saved because they had received the Holy Spirit.

God had shown Peter a vision to convince him that Gentiles could be saved. But these visitors had seen no vision, like most other Jews who doubted that salvation was really for Gentiles as well as Jews.

Finally, the people at the church in Antioch decided that Paul and Barnabas would go to the church in Jerusalem and talk with the apostles and teachers there about whether Gentiles could be saved. As they went, they stopped at some other churches along the way. They told the people at those churches how God had blessed them by allowing so many people to be saved during their last missionary journey.

The believers in Jerusalem were glad to receive the visitors from Antioch. Soon they explained the reason for their visit. Some of the teachers were strict Pharisees, like Paul had been, and they did not understand what Paul and Barnabas understood because they had not seen what they had seen by traveling among the Gentiles. Paul and Barnabas spoke, and they explained that many Gentiles had been saved and also received the Holy Spirit.

Then James, the brother of Jesus, spoke. Everyone listened carefully because they thought that he was given wisdom from God to speak to them. He urged them to stop troubling the Gentile believers about keeping the Laws of Moses. James said that they could write a letter to the Gentile believers, telling them to be careful not to do certain things that they had always done while worshiping idols.

James's advice pleased all of the assembly. The apostles and teachers in the church at Jerusalem decided to write such a letter and send it with Paul and Barnabas to the Gentile Christians at Antioch. They sent the letter, and they also sent two preachers from Jerusalem named Judas and Silas.

A large gathering of people was waiting for them to return to Antioch. They listened carefully to the letter when it was read to them. They were very happy to hear that they would not be required to follow all of the Law of Moses. They continued to worship God with pure hearts, obeying the teachings of the gospel.

Judas and Silas, the two preachers from Jerusalem who traveled with Paul and Barnabas, spoke to the people and encouraged them to remain strong in their faith in Jesus. After many days, Judas returned to Jerusalem, and Silas chose to remain with the people in Antioch.

H-17 A CALL FOR HELP FROM FAR AWAY
ACTS 15:36 – 16:15

One day Paul told Barnabas that he thought it would be a good idea for both of them to return to the people they had visited while traveling and teaching as missionaries. Barnabas agreed, and they prepared for their journey.

John Mark had come to Antioch, and he wanted to travel with Paul and Barnabas. He had started with them on their first missionary journey but ended up turning back, and Paul did not care to take him this time.

Barnabas said that he would allow John Mark to travel with him, even though he had turned back the first time. Paul ended up choosing Silas, the preacher from Jerusalem, to travel alongside him. Barnabas and Mark went to the island of Cyprus while Paul and Silas went as far as the churches in Asia Minor.

When Paul and Silas arrived at Lystra, where Paul had been stoned, they met a young man named Timothy. His father was a Gentile and his mother was a Jew. Timothy believed very strongly in Jesus, and Paul was pleased with him. Timothy joined Paul and Silas, going from Lystra to other cities where the gospel had been preached. Paul became like a father to him, and years later Paul wrote letters to Timothy while he was locked in prison.

The missionaries did not stop at every town because some people were not yet willing to listen to them. Eventually they arrived at Troas, a city on the coast where ships docked. Paul preached to some of the people traveling on those ships from faraway lands where the gospel had never been heard.

Paul Preaches at Troas

One night Paul had a dream. He saw a man standing on the shore across from Troas calling to him and asking for help.

Paul knew that the man was from Macedonia, based on his appearance. He told his companions about the dream, and they also agreed that it meant God wanted them to travel to Macedonia and preach the gospel to the people there. They all paid to travel aboard the next ship leaving for Macedonia.

Another disciple, a doctor named Luke, joined Paul, Silas, and Timothy, and they all sailed for Macdeonia. Luke eventually wrote the Gospel of Luke and also the book Acts of the Apostles, both books of the New Testament.

Philippi was the first city they visited in Macedonia. There were very few Jews there and they had no real synagogue. The people met on the Sabbath day at a place near the riverside, outside the city. Paul and his companions decided to go there on the Sabbath and preach to the people.

Only a few people were there, and they were all women. Paul told them about Jesus, a gift from God for all people. One woman, Lydia, believed his words and knew that her sins were forgiven. Then she was baptized in the name of Jesus. Her family also became believers.

Lydia, the first Christian in this land, invited Paul and his companions to stay at her house. She was rich, and she was able to provide food and shelter for them while they stayed in Philippi.

534

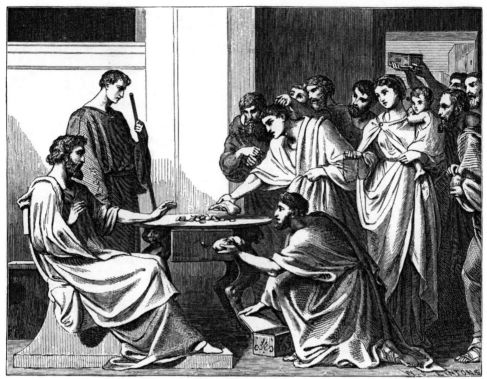

Lydia Presents Food and Gifts to Paul and His Companions

H-18 A Prison Prayer Meeting
Acts 16:16-40

One day a mob of people led two men down the streets of Philippi to the city prison. These men had just received severe beatings in the public square, and they were wounded and bloody. As they were dragged along the streets, they suffered more and more. When they reached the prison, the jailer quickly brought the men inside and locked the prison door to keep the angry mob away.

The two men were Paul and Silas, the Christian missionaries in Philippi. They had done nothing wrong, and they were beaten only because the sinful people there had not liked what they preached.

Trouble began for Paul and Silas when a young slave girl began following along behind them as they walked through the streets. She yelled to everyone that they were servants of God who had come to show everyone the way to salvation. This girl had an evil spirit living inside her. The spirit told her things that would happen in the future, and people came to her to ask her questions about things that might happen. The men who owned the slave girl charged the people money for her to answer their questions, and in

Paul in Prison

this way the men had become very rich.

Paul felt sorry for the poor slave girl. He could tell that an evil spirit possessed her. One day he turned around while she was following him, and he commanded the evil spirit to leave her body. Immediately the evil spirit obeyed, and the girl was set free. However, she could no longer predict the future without the spirit's help.

The masters of the slave girl were angry when they learned what had happened. They knew they would no longer be able to charge people for her to answer their questions because she could no longer predict the future. They grabbed Paul and Silas and brought them before the rulers of the city. They told the rulers that Paul and Silas were Jews who were teaching things that should not be taught to Romans.

The rulers decided that Paul and Silas were troublemakers who should be beaten and imprisoned. The rulers told the jailer to keep the men safe and secure inside the prison. The jailer put them in an inner room and even secured their feet in stocks to keep them from escaping. Then he left them alone.

Paul and Silas did not complain like other prisoners. They talked to each other about God and began to pray. At night, they could be heard singing songs of praise.

The Earthquake at Midnight

Suddenly at midnight, the prison began to shake violently from an earthquake, and all of the prison doors swung open. Even the stocks that held the feet of Paul and Silas popped open. The jailer heard the great noise when the earthquake shook the prison, and he was afraid that the prisoners were escaping. He knew the rulers would kill him if he allowed even one prisoner to escape. When he saw the doors open, he drew his sword and prepared to kill himself instead of allowing the rulers to torture him to death.

Paul and Silas saw what the jailer was about to do, and they yelled to him, "Do not harm yourself! We all are here!" The jailer found a candle and went into the prison. He could see all the prisoners, with Paul and Silas among them.

The jailer was sure these men were not dangerous. He believed that they were good men who had taught the way of the true God, which the slave girl had told everyone. He asked Paul and Silas how to receive the gift of salvation. They told him about Jesus and how he died for everyone's sins, and that if he believed this he would be saved.

Paul and Silas at the Jailer's Home

This news brought joy to the jailer's heart, and he believed the message of salvation. He took Paul and Silas into his home and cared for them. Soon the missionaries baptized the jailer and everyone in his household in the name of Jesus.

When the rulers heard what had happened that night, they sent orders for Paul and Silas to be set free. Paul and Silas replied that they were Romans and should not have been punished the way they were, and they wanted the rulers to personally set them free. The rulers were frightened to learn that Paul and Silas were Romans since legally they were not permitted to punish Romans. They went to Paul and Silas and begged them to leave the city.

Before leaving Philippi, the missionaries returned to Lydia's house to speak words of comfort to the other Christians. Then they said goodbye and left. Years later, Paul wrote a letter to the church at Philippi, and this letter is part of the New Testament: the Epistle of Paul to the Philippians.

H-19 Preaching in Other Cities of Macedonia
Acts 17:1-15

Paul and Silas were not discouraged when they left Philippi. They were excited to be able to carry the news of Jesus to people in other towns and cities.

Many Jews lived in a large city called Thessalonica, and there was a synagogue there. Paul and Silas went to the synagogue each Sabbath day and taught the people the story of Jesus. Some of the Jews who listened were convinced that Jesus really was the Savior. And many Greek people who listened decided to become believers.

The Jews who refused to believe in Jesus were jealous of the missionaries because so many people gathered to listen to them preach. They decided to get rid of Paul and Silas. They gathered together a group of rough men and made a loud disturbance in the city, but Paul and Silas did not come. Then they searched the home of one believer, Jason, trying to find Paul and Silas. They did not find them at Jason's house, and they dragged Jason before the rulers of the city and told them that he had been letting people stay at his house who taught beliefs that were contrary to Roman beliefs, including teaching about another king named Jesus.

The rulers were troubled after they heard this, but they did not punish Jason severely. The believers in the city were afraid something bad would happen to Paul and Silas if they remained in Thessalonica. At night, they sent them to a different town, called Berea.

In this town they also found a synagogue, and they preached there on the Sabbath, telling the people that Jesus was the Savior promised to them in the Old Testament. The Jews there researched the writings of the prophets, and many of them were convinced that Jesus was the Messiah or Savior. Many Greeks also believed, and soon a large congregation was gathering to hear Paul and Silas speak.

Eventually the sinful Jews in Thessalonica heard that Paul and Silas had been preaching in Berea. They tried to make trouble for them there. The believers hid and protected the missionaries from the men who were looking to harm them. Then they sent Paul to a different city, but Silas and Timothy remained in Berea to encourage the Christians in their church.

From Berea, Paul left the country of Macedonia and went to Greece. He went to a large city called Athens, and he waited for the arrival of Silas and Timothy.

Athens in the Time of Paul

H-20 PAUL TELLS THE WISE MEN OF GREECE ABOUT THE UNKNOWN GOD

ACTS 17:16 – 18:23

While Paul waited in Athens for Silas and Timothy, he walked around the city streets and saw idols in various places. He could see that the people there worshiped many different gods. They even had an altar for the Unknown God.

There were Jews in this city also, and Paul visited their synagogue to tell them about Jesus. In the streets, he met many thoughtful men who were eager to listen to him preach. Others listened simply because they were curious. When they heard Paul speak about Jesus and his resurrection from the dead, some of them thought that Jesus was a strange god from a foreign land.

There was a placed called Mars Hill in the city. This was the place where the wisest men met and discussed many important matters. They brought Paul there and asked him to further explain the doctrine that he was preaching on the streets.

540

Paul on Mars Hill

Paul told them that he had seen the altar to the Unknown God. Paul told them that he knew the Unknown God, and that was the God who had created everything, including all living creatures. Paul said this God did not live only in a temple but lived everywhere. He told them that the time would come when God would judge everyone for their sins. He said that they should repent from sin and ask forgiveness, before it was too late.

Paul then told them about Jesus and how he rose from the dead. But the wise men did not believe that this could be true, and they told Paul to come back some other day and tell them more. Paul left Mars Hill and went back into the city.

Some people who had heard Paul preach followed him and asked him some questions. One of these men was a leader in the city. He and a few others decided to stop worshiping idols, and they started believing in the true God and his son Jesus.

From Athens, Paul went to another city in Greece called Corinth. He met a Jewish man and his wife who were strangers in the city. They were tent makers. Paul also knew how to make tents, and he worked with them to earn money. He continued to preach in the synagogue on the Sabbath days. The tent maker, Aquila, and his wife, Priscilla, were Jews who believed in Paul's teachings.

Silas and Timothy arrived in Corinth from Philippi, and Paul was relieved to be with them once again. Paul began to speak more boldly about Jesus, and many of the Jews started to oppose him. Then he focused on preaching to the Gentiles once again.

The chief ruler of the synagogue and those in his household believed in Paul's teachings, as did many others. They were baptized in the name of Jesus. Because most of the Jews in the synagogue did not believe, those who believed in Jesus began worshiping at the home of a man named Justus.

One night while Paul was in Corinth, God spoke to him in a dream. God told him that he would protect him and not to be afraid, and God said that there were many people in Corinth who needed to be saved. After this dream, Paul stayed in Corinth for a long time, preaching the gospel to all who would listen. Many believers were added to the church in Corinth.

After Paul had been there for many months, some sinful Jews who hated the believers planned to make trouble for them. They abducted Paul and brought him before the leaders of the city, and they accused him of doing wrong. The rulers did not even listen to them and they set Paul free. Some Greeks beat up one of the men who had falsely accused Paul.

Paul decided to return to Jerusalem. He took Aquila and Priscilla with him, and they sailed from Greece to Asia Minor. He left his friends in the city of Ephesus, and Paul continued on to Jerusalem to attend the Feast of the Passover. After he left Jerusalem, Paul returned once again to visit the believers in Antioch.

H-21 HOW THE PEOPLE OF EPHESUS HEARD THE GOSPEL
ACTS 18:24 – 19:20

Ephesus was a large city in Asia Minor, not far from the sea. There were many people in Ephesus who worshiped an idol or goddess called Diana. A great temple had been built to worship Diana, and many people traveled

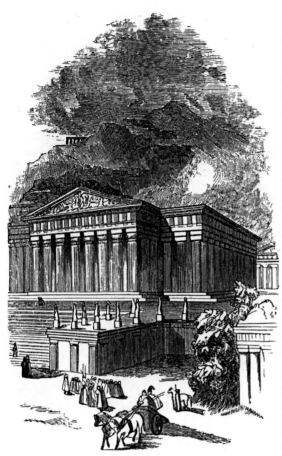
The Temple of Diana

there to worship her and had donated money to help with the temple's construction. It was so beautiful and grand that it is considered one of the seven wonders of the ancient world.

Not everyone who lived in Ephesus worshiped the goddess Diana. Some Jews lived there, and they had built a synagogue. They met there on Sabbath days to study the Old Testament Scriptures.

One day a Jewish man named Apollos came to Ephesus from Alexandria, a city in Egypt. He believed John the Baptist was a prophet, and he taught the Jews in Ephesus about John's teachings. He baptized some of them, after they had repented of their sins. But neither Apollos nor the other Jews had ever heard about Jesus.

Aquila and Priscilla, the friends of Paul who stopped in Ephesus when he went on to Jerusalem, had heard Apollos preach. They thought that he preached well and that he would be a great preacher if he knew all about Jesus and the Holy Spirit. They invited him to their home and told him what they had learned from Paul. Apollos believed their words. Apollos decided to sail to Corinth and found many Christians there.

Shortly after Apollos had left Ephesus, Paul went on his third missionary journey. He met some Jews in Ephesus who believed in the teachings of John the Baptist, and he taught them about Jesus. Many were baptized in the name of Jesus, and many received the gift of the Holy Spirit.

Paul taught for three months in the synagogue at Ephesus. A large number of people there believed him, but many more did not believe, and they spoke unkindly about Paul and Jesus. Paul and those who believed left the synagogue and went to a nearby school. Paul taught there every day for two years, and many more people received the gift of salvation.

Ancient Ephesus

Paul also worked many miracles in the name of Jesus. He healed the sick and cast out evil spirits. Some people were too ill to travel to Paul. Their friends would bring a handkerchief from Paul to the sick persons, and they were healed when they touched the handkerchief.

Many people realized the power of God as shown through Paul. But there were seven brothers who were very sinful. They were able to cast out some evil spirits using spells and charms. They had heard that Paul had great success casting out evil spirits in the name of Jesus. They tried to do this themselves, but because they were sinful, a possessed man leaped up and badly beat the brothers. They ran away in shame.

Other people heard what had happened to these brothers, and they respected the great power of Jesus. Many of those who had practiced magic and spells decided that the power of Jesus was much greater, and they gave up their magic.

Burning Magic Books at Ephesus

In Ephesus, there were many books that taught people how to work wonders by magic. These books were very expensive, but the people built a large fire and burned all of them in the street after they understood the power of Jesus.

The Temple of Diana at Ephesus

Not everyone in Ephesus believed in the power of Jesus when they heard Paul preaching and saw him performing miracles in the name of Jesus. Many still went to the temple of Diana to worship the image of the goddess they believed had fallen from the sky.

Some people couldn't go to the temple to worship Diana. They had their own idols in their homes. Visitors from faraway lands usually wanted to take an idol home with them when they visited Ephesus. Men in the city knew how to make idols of Diana using silver. These silversmiths made a lot of money selling idols to those who wished to buy them.

One silversmith was named Demetrius. He became nervous when he heard about the miracles Paul was performing in the name of Jesus. He feared that more people would stop worshiping Diana and start worshiping Jesus, and he wouldn't be able to sell as many idols. He knew no one would pay for images of Jesus.

When he heard that the people had burned their expensive magic books, he became even more fearful. He contacted all the other silversmiths who made idols of gods and goddesses and told them that Paul was damaging their business in many different lands.

The silversmiths ran through the streets yelling, "Great is Diana of the Ephesians!" A mob began to follow them. They grabbed two of Paul's companions and dragged them into the theater.

Paul heard what had happened and wanted to try to save them. However, his friends wouldn't let him go because they thought that he would be killed by the mob.

The excitement continued for over two hours, and finally an official of the city told the people to be quiet. He told the people that they should not have bothered Paul and his friends because they had done nothing wrong, and he sent everyone home.

Paul was ready to leave Ephesus by this time. He said goodbye to his friends and sailed for Macedonia. He visited the believers in Philippi, where he and Silas had been imprisoned and God had caused an earthquake to open the prison doors.

He passed through Thessalonica and Berea, where he had preached the gospel before, and he went on to Greece. He stayed there for three months, and then he prepared to return to Jerusalem. Before leaving Greece, he heard that his enemies were planning to kill him. He traveled by a different route than the one he had been planning to take, and he was safe.

H-23 The Faithful Missionary's Last Farewell
Acts 20:5 – 21:17

From Macedonia, Paul sailed across the sea to Troas, where he had been when he had the dream about the Macdeonian man calling to him. He stayed there for several days, and then he prepared to start his journey toward Jerusalem once again.

The night before leaving Troas, Paul preached a farewell sermon to the believers there. It lasted until midnight; Paul knew that he would never see them again and he had much to say.

While Paul was speaking, a young man named Eutychus sat in an open window listening. After a while he became sleepy and started to nod off. Then he fell into a deep sleep and sank down on the windowsill. He fell off the windowsill as he slept, and his friends found his dead body below. Paul saw his friends holding his body and crying. Paul told them not to worry because he still had life left in him, and he came back to life after Paul embraced him.

After this happened, Paul returned to the group of believers upstairs where he had been preaching, and he ate with them while he continued his talk. Paul talked with some men who had traveled from Ephesus to meet him at the coast. They were leaders in the church. Paul told them that they would never see him again and that the Holy Spirit was warning that they should prepare for possible danger. Paul urged them to remember that it is more blessed to give than to receive. The men cried as he was leaving, and they went with him aboard the ship before it sailed for Jerusalem.

The ship stopped for several days at the coastal town of Tyre. Paul and his companions met some Christians and worshiped with them. Before he left this town, the believers told Paul that the Holy Spirit had warned them that bad things would happen if he went to Jerusalem, but Paul thought God wanted him to go.

While Paul and his companions were visiting the church in Caesarea, an old man named Agabus arrived from Jerusalem. He was a prophet, and sometimes God told him things that were going to happen. When he saw Paul, he took off a piece of Paul's clothing and tied it around his own hands and feet. He told Paul that the sinful-minded Jews in Jerusalem would tie his hands and feet and turn him over to the Gentiles.

Paul's friends were troubled when they heard this. They gathered around him and begged him not to go to Jerusalem. Paul said that he was ready not only to be tied up, but also to die in Jerusalem for the name of the Lord Jesus Christ. The people realized that they could not stop Paul from going.

Not long afterward, Paul and his companions went over the mountains toward Jerusalem. Other Christians from Caesarea joined them, and when they arrived at Jerusalem the elders of the church welcomed all of them.

H-24 HOW THE PROPHET'S WORDS CAME TRUE
ACTS 21:18 – 23:10

In the years since Herod had tried to kill Peter, the church in Jerusalem had grown very large. Some of the people who had killed Jesus were still alive and they hated the Christians, although they didn't trouble them as much as they had in earlier days.

All of the believers in Jerusalem were Jews. They had not yet learned that God wanted salvation to be for all people, and most of them did not approve of Paul's missionary work among the Gentiles.

The leaders in the church at Jerusalem understood that God had chosen Paul to be a missionary to the Gentiles. But they also knew that many in their church did not understand this, and they encouraged Paul to explain it to everyone.

Paul wanted to show the people that he still had respect for the Law of Moses. He performed a cleansing ceremony at the temple. A week later,

Paul Is Bound by the Roman Soldiers

some Jews from Asia Minor saw Paul at the temple. They became excited because they knew he taught that Gentiles could also become believers, and they didn't agree with this.

Soon the old enemies of Jesus heard about the excitement, and they rushed inside the temple to seize Paul. They dragged him outside the temple and began beating him. They would have beaten him to death if a Roman captain had not arrived with his soldiers to investigate the disturbance.

Thinking he must be a troublemaker, the captain ordered his soldiers to restrain Paul with chains. He then asked what Paul had done. So many people were yelling different things that he could not understand any of them. The captain took Paul away to the castle, where the prisoners stayed.

The angry mob followed, and the soldiers had to carry Paul to protect him from them. Paul asked to speak to the Roman captain. The captain was surprised because he did not know that Paul could speak his language. Paul asked for permission to speak to the mob of people from atop the stairs, and the captain agreed.

Paul Is Rescued From the Mob

Paul motioned with his hand for everyone to be quiet. He began speaking to the people about his early life and training. He reminded them that he was once a Pharisee who had hated Jesus and all his believers.

Paul talked about his journey to Damascus, where he planned to persecute Christians. He told the mob about the bright light and vision he had seen on the road and how God had spoken to him. He told them how he had been baptized, and how God had told him in a vision to preach the

550

gospel to the Gentile countries.

The people became angry again when Paul started talking about preaching to the Gentiles. They began shouting that he was dangerous and should be taken away.

Because they did not speak Hebrew, the Roman captain and his soldiers could not understand what Paul had said to the people. They assumed that he must be dangerous and brought him into the castle. They began to torture him in order to find out why everyone hated him so much. Paul informed the soldiers that he was a Roman citizen and that it was illegal to treat a citizen in this horrible way.

The soldiers told the captain. He asked Paul if he really was a Roman citizen, and Paul told him that he really was. Everyone was frightened because they had treated Paul badly. Still they were confused because they did not know the crimes Paul was guilty of.

The next day, they called the rulers of the Jews together and brought Paul before them. But the rulers could not decide what to do with him. Some wanted to set him free and others wanted to kill him. The captain ordered the soldiers to take Paul away from there for his own safety.

H-25 A YOUNG MAN SAVES HIS UNCLE'S LIFE
ACTS 23:11 – 24:27

Paul understood why he had been warned of danger in Jerusalem. Christians were routinely killed by soldiers working under the Emperor Nero, often by burning and other very painful methods. This happened mostly in Rome, but still Paul knew that he was in a precarious situation.

He knew he was not safe among his own people, and this made him sad. While Paul was sleeping in the castle, God appeared to him and told Paul to go to Rome to preach instead of preaching in Jerusalem. Paul had wanted to go to Rome to preach, and he was excited to hear God tell him to go.

Forty men planned to kill Paul when he was brought down from the castle, when the rulers would hear his case again. Paul's nephew heard about this plan, and he hurried to the castle to tell his uncle.

Paul arranged for the young man to meet with the chief captain. The chief captain knew that Paul was a Roman Jew, and he understood that the other Jews wanted to kill him without a good reason. He told Paul's nephew to tell no one that he had told him about the plan to kill Paul, and he sent the young man away.

The chief captain called two centurions, and he told them to prepare to take Paul to Caesarea that night. Fearing for Paul's safety, he told them to

The Persecution of Christians

prepare 200 soldiers, 70 men on horseback, and 200 men with spears. And Paul was to be given his own horse to ride.

The captain wrote a letter to the Roman governor Felix, who lived in Caesarea, explaining why he was sending the prisoner from Jerusalem to him.

Everyone arrived at the castle at about nine o' clock that night. Paul was led down and put on his own horse, and the small army began to travel down the street. None of the Jews who wanted to kill Paul had heard about the plan.

The next afternoon when Paul was in Caesarea, he was taken to the governor Felix, and the chief captain's letter was delivered. The letter explained that many Jews wished to kill Paul for no good reason, and he was being sent away for his own protection. It also said that Paul's accusers would be told to come before Felix for Paul's trial. Paul was placed in the palace that belonged to Herod, to wait there until his trial.

Paul's enemies were very angry when they learned that Lysias, the chief captain, had ruined their plan to kill Paul. They arranged to go at once to Caesarea and speak to Felix.

Felix arranged for Paul to appear before his accusers. The high priest and Tertullus, a lawyer, were Paul's accusers. Tertullus said many things about

552

Paul that were not true. He accused Paul of being a troublemaker among the Jews, wherever he went. Tertullus also accused Paul of being the leader of a new religion, which he called the sect of the Nazarenes.

When the lawyer had finished making his complaints against Paul, Felix motioned for Paul to stand up and answer the accusations. Paul said that they could not prove anything they said. They had taken him while he was alone in the temple, worshiping. Paul said he followed the Laws of Moses and believed the writings of the prophets.

Felix then spoke. He said that he would wait until Lysias, the chief captain, arrived in Jerusalem, and then he dismissed the council. He turned Paul over to a centurion and instructed his guards that Paul was allowed to have his friends visit him in the palace.

Several days later, Felix called for Paul again. Felix's wife, Drusilla, was with him, and they wished to hear Paul preach about the gospel of Christ. Paul spoke to them, and Felix trembled because he became aware of his great sins. He knew that he was guilty before God and he became afraid. He did not wish to appear weak in front of Paul, so he sent him away and told him that he would call for him again on a different day.

During the next two years, Paul was kept in Caesarea as a prisoner. He was given many privileges, and Felix often called for him, hoping that Paul's friends might offer money to have Paul set free. He knew that Paul did not deserve to be in prison, but still he refused to let him go. After the two years had passed, a new governor was sent to Caesarea. Wishing to please the Jews before leaving their country, Felix left Paul in prison.

H-26 A KING LISTENS TO PAUL'S STORY
ACTS 25, 26

After Felix went to Rome, a new governor was sent to take his place. The new governor's name was Festus. He was Roman and knew little about the Jews and their religion and customs. Three days after he arrived in Caesarea, he went to visit Jerusalem to learn more about the people he was to govern.

Several days later, after Festus had returned to Caesarea, he called for Paul, who was still in prison. Men who had come from Jerusalem stood up and spoke false accusations against Paul, but they couldn't prove anything. The Jews still wished to have Paul taken to Jerusalem, hiding their reason. Festus wished to please the Jewish people, and he asked Paul if he was willing to go to Jerusalem to be judged.

Paul said he had done nothing to be judged for, and that he would gladly die if he had done anything worthy of death, but he had done nothing. Paul asked to appeal to Caesar, the ruler of the Roman Empire, which was the right of every Roman citizen. Festus told him his request would be granted.

Around this time, some visitors came to Caesarea to see the new governor. They were Agrippa, the governor of the country east of the Jordan River, and Bernice, his sister. During their visit, Festus told them about Paul and how the Jews had accused him of a crime against their religion. He told them that during his trial before the Jews, Paul had spoken earnestly about a man named Jesus whom he said had arisen from the dead.

Paul Appears Before Agrippa

554

The next day, Agrippa and Bernice entered the judgment hall with Festus. Festus ordered that Paul be brought before them. Festus introduced Paul. He explained that the Jews wanted to put him on trial, but he didn't know what for. He said that Paul had asked to be brought before Caesar, but he had no charges to make against Paul. He asked King Agrippa to help him figure out why he was even being held as a prisoner.

Agrippa told Paul that he was permitted to tell them what had happened. Paul told how he was raised as a Jew and lived among the strictest Pharisees. He told them that the Jews were accusing him because he believed the what the prophets had written concerning the Messiah, who was Jesus.

Paul explained that he had persecuted many Christians himself. He told them how he was on his way to Damascus to persecute more Christians when he saw a vision from God. He heard a voice, asking, "Why are you persecuting me?" and the voice answered that he was Jesus, after Paul asked. Then the voice told him to preach the gospel not only to the Jews but to the Gentiles as well.

Paul told them that because he had obeyed this command, the Jews who refused to believe in Jesus were persecuting him. Now they were trying to kill him for believing that Jesus was the Christ that Moses and the prophets had written about.

Festus stopped him and told Paul that he must be crazy. Paul answered calmly that he was not crazy but was speaking words of truth and soberness. Paul told Festus that King Agrippa already knew about Jesus, which was why he was speaking openly with him. Paul appealed to Agrippa for help.

Agrippa answered that he was almost convinced to become a Christian, but he was too proud to humble himself. Agrippa discussed Paul with Festus and the others. He said to Festus, "This man has done nothing worthy of death or even imprisonment. If he had not asked to be sent to Caesar, he could be set free at once." But it was too late to change the plans, and Paul could not be set free.

H-27 A SHIPWRECK
ACTS 27

Paul was aboard a ship as it left the port at Caesarea and other prisoners were traveling with him. A Roman centurion named Julius was in charge of Paul and the other prisoners. Festus had commanded Julius and his soldiers to take the prisoners to Rome and safely deliver them to Caesar.

Paul was not the only Christian on the ship. Two of his friends, Luke, the doctor, and Aristarchus, who had gone with Paul on his third missionary

Paul's Ship Heads for Rome

journey, were also going to Rome with him.

The next day after leaving the port, the ship stopped at Sidon, a seacoast town of Phoenicia, to the north of Jerusalem. Paul had some friends in this city, and the soldiers allowed him to go ashore with Luke, Aristarchus, and a Roman soldier. They visited with the Christians who lived in Sidon, and then they returned to the ship.

Their next destination was Myra, a city on the southern coast of Asia Minor. The ship they had started their journey on was not going all the way to Italy, therefore they found a different ship headed that way and boarded it. Luke and Aristarchus went with Paul.

From Myra, the ship left the shore and traveled into the Mediterranean Sea. The wind was very strong and the ship made little progress. After sailing for many days, the passengers were relieved to see the Island of Crete. They stopped at a harbor called Fair Havens.

After resting for some time, the captain wished to begin the journey again, but Paul warned him that sailing at that time of year could be very dangerous. Paul urged them to remain in the port for the winter. But the centurion believed that they could reach another port that was not far away. No one liked staying at Fair Havens because it was not a nice place, and the captain and many of the other passengers were eager to go further before stopping for the winter. When the weather seemed better, the ship left the harbor and returned to the sea.

They had not gone far when suddenly a great wind began to blow. They could not go on to the next port, and they could not turn back. All they could do was hold on and pray as the ship was being tossed about in the waves.

Paul Speaks to Everyone Aboard the Ship

The captain and the centurion knew that Paul had spoken wisely when he urged them to stay at the Fair Havens harbor. They began to throw anything

557

Paul Is Shipwrecked

they did not need overboard in order to lighten the ship. They waited for the storm to stop, but it raged on, day after day and night after night.

One morning Paul spoke to everyone. He had to shout to be heard over the winds. He told them that an angel had appeared to him and told him that the ship would be lost, but everyone aboard would be safe after they were cast onto an island. Paul said that the that angel had told him it was very important that he appear before Caesar.

After two weeks in the storm, the sailors saw land in the distance one night. They had no idea where they were, but they dropped their anchors. When morning came, the sailors planned to leave everyone else aboard the ship and try to save themselves. They pretended to lower a smaller boat into the water in order to drop more anchors, but Paul knew that they were lying. He told the centurion that they would all die if the sailors did not stay on the ship.

The Roman officer believed Paul, and he quickly cut the ropes that held the boat, allowing it to drift away into the darkness. When daylight was breaking, Paul urged those on board to eat some food. They were weak from not taking the time to eat, and Paul knew that they would need all their strength. He reminded them all of what the angel had said: that no one would be harmed if they all stayed together. Paul blessed some bread, and everyone ate. After they had eaten, they threw overboard the wheat they were transporting to Italy. Everything else that was not totally necessary was thrown overboard in order to lighten the weight of the ship.

It was daylight, and they could clearly see the land nearby. They did not recognize the land, but they saw a sandy shore, and the sailors tried to steer the ship in that direction after lifting the anchors out of the water. As they were moving, swirling waters caught the ship in a narrow place. It struck a hidden rock and became stuck there. Then the rear of the ship was broken to pieces by the violent storm.

The soldiers on board knew that they would be killed if the prisoners escaped, and they urged the centurion to allow them to kill all of the prisoners immediately. Because the centurion liked Paul, he refused to let this happen. He commanded everyone who could swim to jump overboard and swim to land. He commanded those who could not swim to take broken pieces of the ship and use those to float to the shore.

Everyone made it safely to the sandy beach. All 262 people aboard were saved.

H-28 PAUL'S VISIT TO THE ISLAND OF MELITA
ACTS 28:1-11

On the shore of the island where Paul's ship was wrecked stood a group of men anxiously watching everyone swim and float to shore. These men were natives of the island, and they felt sorry for the strangers. They hurried out to meet them and helped them reach land. Then they built a fire because everyone was wet and cold. The shipwrecked strangers gathered around the fire, and they were glad for the kindness of the natives. They learned that they were on an island called Melita, south of Italy.

The natives could see that some of the men were soldiers and others were prisoners, but they treated everyone kindly. Paul wished to be helpful, and he gathered some sticks to keep the fire burning. As he laid the bundle of sticks on the fire, the heat from the flames awakened a venomous snake that was hidden among the sticks. Suddenly the snake bit Paul and held onto his hand with its deadly fangs.

The natives knew that Paul was a prisoner. When they saw the snake biting him, they decided that he must be a very wicked man that the gods wanted to kill, even though he escaped from the stormy sea. They were surprised to see Paul shake off the snake without anything else happening. His hand did not swell and he did not become sick. They decided that Paul was a god, since even a venomous snake could not harm him.

Not far from there lived a man named Publius, who was the ruler of the island. He was kind to the shipwrecked strangers, and he invited Paul and his friends to his home. For three days they stayed there and were entertained by Publius and his friends.

Publius's father was very ill with a fever. When Paul heard about this, he visited him, prayed for him, and healed him. The news of this healing spread quickly all over the island, and others who were suffering from diseases went to Paul, asking to be healed.

Paul preached the gospel wherever he went, even though a heavy chain bound him. Everyone was interested to hear him preach and many became believers. Everyone saw that God's power was with Paul and they respected him. Paul and his companions stayed on the island of Melita for three months.

H-29 Paul's Last Journey and His Life in Rome
Acts 28:11-31; Philemon; Colossians; 2 Timothy

When spring came, the Roman centurion, Julius, led his soldiers and prisoners aboard a ship that had been in the harbor of the island all winter. This ship was headed for Italy, and the centurion planned to finish the journey to Rome on foot, once the ship had taken them as far as they could go by sea.

Paul's two friends, Luke and Aristarchus, continued on the journey with him. When the ship was ready to leave the island, the natives brought gifts of food and supplies for their new friends who had taught them about God and his Son, Jesus.

Sailing for Italy

The last place the ship stopped was a city in Italy called Puteoli. Everyone left the ship, and those planning to go to Rome started to prepare for the last stretch of their journey. Some Christians were living in this city, and they were glad to see Paul and his friends. The Roman centurion allowed Paul to remain with these Christians for one week.

Paul Leaves the Ship in Chains

The Roman Highway - The Appian Way

The men journeyed on foot from Puteoli to Rome, traveling a well-built highway. Paul was glad that he was going to Rome, but he did not know whether he would be able to preach there. Paul had written a letter to the Christians in Rome before he was captured, telling them of his desire to visit Rome and preach the gospel there.

When the Christians in Rome heard that Paul was on his way there, they were very happy. Some of them went down the highway to meet him. Even though he was a prisoner, he was welcomed to their city.

Paul was encouraged by the number of people wanting to meet him. He was no longer sad, and he thanked God for bringing him there. He knew that he had true friends there.

Julius the centurion turned over his prisoners to the captain of the guards once they reached the city of Rome. Julius told him that Paul did not deserve to be a prisoner, and Paul was allowed to live in a rented house instead of a prison. But Paul still had to wear his heavy chain, and a soldier always stayed with him to guard him as a prisoner.

For two years he lived in the rented house, and all the soldiers who guarded him learned about Jesus. Anyone who wanted to could come and see him. When he had been there for only a few days, he sent for the chief Jews in the city. They arrived, and he told them how the Jews in Jerusalem had falsely accused him and caused him to be treated like a criminal. The Jews in Rome knew nothing of this, and they asked Paul to tell them of the

The City of Rome

new religion he preached about. Paul was happy to do this.

Many Jews who lived in Rome went to Paul's house to hear him tell the story of the gospel. They had heard about Christians for a long time, but they had never heard the teachings of the new religion.

Paul explained to them how Jesus fulfilled the predictions of the prophets by the way he was born, lived, died, and arose from the dead. The Jews listened carefully. Some of them believed but many others did not. Paul told them that even though they did not believe, many Gentiles did.

While a prisoner in Rome, Paul taught many people about Jesus. He also wrote letters to the Christians who lived in other cities where he had preached. Some of these letters are the epistles of Paul, in the New Testament.

One day while in Rome, Paul happened to meet a runaway slave named Onesimus. This slave belonged to Philemon, a friend of Paul's who lived in Colosse, in Asia Minor. Paul treated Onesimus kindly and taught him about God. He was eager to learn about salvation and Jesus. He wanted to stay with Paul and learn more about Jesus. But Onesimus knew that he belonged to Philemon, and he decided to return to his master.

Paul liked this slave. He knew that runaway slaves were often treated very harshly, but he believed that Philemon would not treat Onesimus so

Paul Preaches in Rome

unkindly. He wrote a letter to Philemon and sent it with Onesimus. In the letter, Paul told Philemon how the slave had helped him so much while he was in Rome. He urged Philemon to welcome him as a brother instead of as a runaway slave since he was now a Christian and God had forgiven him for his sins. Paul's letter to Philemon is part of the New Testament. Onesimus delivered the letter Paul wrote to the church at Colosse, which is also part of the New Testament in the Bible.

Paul Writes One of Many Letters

The Acts of the Apostles does not tell us any more about Paul or the other apostles. But history tells us that the wicked Nero, who was ruler of Rome, finally killed Paul. Perhaps it was by burning, the method used to kill many other Christians. Not long before he was killed, Paul wrote a letter to Timothy, the young man whom he loved as his own son. In this letter, he told him that he knew he would die soon, but he was not discouraged because he had worked faithfully for God. He told Timothy that a crown of righteousness was waiting for him in heaven, and also for everyone else who loves God. This letter to Timothy is also found in our Bible.

H-30 THINGS WE LEARN FROM THE EPISTLES
THE EPISTLES

Paul did not write all the letters or epistles in the New Testament. Two were written by Peter, three by John the disciple of Jesus, one by James, and one by Jude.

These epistles teach us about the preachers in the early church. We learn from them how they depended on God to help them teach correctly. And we learn that the letters are to be read by everyone who reads the Bible, including people today.

These letters also tell us more about God's plan for salvation. We learn

Early Christians Read One of Paul's Letters

that all people are sinners. We learn that God loves sinners and wants to help them, even though they deserve to be punished. God gave his only son, Jesus, to be punished in place of the sinners who believe in his plan of salvation. Those who do not believe in Jesus and God's plan for salvation will still be punished, whether they believe it or not.

Another letter teaches us how Christians should live. Christians are honest, treat the poor well, and are willing to suffer for Jesus's sake. They are kind to those who treat them badly, are always ready to forgive others, and they love each other. They also try to lead others to Christ whenever they can. We learn that Christians are happy because God fills their hearts and spirits with joy. Those who do not believe can never have the joy that comes from knowing that their sins are forgiven.

We learn in these epistles that Jesus will return again someday. When he returns, he will take all the believers with him, and they will live with him forever. Even the dead believers will come up out of their graves when Jesus returns. Those who did not believe, both alive and dead, will face great judgment and punishment from God.

No one will know when this great day will be, and it will be as a thief comes in the night, without being expected by anyone. Just as Jesus warned his disciples about this, the epistles warn us.

Today, many people do not believe in Jesus and laugh at the idea that he will return. This is just as the epistles predicted. These people do not believe that God will destroy the world with fire, just as the people of Noah's time did not believe that God would destroy the world with water. No one will be able to hide, and everything will be burned up – except for the believers.

The epistles also tell us much about God the Father, God the Son, and God the Holy Spirit. They are what we call the Trinity, or the three parts of God. We can pray to any of them because they are all the same God.

H-31 WHEN JOHN WAS OLD AND ON AN ISLAND
THE BOOK OF REVELATION

John on the Island of Patmos

An old Jewish man sat on a lonely island, far from his friends and homeland. He had been a fisherman in his younger days, and his home had been near the Sea of Galilee. But one day he left his fishing nets to follow

Jesus and become one of the twelve apostles, and he never went back to fishing after that day. Jesus died, arose, and went to heaven; and he became a preacher of the gospel.

This old man was John. He was on the lonely island because a wicked ruler had sent him there as a prisoner. He was not unhappy, although he missed his old friends. He knew that he would die soon and then he would be with Jesus – his old friend, master, and Lord.

One day while John was on the Island of Patmos, he was thinking about God. He remembered how the Christians always met together to worship on the first day of the week, called the Lord's Day, since Christ had risen on that day. While he thought about these things, he heard a voice that sounded loud like a trumpet: "I am Alpha and Omega, the first and the last: write what you see in a book, and send it to the seven churches in Asia."

John turned around to see where the mighty voice was coming from. When he turned, he saw seven golden candlesticks, and amid them stood a person who looked like Jesus. John had never seen Jesus looking like this before. He was dressed in a long garment that reached his feet. A girdle of gold was about his chest, and in his right hand were seven stars. The face of Jesus shone like the sun on a summer day, his eyes like flames of fire and his feet like polished brass. His voice sounded like a rushing torrent of water.

John fell down at the feet of Jesus as if he were dead. Then he felt a touch, and looking up he saw Jesus bending over him and saying, "Do not be afraid; I am the same one who was crucified and who died, but I am alive forevermore. Write the things that you see and hear, and the things which shall be hereafter."

Jesus then told John that the seven stars he saw were the seven ministers who preached to the seven churches in Asia. The seven golden candlesticks were the seven churches, and to these seven churches John should write letters. Jesus told John what to put in each letter. One of these letters was intended for the church at Ephesus, where Paul had preached the gospel during his missionary journeys.

John faithfully wrote the letters. They were kept safely and finally copied in other books. Today we have each one of them written in the Book of Revelation, which is the last book of our Bible.

After John had written these letters, he had a vision of the throne of God in heaven. He saw a door open in heaven, and he heard the voice like a trumpet, calling him to come up and enter the door. When he had entered, he saw the great throne of God. Around this throne sat twenty-four old men, dressed in white and wearing crowns of gold. Other heavenly beings were there, and they all were worshiping the one who sat on the throne.

The Vision of the Candlestick

While John was looking at this wonderful sight, he noticed a sealed book in the hands of God. Then a strong angel cried out with a mighty voice, "Who is able to break the seals and open this book?" A search began in heaven, but no one was worthy to take the book, break the seven seals, and open it to see what was written inside.

John wept when he saw that no one could do this. He wanted to know what was written in God's book. While he was crying, one of the old men who sat near the throne spoke to him and said, "Do not cry, because the Lion

The Angel With the Book

of the tribe of Judah has been able to open the book." John looked quickly and saw one being who looked like a lamb. He knew it was Jesus, who had been killed like the lambs at Passover and whom John the Baptist had called the Lamb of God. This being approached the throne and took the book.

The heavenly beings now stood around the throne now rejoiced greatly and fell down to worship before the lamb that had taken the book from the right hand of God. They sang a song praising the one who took the book –

The Vision of Diseases and Deaths

because he had given his own life to redeem them from sin and make them pure so that they might enter heaven.

When the Lamb of God opened the book, John saw the strange things that were in it. He wrote these things down for others to read and know what he had seen. He saw many horrible diseases and deaths, and of course those who believed in Jesus were saved from these horrors when Jesus returns to

Babylon Fallen

Earth. He saw the greatest nation – Babylon – destroyed.

The Earth was eventually destroyed by fire. Afterward, John saw a new heaven and a new Earth, and the old Earth on which he lived seemed to pass out of sight.

Then, in the clouds, he saw the great city of God coming down to dwell in the new Earth. He heard a great voice out of heaven, saying, "Behold, God's house is with men and he will dwell with them. They will be his

The City of God on Earth

people, and he will be their God. And God will wipe away all the tears from the eyes of his people. Never again will they cry from sorrow or pain, because sorrow, pain, and death will no longer be problems for them."

John saw the beautiful city of God, which was far more beautiful than anything he had seen on Earth. He saw that God himself provided light for his people, instead of light from the sun. It was always daytime there.

The City of God

John saw that people from every nation on Earth lived there in that city, people whose sins had been forgiven because they believed in Jesus. He saw that nothing unclean or impure entered the city, and only those whose names were written in God's book were allowed to enter.

John saw a pure river of crystal water flowing through the city. Along the banks of that river he saw the Tree of Life, with fruit that is always ripe. The leaves of the tree were used for healing and staying well.

When John saw all these things, he fell down to worship at the feet of the angel who showed them to him. The angel picked him up and said, "Do not

The Last Judgment

worship me, for I am just a servant. Worship God. And blessed are they who obey his commands, for they shall be able to enter the gates of the beautiful city and eat the fruit of the Tree of Life that grows by the river."

Jesus said to John, "I have sent my angel to tell you these things in the churches. And whoever wishes may come and drink of the water of life freely; the invitation is to everyone. But only those who hear and obey the

575

words of God may share in the blessing of the heavenly city."

"Anyone who tries to add more words to the book of God shall be punished, and anyone who tries to take away any part from that book shall have his own name taken away from the Book of Life and shall never enter the holy city."

Then Jesus said, "Surely I will return quickly."

John, the elderly prisoner, replied, "Come now, Lord Jesus." And all of those who love God and whose hearts have been made pure by the blood of Jesus feel the desire for the return of the Lord, just as John did.

THE END

*This work is not intended as a substitute
for reading the complete text of the actual Bible.*

INDEX OF STORIES

STORIES OF THE OLD TESTAMENT IN SIX PARTS

PART A: THE PATRIARCHS
GENESIS, JOB

PART B: MOSES
EXODUS, LEVITICUS, NUMBERS, DEUTERONOMY

PART C: JOSHUA AND THE JUDGES OF ISRAEL
JOSHUA, JUDGES, RUTH, 1 SAMUEL 1-8

PART D: THE THREE KINGS OF UNITED ISRAEL
1 SAMUEL, 2 SAMUEL, 2 KINGS, 2 CHRONICLES

PART E: THE DIVIDED KINGDOM
1 KINGS, 2 KINGS, 1 CHRONICLES, 2 CHRONICLES, JONAH, JEREMIAH

PART F: STORIES ABOUT THE JEWS
DANIEL, NEHEMIAH, HAGGAI, EZRA, ESTHER, MALACHI

PART G: STORIES ABOUT JESUS
MATTHEW, MARK, LUKE, JOHN, ACTS 1:1-15

PART H: STORIES ABOUT THE APOSTLES
ACTS, THE EPISTLES, THE BOOK OF REVELATION

List of Illustrations

CPSIA information can be obtained at www.ICGtesting.com
227852LV00002B/102/P